Louis Auchincloss

ALSO BY CAROL GELDERMAN

Henry Ford: The Wayward Capitalist
Mary McCarthy: A Life

Louis Auchincloss

A WRITER'S LIFE

Carol Gelderman

Crown Publishers, Inc.
New York

This book includes quotations from *Matters of Fact and of Fiction* by Gore Vidal.
Copyright © 1973, 1974, 1975, 1977 by Gore Vidal. Reprinted by permission of
Random House, Inc.

Copyright © 1993 by Carol Gelderman

All rights reserved. No part of this book may be reproduced or
transmitted in any form or by any means, electronic or mechanical,
including photocopying, recording, or by any information storage and
retrieval system, without permission in writing from the publisher.

Published by Crown Publishers, Inc., 201 East 50th Street, New York,
New York 10022. Member of the Crown Publishing Group.

Random House, Inc. New York, Toronto, London, Sydney, Auckland

CROWN is a trademark of Crown Publishers, Inc.

Manufactured in the United States of America

Library of Congress Cataloging-in-Publication Data
Gelderman, Carol W.
Louis Auchincloss: a writer's life / Carol Gelderman.
p.   cm.
Includes bibliographical references and index.
1. Auchincloss, Louis—Biography.   2. Authors, American—20th
century—Biography.   3. Lawyers—United States—Biography.
I. Title.
PS3501.U25Z68   1993
813′.54—dc20

[B]   92-17324
CIP
ISBN 0-517-58720-3
First edition

10   9   8   7   6   5   4   3   2   1

For Margot, Tony, and Katherine

Contents

Contents

Preface

Louis Auchincloss has written a handful of books that rank among the best in American literature. Yet, from the mid-1960s, when he did not even rate a mention on a list issued by two hundred of the nation's critics of the top twenty post–World War II American writers—and this after the publication of three extraordinary novels as great or greater than the best of Edith Wharton, to whom he is often compared—to this day, he has been consistently underrated and inaccurately "associated with the tinkle of silver on teacups."

Auchincloss's subject matter, the upper echelons of the Protestant Establishment, accounts for his never having received his due. His books take on a whole society—a society referred to in shorthand since the 1960s as WASP—and its decline as a ruling class. "I especially want to portray things into which I've been fortunate enough to gain insight," he told an interviewer in 1964, "that is, a decline of a class. WASPs have not lost their power, but they have lost their monopoly on power." A fictional character from a 1983 collection of short stories specifies just how monopolistic this power had been.

> In my youth American society and government were almost entirely in the hands of big business and the legal profession, and both of these were very white and very Protestant. What we now call ethnic groups, Jews, Irish, and Italians, had managed to get hold of political organizations in the larger cities, but even there the financial districts—the real centers of power —remained predominantly WASP. I do not mean that there

was not plenty of opportunity in New York City for a young lawyer of Italian-American origin, but if he wanted to join the Union Club or Piping Rock, if he wanted to send his sons to Groton or Andover, if he hoped ever to be president of the American Bar Association or achieve high federal office, it was going to be a lot easier for him if he became Episcopalian and treated his homeland as an exotic memory rather than a present-day inspiration.

Auchincloss has often said that everyone has a story, and his tells of the loss of upper-class authority, which he observed first-hand. He grew up under circumstances that offered him "a wider than ordinary perspective of the great public events of the day," he told a Russian audience recently. "As a child in the financial capital of the world I had a front row seat from which to view the ebullience of the new rich in the hectic nineteen-twenties and the violent reversal of their fortunes in the great depression that followed." He spent six years at Groton, a small New England church-affiliated boarding school that was the breeding ground of the Establishment. Here and at Yale, which he attended after Groton, he made friends with men who themselves became the managers of society, members in good standing of the Great World, as centers of power are referred to in his fiction. As a Wall Street lawyer himself, he worked within the ruling circle of American capitalism and used this setting in story after story in which he scrutinized the moral or ethical limits on the exercise of self-interest (the pursuit of happiness), one of the few American novelists to recognize and deal with this eminently American dilemma.

Few of the country's writers bother about business, and when they do, they manage to get no closer to the doings of an actual office from a businessman's point of view than the wrong side of a closed door to the executive suite. America is, after all, a country of romantics who apotheosize the loner—the deerslayer, whaling captain, riverboat gambler, the private eye, the Lone Ranger, the rebel. The great law firms and corporations of this country neither spawn nor nurture loners or rebels. Louis Auchincloss goes against the literary grain, being in no way a romantic but, rather, a tough-minded realist who takes the wealthy and powerful as his dramatis personae. He "is the only serious writer seriously writing about the American business world—our ruling class, after all," says critic John Leonard.

Although mythically America is classless, the obsession of Americans with class distinction belies the myth. From the 1830s, when Alexis de Tocqueville observed in *Democracy in America* that the driving force of American life was the unleashed energy of individuals with a ruling passion for equality, until the 1990s, when Benjamin de Mott in *The Imperial Middle* makes the valid point that Americans deny the existence of classes, the American novelist who relentlessly reminds us of their existence will be resented for it. Edith Wharton was also subjected to carpings that her scope was too narrow, and she felt frustrated by such criticism. "The assumption that the people I write about are not 'real,' " she said, "because they are not navvies and char-women, makes me feel hopeless." Auchincloss, too, feels "constantly downgraded as a specialist in the small and presumably unimportant colony of privileged folk who live in New York City."

A critic writing for *The New York Review of Books*, for example, wrote, "I can believe the upper class is human . . . but fiction seems the wrong medium for the privileged life, which belongs, if anywhere, in the spreads in *Country Life* or *The New York Times* society page, or in the moments of awed intrusion that TV likes to purvey." Other critics have called Auchincloss's "thin slice of privileged rich in American society" "anachronistic"; "that little world" that "exists like Shangri-La, lost to habitation"; "claustrophobic and rigid." His "characters called WASPs are not fashionable" and Auchincloss himself is "an arrogant neo-aristocrat," whatever that is. The reviewer Granville Hicks routinely castigated Auchincloss not for literary technique, which he acknowledged and praised, but for his subject matter—a "little world" absolutely "detached from the real world." "What bothers me," Hicks pronounced in a book he called *Literary Horizons: A Quarter Century of American Fiction*, "is not that he writes about this little world but that he seems to be aware of no other." Gore Vidal blames the critics' attitudes on ignorance. "Such is the vastness of our society and the remoteness of academics and book-chatterers from actual power that those who should be most in this writer's debt have no idea what a useful service he renders us by revealing and, in some ways, by betraying his class."

It is true that in Auchincloss's career, other members of his class sometimes have felt he has betrayed them, for he is no uncritical booster of the world he inhabits. He is an insider with an outsider's perspective, casting an unerring eye on the hypocrisies and failings, as well as the virtues, of that world. As a consequence, there is an undercurrent of wistfulness throughout his work, a recognition that despite the imperfections of the past, an authoritative Establishment secured order, whereas today, when all values are equal, no values have authority, resulting in social conflict. His work reflects a dichotomy in himself that goes back to his childhood, between the observer and the doer, between the artist and the man of affairs, and, in a way, between his mother and father. His life and fiction coalesce: To know one is to understand the other.

There is no ecstasy like that of creation.

The House of the Prophet

Louis Auchincloss

CHAPTER 1

Ancestry

When I am told that I have confined my fiction to too small a world, I find it difficult to comprehend. For it seems to me as if I should never come to the end of the variety of types represented by my relatives alone. Auchinclosses, Russells, Dixons, Stantons, how could anyone lump such people into one mold?

LOUIS AUCHINCLOSS

Jabbing his finger at a framed document in his collection of marriage contracts from the court of Versailles, Louis Auchincloss all but shouts at the visitor. "See that? Look at that! What is it? Marie-Anne de Bourbon. Nobody signs anything after Bourbon. What did she write? *Légitimée*. She added the word *légitimée*. There it is, *légitimée*."

As a student of French royal ancestry and peer precedence, the novelist knew that Marie-Anne de Bourbon was Louis XIV's daughter by his first mistress, Louise de la Vallière. He also knew the king had "legitimated" her, as well as the four other bastards, children by his second mistress, Madame de Montespan, and in so doing had threatened ancient prerogatives concerning heirship to the throne and gave grave offense to the peers who were sticklers in matters of rank. Thus for a long time, Auchincloss puzzled over why Marie-Anne de Bourbon had called attention to this smoldering court resentment by signing *légitimée* after her name. "I checked every reference to Saint-Simon, and I got it!"

From Saint-Simon, he learned that Marie-Anne de Bourbon

had used *légitimée* only when she signed her name on a document with her two half sisters, the children of Montespan. They were supposed to use it, too, but did not for the obvious reason that to write *légitimée* accentuated their bastardy. Marie-Anne de Bourbon must have done it to humiliate her half sisters, Auchincloss reasoned.

Explaining his discovery, he says, only half-facetiously, "I felt as if I had found a cure for cancer." Then later, when he found a contract on which she had not signed *légitimée*, he felt fully vindicated. "Obviously the king had caught on, and said, 'knock it off.' "

Louis Auchincloss has always enjoyed probing family histories. "Genealogy amuses me," he says. As a ten-year-old, he collected cards illustrating royal French lineage, and at eleven, he wrote two plays—one about the Tudors under Henry VIII, the other about the Bourbons during the Reign of Terror—that display the perils of pedigree. He developed just as keen an interest in old New York's family trees from the stories he heard about them from his mother, "a chest of information on New York families," for she had grown up in a time when the mid-Manhattan bourgeoisie all knew one another. "My mother told me that in the very early 1900s she and her mother, engaged in leaving calling cards, might have as many as half a dozen to drop in a single street," Louis remembers. "I was fascinated by New York families and loved to push back into the past for the origin of each. I became something of a joke for my cultivation of the ancient, and I remember being seated, at a dinner before the Tuxedo Ball, at a tiny table with old Mrs. Tilford, its founder. And at a coming-out party at the Breakers in Newport, I spent a large part of my evening talking to an elderly man who recalled a dance given in the same hall by the Vanderbilts at the turn of the century when footmen in maroon livery had lined the whole of the great marble stairway."

Several decades later, he organized an exhibition of portraits called "Three Hundred Years of New York Families." The opening night of the show in January 1966, when five hundred formally attired guests passed through the three upper rooms of the Wildenstein gallery to view the fifty-eight family paintings of New York's elite from 1690 to 1960, prompted a *New York Times* reporter to observe that not since Mrs. Astor's famous parties in the 1880s had so many old New York families gathered under one roof. And even today, Auchincloss's shelves are lined with books such as *Old New York*, *Prominent Families of New York*, and *First Families*. (Inside the latter is a penciled notation in his hand that his father was a third cousin of Franklin Delano Roosevelt and an explanation of how he figured the sequences of relationships.)

Quite naturally, his own family provided considerable drama. "Years before I dared to speculate that I might do anything as different as becoming a writer, I was beginning to see my family . . . in terms of stories. . . . I enthusiastically noted which were the richest cousins, which the richest ancestors, I counted divorces and infidelities in the family tree with glee; I strained for foreign titles and financial scandals." His parents were genuinely appalled at what they saw as his vulgarity. "It became a rather sour family joke," the author admits, "that I had inherited the characteristics of mother's paternal grandmother, a comic legend in the family for the naïveté of her worldly values. 'Don't speak ill of Mrs. Kingsland,' she had told a grandchild, 'she has three million dollars.' " With the born novelist's sharp eye, he mentally filed away all her interesting family vignettes and characters for later fictional and nonfictional treatment. By an early age, he had mastered the complicated Auchincloss, Russell, Stanton, and Dixon lineages.

J. Howland Auchincloss, Louis's father, showed little interest in his family's history, but his maiden sister, Joanna—Aunt Josie to Louis—did, assembling scrapbooks of Auchincloss pictures and memorabilia with the help of her nephew. "Louis is very proud of the family ancestry," says his cousin Gordon Auchincloss, yet Louis pondered the meaning of family. "Looking for my answer in the pages of Aunt Josie's photograph album, staring at the sober Presbyterian countenances of those early Auchinclosses with their great aquiline noses and gravely staring eyes," he wrote in an introduction to her privately printed genealogy, he concluded that family is little more than "a certain proportion of males with the family surname." Because the Auchincloss family by some genetic quirk has had a preponderance of male descendants, most of whom stayed in or near New York City, "you have the beginnings of a clan," Louis has written. His parents, four grandparents, and eight great-grandparents were all New Yorkers, though two, the Dixons, dwelt in Brooklyn, which did not become part of the city until after their time. As late as the 1930s, Louis's great-aunt Emma assembled the clan in the ballroom of the Colony Club for a dinner, "but that was a tremendous feat," the novelist remembers, "more like a stockholders' meeting than a family gathering." Another such dinner was given some twenty years later by Charles Auchincloss, "but he had to lop off several branches as the party would have been too big. Of course, we always had reunions within the branches." Now the family, numbering in the hundreds, meets rarely. The last time, in the mid-1970s at the Darien Country Club, Louis's cousin Sam Auchincloss, an electrical engineer, had designed a mechanical eagle—the eagle being the most prominent feature of the family crest—to hang over the bandstand. As Louis spoke to the gathering, Sam pressed a miniature device concealed in his pocket, bringing the eagle to life by a flapping of wings and dissonant *awk-awking*. A not-so-amused Louis was forced to cut short his exposition of the family tree.

His in-laws must have been amused. Gore Vidal, a former Auchincloss family in-law, wrote that although Louis is "realistic about the family's pretensions," he seems unaware of in-law criticism of the family. "I can recall various quasi-humorous rebellions on the part of the in-laws at the clan gathering in New York. What the in-laws could never understand was the source of the family's self-esteem. After all, what had they ever *done?* And didn't they come to America a bit late by true 'aristocratic' standards? And hadn't they been peddlers back in Scotland who had then gone into *dry goods* in New York?" Louis Auchincloss readily admits his family "were really 'Johnny-come-latelys,' " and that they were not especially distinguished. "There never was an Auchincloss fortune," he says; "each generation of Auchincloss men either made or married its own money."

Twenty-three-year-old Hugh Auchincloss, of Paisley, Scotland, arrived in America on the ship *Factor* in 1803 and set up a dry goods business like his father's in the old country. In two years, he had become prosperous enough to be able to pay for a substantial order of yard goods that arrived from Scotland on the ship *Fanny Taylor* and to marry Ann Stuart, the daughter of a Philadelphia merchant. They settled in a house at the tip of Manhattan on the northeast corner of Pearl and Pine streets. Seven years and three children later, Hugh, who had not renounced his British citizenship, was pronounced an enemy alien when war was declared against Great Britain on June 18, 1812, and forced by presidential proclamation to go at least "forty miles from tidewater so that [he] might not be able to render aid or give comfort to the enemy." Enterprising and industrious, he outfitted a team of mules and a wagon as a traveling dry goods store to take his business on the road. When the war was over, he returned to New York richer than when he had left. He continued to prosper, becoming president of the American Wholesale Dry Goods Association.

The third of Hugh and Ann's children, John, was Louis Auchincloss's great-grandfather, and it is he who first demonstrated the family's proclivity for marrying "up." John's wife, Elizabeth Buck, "provided the family with respectable Colonial ancestors," Louis says with a laugh. And when his son, John Winthrop Auchincloss, Louis's grandfather, married Joanna Hone Russell, he, too, allied himself with several distinguished families. One of Joanna's maternal forebears, John Howland, whose surname Louis's father bore, had come to America on the *Mayflower* in 1620 and was one of the founders of Plymouth Colony. The Russells were the founding family of Woburn, Massachusetts.

Through these and subsequent marriages, the family became kin to the descendants of the great Colonial families—the Winthrops (also the middle name of Louis's brother and oldest son and the family that unifies the nine stories that make up *The Winthrop Covenant,* Louis's 1976 study of the Puritan ethic in American history), Dudleys, Wainwrights, Mainwarings, and Saltonstalls; of Aaron Burr; of Oliver B. Jennings, a founder of Standard Oil; of the Colgate family; of the Smedbergs, the Frelinghuysens, the Van Rensselaers, the Cuttings, the Reids, the du Ponts, the Sloans (with and without the final *e*), the Grosvenors, the Truslows, the Tiffanys, the Bundys, the Adamses, the Burdens, and the Vanderbilts, among others.

"It's not exactly the family next door," Gore Vidal wryly observed. "Sooner or later the Auchinclosses pick up one of everything, including the chicest of the presidents," he said, alluding to John F. Kennedy. And he should know. His mother married Hugh Auchincloss II; for six years, Vidal was step-something to every family member, as well as to Jacqueline Bouvier Kennedy Onassis, whose mother also married Hugh Auchincloss. (Louis Auchincloss has written two books under Mrs. Onassis's editorship and dedicated another to her.) Since the Kennedy/Onassis connection, the family, previously prominent in the *Social Register* sense, became highly visible and widely known, though few people can identify precisely the source of their renown or pronounce their name (AWK-in-closs). "For idle hypergamy and relentless fecundity," Vidal says in summation, "there has not been a family like them since those much less attractive *Mittel-Europa* realtors, the Hapsburgs."

The Auchincloss marriage that most engaged the future novelist was that of his great-grandparents on Joanna Russell Auchincloss's side. Charles Handy Russell, Joanna's father, is the model for the father-in-law in his great-grandson's 1982 Civil War novel, *Watchfires*. In the book, Charles Handy is a prosperous burgher, already retired—like the Auchinclosses, the real-life Charles Handy Russell was in the wholesale business of importing and selling foreign dry goods—and a reluctant Union partisan in an impending Civil War. "No Handy ever owned a slave, even in the days when half your old New York families did," the fictional Charles Handy brags. "Oh, our record is pure! But that doesn't mean I believe in telling our Southern friends and neighbors how to run their lives." Charles Handy Russell was never so lukewarm. According to his son's privately printed biography of his father, he hated slavery and worked ceaselessly during the Civil War to raise regiments. President Lincoln expressed his appreciation once in person and again by letter, a letter Russell framed and carried with him between New York and Newport, where he kept homes, both of which are pictured on the dust jacket of *Watchfires*. One home, at Thirty-seventh Street and Fifth Avenue, was "a square brown-stone mansion with a four-window frontage on the Avenue, and it boasted every modern convenience, including a picture gallery."

Oaklawn, Russell's Newport house, was designed by the architect Richard Upjohn—noted for Trinity Church in New York and Kingscote in Newport—and finished in 1853, three years after his marriage as a fifty-four-year-old widower to Caroline Howland. "The Russells and the Howlands," Louis Auchincloss writes in his memoir, *A Writer's Capital*, "were of English origin and had once held themselves very high, having belonged to the richest class of merchants and bankers before the American Civil War," but by the time the novelist was born they were in decline, in sharp contrast to the "rising" Auchinclosses.

Joanna Auchincloss was one of Charles Handy Russell and Caroline Howland's children. During her childhood, Russell entertained frequently, giving garden parties at which Newport specialties such as "soft-shell crabs, corn-roasted on the cob, and johnny cakes" were served and receptions with music and dancing inside the house and croquet and archery on the lawns outside. Edith Wharton, who obviously had Oaklawn in mind for Julius Beaufort's home in *The Age of Innocence* (a square, wooden, chocolate-colored house "with the tin roof of the verandah striped in yellow and brown to represent an awning"), probably attended one or more of these parties. General and Mrs. Ulysses Grant and President Rutherford B. Hayes most certainly did attend.

Accounts of balls and weddings in Russell's Fifth Avenue house show up in the diaries of his friends, one-time New York mayor Philip Hone (whose son married one of Russell's daughters, making Hone a great-great-great-uncle of Louis Auchincloss) and Charles Templeton Strong. Auchincloss has been a lifetime reader of the diaries and once told historian Allan Nevins that he set out to chronicle post–World War II New York fictionally just as Hone and Templeton had nonfictionally brought to life the decades just before and after the Civil War. Auchincloss's edited excerpts, *The Hone & Strong Diaries of Old Manhattan*, appeared in print in late 1989.

Russell had retired from business fully eight years before he commissioned Oaklawn, but he remained active in New York's civic affairs. He was one of the original commissioners of Central Park, from the time the board was organized in 1857 until it was dissolved in 1879 by the Tweed Ring, then in control of the legislature and city government. The number of portraits of Russell—among them one painted by William Sidney Mount that hangs in his great-grandson's Park Avenue dining room, and another, painted by David Huntington, that shows a marked resemblance to Howland Auchincloss, Louis's father—attests to his eminent standing. His scrapbooks, "filled with decades of newspaper clippings recording his noted presence at august occasions and the pasteboard invitations, reverently glued in, of the socially great," Louis writes, fill a shelf at the Newport Historical Society. When he died, his beloved Newport house was sold.

Eight years later, his daughter Joanna returned to Newport to her own house. Her husband, John Winthrop Auchincloss, built a twenty-eight-room house on seventy-five acres, not on Bellevue Avenue (Newport's ocean side) as his father-in-law had done, but on Narragansett Bay. Started in 1887 and finished in 1892, the sprawling house was designed in the Shingle Style with a collection of turrets and gables, dormers and dramatic windows with views of the sea and of rolling lawns. Business reverses forced John to sell the estate to his brother Hugh. The brothers had been agents for the Scottish thread manufacturers J. and P. Coats, but they lost the business in 1897. Their much older sister Sarah had married James Coats. When Sarah and James's daughter married Theodore Frelinghuysen, they wanted their son-in-law to be brought into Auchincloss Brothers as an equal partner. For reasons now unknown, John and Hugh said no. Their refusal finished them as factors for the Coats and as partners in a prosperous firm; it nearly finished John. Hugh, as the son-in-law of Oliver Jennings, a co-founder with John D. Rockefeller of Standard Oil, had ample funds to buy his brother's estate, called Hammersmith Farm, which remained in his family until 1977. Today, Hammersmith Farm is best known as the setting for the 1953 wedding of John F. Kennedy and Jacqueline Bouvier.

John Winthrop Auchincloss was far from broke. According to his son Howland, he had financial acumen, advising a number of his relatives on their investments, and an unusual understanding of the complicated operation and financing of railroad corporations. For forty-five years, he was a director of the Illinois Railroad and chairman of its finance committee. He was also a director of other companies, including a Florida phosphate company of which he was president. He and Joanna had six children; their third and fourth were twin boys born in 1886. John Winthrop died in infancy; Joseph Howland (Louis Auchincloss's father) lived eighty-two years. Growing up, Louis lived near his grandparents in New York and in Bar Harbor, where his grandfather had built a more modest edifice than Hammersmith Farm. Miramichi, as it was called, was a large Shingle Style villa atop a wooded hill that provided dazzling views of Frenchman's Bay. One of Louis's favorite photographs in his Aunt Josie's album is of a 1925 reunion of Howland's siblings with their families. "Only Uncle Russell's daughter is missing," the novelist tells an interviewer, not mentioning that he had recently fictionalized the drama surrounding her absence in the first story of *Fellow Passengers*. She had been "living in Paris under circumstances . . . evidently reprehensible, as for once mother and grandmother agreed on a subject," according to the story's narrator.

Like many Auchinclosses, including two cousins his age, Howland went to boarding school at Groton and then to Yale. There he met Courtlandt Dixon, who introduced him to Priscilla Dixon Stanton. Howland Auchincloss and Priscilla Stanton married in 1911.

Since the dominant influence in Louis Auchincloss's development was Priscilla Auchincloss, it is only to be expected that her family's history stimulated even more intense curiosity and invention in the boy than did his father's. The Stantons came to the United States from England in the mid 1600s, settling eventually in Stonington, an old whaling seaport on the extreme southeast corner of Connecticut. Since the 1850s, they have been New Yorkers, "a polite, agreeable, urbane clan, of no particular distinction or notoriety," Louis Auchincloss has written, yet with a storyteller's watchful instinct, he found the best Stanton stories to write about. His grandfather's and great-uncle's insistence that their mother marry William Tillinghast after his wife died, so the poor woman could respectably continue what had become an annual summer European trip for the three old friends, became part of *Portrait in Brownstone,* for example. One of the sons, the elegant Edmund Stanton, who "sent his shirts to Paris to be cleaned," became Uncle Ed Stillman in a 1966 short story called "The Wagnerians," an imaginative and moving account of Stanton's motives and behavior during the time he was general manager of the Metropolitan Opera from 1886 to 1891. Asked to write an article about his great-uncle for *Opera News,* Louis preferred to make this fictional account, although two decades later, he did write a nonfictional profile for a collection of short sketches he called *The Vanderbilt Era.*

An unlikely combination of influence and chance propelled the nonmusical Stanton to the Met's stewardship. His stepfather (William Tillinghast) and a cousin by marriage were board members of the company that had been formed by William H. Vanderbilt to build a new opera house. Unable to get boxes in the Academy of Music, the established opera venue, they opened their Metropolitan in 1883 and asked Stanton to become secretary to the board. The first season was a financial disaster primarily because the Italian prima donnas made extravagant demands. The board hired Leopold Damrosch, who, since his emigration from Germany in 1871, had founded the Oratorio Society and the New York Symphony—today the New York Philharmonic—to see what he could do with German opera. He died before the end of the second season. Inexplicably, the board chose the thirty-two-year-old Stanton, a man with neither managerial nor musical experience, to run the Met. Nonetheless, he accomplished much in his short tenure. With the help of Walter Damrosch, Leopold's twenty-three-year-old son, he brought four Wagnerian stars to the company—the soprano Lilli Lehmann, the tenor Max Alvary, the bass Emil Fischer, and the conductor Anton Seidl, and he did this without any overbidding of salaries that had been customary for the hard-to-get Italians. Moreover, he firmly and decisively quashed unreasonable demands. Once Max Alvary refused to sing at a dress rehearsal. If Alvary did not sing, Seidl announced, he could not conduct. The general manager was summoned. "I cannot sing today and tomorrow," Alvary said. "Choose." "Sing today," the unruffled manager replied, guessing correctly the tenor would not refuse to sing at the next day's premiere.

Stanton's fatal flaw, apparently, was his love of German opera. During each succeeding year of his tenure, he produced more and more of Wagner's works, pleasing the quarter of a million of New York's Germans but displeasing the wealthy box holders who wanted and then demanded Italian opera. In his last season (he was fired in 1891), he put on five Wagnerian operas in a row. Stanton ended up broke and alcoholic, forcing Mrs. Tillinghast to support his widow and children. His great nephew Louis later acquired Stanton's passion for German opera.

Edmund Stanton's brother, Louis Lee Stanton, was Louis Auchincloss's maternal grandfather. A more prosaic and temperate man than his brother, he became an officer of the Standard Trust Company and married Pauline Dixon of Brooklyn. Their first child, born in 1888, was Priscilla Dixon Stanton, Louis Auchincloss's mother.

"Don't get Dixonized," Joanna Auchincloss told her son Howland when he became engaged to Priscilla twenty-three years later. No doubt she recognized her future daughter-in-law as more of a Dixon than a Stanton. And no wonder: The Dixons of Mrs. Auchincloss's generation were a tight-knit clan. In a foreword to a privately printed Dixon genealogy, Priscilla Auchincloss wrote about what it was like to grow up among the Dixons, who had such a powerful influence on her, and, through her, on her novelist son.

Her Dixon grandparents, whom she never knew, brought up several extraordinarily close children who had to be together at home all the time. "Homesickness," Priscilla wrote, "was always spoken of with a certain pride, as a family failing." Her mother claimed to be too homesick to go to school, so she was educated at home. The first time Willie Dixon spent a night away from home, he "took all his ornaments to lessen the suffering." Homesickness attacked Priscilla, as well. "When I had to return to Southampton, after one night of a visit to East Hampton, I was greeted on my arrival as having shown myself a worthy member of the family." But surely the foremost yearner for home must have been Aunt Pink, "much applauded when, having returned to Brooklyn after her honeymoon with Uncle Tom Sloane, she was driven to the Brooklyn Bridge to go to New York where she was to live, but was too homesick to make the crossing."

Move to Manhattan she did, but so, too, did her brothers and sisters. Six of the seven settled in brownstones on Forty-ninth Street between Fifth and Sixth avenues, a block that became known as Dixon Alley, and a seventh moved around the corner on Forty-eighth Street. Because Dixons hated to be apart, they shared carriages; they did errands together; they took exercise in family groups; their children ate dinner together in a different house each night; they even congregated together in Southampton each summer. The constant arranging this "compulsory cousinship" necessitated was accomplished every morning by telephoning between families. If a line was busy, the operator, in that simpler time, offered to try another Dixon phone.

Dixon coziness conferred considerable benefit. When Priscilla's father died in early middle age of Bright's disease, Aunt Pink helped her mother with school bills for Priscilla's two younger brothers, and when Priscilla went to parties, her male cousins kept an eye on her to make sure she kept dancing and meeting men. It was a cousin who introduced her to Howland Auchincloss. But the greatest benefit, Priscilla Auchincloss implies in her foreword, was intangible, and that was the family's shared values. "Anything in excess (except perhaps homesickness) was disapproved," she wrote. The family's perfunctory churchgoing, for example, discouraged overzealous piety. *Her* daughter Priscilla remembers that the Dixons went to church, "so long as there was nothing better to do." One of them was even dissuaded from "reading the Bible so hard." A coolness toward religious pursuit must not be interpreted as softness on fundamentals such as honor, truth, and loyalty, Priscilla contended, but seen as indicative of a healthy skepticism about human progress.

Pauline Dixon, Priscilla's mother, wrote a piece in 1909, entitled "My Daughter's Friends," that illustrates the approved skepticism. Called old-fashioned by her daughter, she wrote of her observation that human nature did not change from generation to generation, that "all 'foolishness,' 'narrowness of view,' and 'love of detail in feminine vanities' die in mine and spring to life in hers as 'wisdom,' 'broadness of view,' 'grasp of situation,' and 'facing the problems.' " Priscilla's friends—one of whom arrived for a visit with a trunkful of books that required three men to carry to her bedroom, and another, never without her rifle, yet afraid of a mouse—were no different from young girls of any other generation.

Portrait in Brownstone, Louis Auchincloss's 1962 novel of the Denisons, who regard "even a small desire for privacy almost antisocial," is a fictionalized conjuring of the Dixon spirit. Yet Auchincloss remakes his mother's "increasingly idealized memory of Forty-ninth Street" with its "warm, pulsating exchange of love and confidence" into a tale of the crumbling of family tradition. To the shy protagonist, Ida, the Denison morality is absolute, just as the Dixons' was for Louis's mother. Despite the Dixon amiability, or perhaps because of it, a sense of duty weighed heavily on Priscilla her whole life, a constricting outlook she passed on to Louis. He regrets that "she played the role in life that she felt she had to play. She cramped her natural personality to fit into the box that seemed always to be opening in front of her. . . . She seemed to feel that she had to live up to all the standards of the tribe."

She was different from the tribe, however. The tribe admired athletic prowess in its males and popularity and good looks in its females, but Priscilla loved books, reading, studying. She was always the top student at Miss Chapin's School, and when she persuaded her unintellectual family to let her attend Barnard, they agreed only if she was willing to take her Irish maid, Alice Morrissey (who spent her entire life in Priscilla's employ) with her as chaperone. Priscilla never graduated, because her father became ill and she had to stay home with him. She did not mind so much, though, for by this time, she was in love with Howland Auchincloss. For the rest of her life, however, she read seriously, omnivorously, and perceptively. People who knew her as an adult feel she might have been an outstanding scholar or teacher or writer. Her familial reminiscences certainly bear this out. But it was a different era, and Priscilla Dixon Stanton was dutiful above all else.

His mother's warning to the contrary, when Howland Auchincloss married Priscilla in 1911, he moved into his just-widowed mother-in-law's Forty-ninth Street brownstone, occupying an entire floor. Just as his new wife had books, he loved music. Surely Priscilla had warned him, if he had not observed it himself, of her family's complete lack of interest in the arts. She herself told of "hearing one end of a telephone conversation of Aunt Pink's, something about Paderewski, and yes there would be 'playing,' and her turning to assure Uncle Jim that the playing would be cards, and not the piano." But if Howland played the piano and violin, and if he enjoyed concerts and operas, he enjoyed them, as his wife did her books, as avocations. There was no idea of vocation in the arts for either of them. The family may have looked on their interests as a little highfalutin, but what was lost if Priscilla and Howland bowed to duty as the Dixons saw it—the downtown world for him and family for her.

As a graduate of Harvard Law School, Howland took his rightful place in the firm of Stetson, Jennings & Russell, the predecessor of the present Davis Polk. No one thought it odd that Russell was his maternal uncle or that Jennings was his sister's father-in-law. As a young matron, Priscilla wholeheartedly accepted the expected pattern of her tribe's mores. Both found unusual happiness and usefulness in the expectations and rituals of their era and background, and they passed these on to their four children. In the ensuing years, these very expectations stifled the sensitive writer-to-be, who agonized over finding his proper place in the world of the Dixon great-aunts and great-uncles. Not until 1962, when the Dixon Association, a periodic family gathering akin to Auchincloss reunions, awarded Louis a small silver cup as the family member with the most outstanding achievement was the writer certain about his place. Asked how he felt when the cup went to him, he said that what pleased him most was to have gotten it from Palmer Dixon, "the symbol of that world, that generation who had no use for the silly writer."

CHAPTER 2

Family

It has been said that his childhood is a writer's entire capital.

LOUIS AUCHINCLOSS

L ouis Stanton Auchincloss was born in Lawrence in his parents' weekend house on Long Island's South Shore on September 27, 1917. He weighed eight pounds and ten ounces. Two days later his maternal grandmother died. The younger Auchinclosses, who had been occupying a single floor in Pauline Dixon Stanton's Forty-ninth Street brownstone, took over the whole house and the care of Priscilla's two younger brothers, Louis Lee, twenty, and William, eighteen. A few short months later, Priscilla, with five-and-a-half-year-old John and two-year-old Priscilla, baby Louis, and four Irish maids, moved to Louisville, Kentucky, to be with Howland at the Field Artillery Officers Training School at Camp Zachary Taylor. Howland completed his studies and was commissioned as a second lieutenant, but World War I ended before he could be sent overseas. Back in New York, the family, which in 1921 was completed with the birth of a fourth child, J. Howland, Jr., settled down to an ordered and inflexible routine of winters in Manhattan (in 1922, they moved to East Ninety-third Street and in 1923 to East Ninety-first Street), weekends and early summers in Lawrence (until 1927, when Howland and Priscilla built a house in Locust Valley on Long Island's North Shore), and two months each summer in Bar Harbor, Maine. When

Howland's father died in 1938, they occupied Miramichi until it could be sold. Later, they stayed in a succession of summer houses, rented and owned. The first that they had bought burned in the 1947 Bar Harbor Fire and the second had been built by William Ralph Emerson, a distant cousin of Ralph Waldo Emerson and one of the earliest and finest designers of that uniquely American structure, the Shingle Style country house.

Despite the continuous moving from house to house, Howland Auchincloss spent every night with his family except for one month in the summer, when he stayed in the city. Even then, he took the 5:00 P.M. Friday Bar Harbor Express to be with them Saturday and Sunday. Running several households costs considerable money, which Howland provided not from inherited wealth but by a steady rise in his profession. When he joined Stetson, Jennings & Russell in 1911, the firm was distinguished and old, dating from the 1850s, but small, never exceeding seven partners. By the time Howland had come back after his stint in the army, Stetson was senile and Jennings and Russell were in partial retirement. Allan Wardwell took over, hiring Frank Polk and John W. Davis, a former congressman and ambassador to England. In 1921, Howland became a partner. From that time until his death forty-seven years later, he was extremely happy in his association with the firm. As his son says in *A Writer's Capital*, "It was his fraternity, his club, almost, in a way, his church. . . . Nothing meant more to him than the concept of friendship united with professional association." Even when the firm got large, he knew everyone and had time for anyone. In return, he was trusted and beloved.

Two years after Howland became a member of the firm, senior partner John Davis won the Democratic party's nomination to run against Calvin Coolidge on the 103rd ballot, after nine days of balloting and fifteen days of the longest convention in history. After he lost the election, the partners renamed the firm Davis Polk Wardwell Gardiner & Reed, and it has, ever since, been known as Davis Polk. A high proportion of its predominantly Anglo-Saxon partners (not until 1961 did the firm have a Jewish partner) was listed in the *Social Register*, making it the most "social" office on Wall Street. Its chief client was J. P. Morgan and Company.

While still in his thirties, Howland was recognized as an expert in the functions of banks acting as trustees of corporate debentures. As his sister-in-law remembers, "He was always bringing out bond issues." He was meticulous and thorough, which earned him an enviable reputation on the street, and the respect of a nephew, now a federal judge.

> When you asked Howland a question, he always started talking about the answer and kind of talked around. He told you a lot of things you felt you didn't need to know, and you'd get impatient. When he was finished, you realized he'd covered the question from every point of view and you'd gotten an answer far more valuable than the shorter one would have been. He answered questions in a neutral and objective way. Howland left you thinking about the questions in different ways. This is the key to good judgment. This is what a lawyer should do, think of the question from a lot of different angles.

The same meticulousness that Howland Auchincloss showed at work was evident at home, too. He kept detailed records of household expenses, servants' salaries, club dues, even church donations, carefully writing each expenditure in a book. Yet he was not a stickler or autocrat to his family, discarding much of the discipline that had been meted out to him as a child. Reared a strict Presbyterian to the extent of having to go to church twice on Sundays, as an adult he treated churchgoing in a perfunctory way. The family belonged to the Madison Avenue Presbyterian Church, and the children were baptized as Presbyterians, but Howland never thought it mattered whether the family attended an Episcopal church, as they did occasionally on Long Island, or no church. None of the enforced eating he had endured—if, as a boy, he did not eat his breakfast eggs, they were presented again at lunch and had to be eaten if he wanted anything else—was visited on his children. They remember him as fair—stepping in to protect Howland when older brother Louis bargained away his brother's wooden animals or otherwise took the upper hand his additional four years gave him. "My older brother [John] was an absolute saint to me when we were growing up," Louis remembers, "and I returned that by being horrid to my younger brother." His sister, Priscilla, corroborates this memory. "Howlie adored Louis and was a virtual slave to him. Louis took advantage of this to the hilt," which is why Howland kept a watchful and protective eye on his youngest son. Once he had to step in to protect young Priscilla, because Louis had locked his sister and her nurse in a room and then had thrown the key out the window.

Howland spent time with his children, throwing balls with them, taking them out in rowboats, walking with them, and teaching them golf and tennis. Every Saturday morning, he played eighteen holes of golf with the same three men at the Piping Rock Club, one delirious day making a hole in one, and in the afternoon, he cajoled his sons into a game of tennis. Louis thought of him as "quite a jock." Although he had been a good athlete at Groton and at Yale as well, he never criticized his decidedly unathletic sons for not following in his footsteps. Asked to list the sports Louis liked on his Groton application, Howland stated simply, "not . . . interested in any sport." Criticism generally came from their mother. Louis remembers that "Mother would protest loudly when she found me on a beautiful summer afternoon hiding away in the darkest corner of the library reading *The Martyrdom of an Empress* or some similar trash. Not Father. He would try, charmingly if unsuccessfully, to build a bridge between my book and the tennis court. I laughed at his arguments but I loved him for trying."

Howland Auchincloss was no pushover, though. He could lose his temper when the occasion called for it. Twice in his childhood, Louis took objects that did not belong to him, and his father exploded both times. Once, after a visit to the dentist, who put prickers on his teeth to prevent his habit of biting his lower lip, he pocketed the books that had been provided for the doctor's juvenile patients. Another time, he took his uncle's watch. When these were discovered, Howland reacted harshly, scaring Louis into tears, even threatening a beating.

On at least one occasion, Louis deliberately provoked his father's anger. For Christmas, when he was eight or nine, he was given a puppy, but he had not wanted one. He had carefully made a list for Santa Claus of expensive toys, which did not materialize on Christmas morning. The dog, he was told, was his principal gift. His disgust, which was all too apparent, turned to outrage when he was made to clean up a puppy mess. Louis caused such a scene that the puppy was given to John. "What do I get in return?" he demanded. John agreed to give him a five-dollar copy of *Safari* by Martin Johnson, which was costly for a book in the 1920s. "A five-dollar book for a seventy-five-dollar puppy," he screamed indignantly. "That really ruins our Christmas," his father said. "Good, I wanted to ruin Christmas for you," he replied, and he remembers thinking, "what sentimental slops his family were." Priscilla thinks the episode illustrates a trait that is at the core of her brother's character. "When Louis wanted things, he wanted them *very* much." While Howland Auchincloss was always enchanting to the outside world, he could be very disagreeable and cross with his secretary and with the servants, but his temper passed quickly. One day, Maggie Kane, the much-loved children's nurse, proudly recounted the latest gossip of the neighborhood's nurses at the Piping Rock swimming pool. "You know, all the nurses think Mrs. Auchincloss is so cross and Mr. Auchincloss is so pleasant-spoken," she told the family. "You see, I told them that if you really knew them, you'd see it's just the other way around." Priscilla laughed and said, "Who comes out ahead on that one?"

Overall, however, Howland Auchincloss was a kind and sweet-natured father who entertained his children with stories—when it thundered, he said the noise was the gods throwing furniture around—and music. He played the piano and violin and for a time belonged to an amateur quartet. Never one to promote his diversions at the expense of his children's, he was nevertheless delighted when Howland junior followed his musical lead, becoming proficient enough as he grew older to perform violin and piano sonatas with his father. Louis inherited his father's love of opera. Howland's was a benign and understated influence—whatever his children got interested in, that was what he became interested in. "He was so patient," Louis recalls. "He never pushed you." John, however, equated his father's tolerance with detachment.

Howland Auchincloss was a well-liked man, not only by his firm and his family but by everyone who knew him, and unlike his sons, he had been popular at Groton and Yale. He showed a sincere interest in other people, not only in his friends and colleagues but in his children's friends, who remember Mr. Auchincloss as an ego-free man with a self-mocking manner. But many people noted a sadness about him.

Louis's father suffered from depressions throughout his life, a condition he inherited from his Russell genes. His mother, Joanna Russell Auchincloss, had had one crippling depression after another throughout her adult life. *Depression* is, however, an inadequate word for the malevolent intensity of the melancholy that sometimes seized her, but it is used today in place of the even more nebulous term *nervous breakdown* that was current in 1903, when Howland had his first attack. This first of his depressions occurred in his last year at Groton, and his father, all too familiar with his wife's "nervous disorder," reacted quickly and took him out of school for two months. Howland's next bout, which was of shorter duration, occurred at Yale. Then he enjoyed a reprieve for thirty happy and successful years, but he was attacked again twice in his early fifties, which slowed his legal career. He might have become one of the major partners of Davis Polk, but not after his illnesses, which not only forced year-long absences from the office but set in motion anxiety about further episodes.

Still, this courtly gentleman managed to live a productive life in spite of illness, owing in no small measure to his happy marriage. According to his son, "he never wavered in his position that Mother was the greatest thing that ever happened to him. Indeed, trying to explain it to me once, he unintentionally aroused my resentment. 'Compared to what your mother and I feel for each other,' he said, 'you children hardly exist.' In his confused sense of what a great emotion he was attempting to put into words, he forgot how this would sound to a boy." Howland and Priscilla Auchincloss were devoted and intimate companions for fifty-seven years.

For Priscilla Auchincloss, the family was the be-all and end-all of life, and for her, her husband was the center of the family. On her sixtieth wedding anniversary in 1971, the year before she died, Louis had dinner with her. He asked her to describe her wedding and reception. After she had re-created the ceremony, which had had to be moved forward because her fifty-one-year-old father had been dying of Bright's disease, and the reception at the family home at 30 West Forty-ninth Street, Louis said, "Father claimed you didn't know the facts of life." "Perfectly true," his mother replied, "but I learned them in a great hurry, and that night. We had a perfectly wonderful time and then your brother John was born." Priscilla Auchincloss's strong attraction to and love of Howland never let up for the more than half century of their lives together. In *A Writer's Capital*, Louis writes that "even after Father's stroke, at eighty-two, when his mind was largely gone, Mother allowed him to mess up all his papers which I had carefully arranged. When I begged her to keep the desk door locked, she simply shook her head, murmuring: 'Those are your father's papers.' . . . She thought of Father and herself as a unit."

For this reason, she was as congenial with her husband's partners and business associates as he was. Although she disliked traveling, she reluctantly accompanied her husband to Belgium in 1928, where he had bond business, leaving her children in care of her brother Lee and his wife, Helen. At home, she subjected herself to the considerable complications of organizing life in three widely separated houses. Louis illustrates just how complicated such arrangements were in *A Writer's Capital:*

> By 1927, when I was ten, we lived in the winter in a brown-
> stone house on 91st Street with two nurses, a cook, a kitchen
> maid, a waitress, and a chambermaid. We had a summer house

on Long Island with a caretaker, later left open for winter weekends. For July and August we rented a large shingle cottage in Bar Harbor. We had a chauffeur and two cars, which rose to four as the children learned to drive. My parents belonged to a dozen clubs.

In addition, there were all the aunts, uncles, first cousins, as well as the considerable number of more distant relatives of Howland's and hers on the New York scene who had to be kept track of, entertained, and visited. Howland's parents, who lived nearby, had the family to Sunday lunch frequently and always to dinner on Christmas Eve, when the grandchildren were expected to recite. Howland junior remembers how much his grandmother was in charge of that household, "one of the great matriarchs who fascinate Louis so much," which accounts probably for the unspoken but patent tension between his mother and grandmother. In a highly autobiographical short story, Louis writes, "Mother was inclined, as I grew older, to become franker about Father's family, of whom, she used to claim, he was the single star." Even so, Priscilla "loved her sense of the tribe all around and close by," her son observes, "because her idea of the most wonderful thing in the world was a large, close, constantly united family."

Life for the Auchinclosses was, owing to Priscilla's organizational bent, extremely structured. She was disciplined and exact in her daily chores. She rose at 5:00 A.M.; in New York, she took her dogs for a walk; in Maine, she climbed a mountain. Then she went back to bed, where she ate breakfast and made her diary entries. Every morning from eight to nine she summoned the help to direct their activities for the day and telephoned her friends. Meals were served exactly on time. (Much later, Priscilla Auchincloss's highly organized ways irritated her daughters-in-law. Sarah, young Howland's wife, recalls not being able to do the laundry in the Bar Harbor house because doing so was too disruptive to the household's regular routine, and Adèle, Louis's wife, complained of her mother-in-law's always having to do things her own way.) Priscilla filled the later mornings and afternoons with charitable committees and with Junior Fortnightly, of which she was a founder. The women's discussion group was patterned after the Fortnightly, to which her mother belonged, and it still meets regularly; its members include Rockefellers, Choates, and Whitneys. In his 1984 short-story collection, *The Book Class*, Louis used the idea of his mother's group to examine fictionally what sort of power the wives and daughters of New York's old families exerted. Although Junior Fortnightly members did not always discuss books, they held "speculative conversations" on topics such as What books changed your life, What is the aristocracy today, When is it permissible to lie. Their monthly meetings elicited much interest on the part of husbands as to what was said and by whom. Because members, who came to meetings prepared to talk about a specific topic, having been sent postcards in advance, were not only cultivated and educated but were exceptionally strong-minded and -willed individuals, the meetings were lively, stimulating, and much looked forward to.

At home, Priscilla Auchincloss did needlework beautifully, and above all, she read. Louis says she was "a quick and omnivorous reader" and that "her literary opinions were pungent, incisive, always interesting." When he wrote a school paper in which he called the cart that carried Marie Antoinette to her death a "repulsive vehicle," his mother criticized the vague description by saying it might have been a greasy airplane, for all the reader could discern. And to a cousin who spent an entire year building a sailboat so he could write a chapter of his novel in which the protagonist does the same thing, she said, "But don't you know that's the chapter everyone will skip?" "She put her finger on every soggy spot," Louis told an interviewer. "For instance, in *Richelieu*, I was writing the chapter about the Thirty Years War, and I was having difficulty getting it right. 'What's the point of something that people are not going to read?' Mother asked. I said that I could not simply leave out the Thirty Years War altogether, but she said that if a chapter was dull, it ought not to be written."

Fellow Junior Fortnightly members have corroborated Louis's assessment of his mother's literary judgment. One member of thirty years said she always "came out with something fresh and original"; another that "the illumination of her mind lit a candle in our minds." She had not only an acute intellect but a remarkable knowledge of books—history, biography, fiction, poetry (despite her comment that poetry was all "yearning"), and philosophy. At one point, she took a small, privately organized philosophy class with Mrs. Learned Hand and Mrs. Gerrish Miliken, for which they got the distinguished Columbia professor Morris Cohen to lecture to them.

Priscilla Auchincloss passed on a love of reading to her children by reading aloud to them, especially Stevenson and Kipling. On his own, Louis tended to choose less serious books. He collected and read all of the Oz books, all of the Peter Rabbit books, and the complete series of books on Bomba the Jungle Boy, but there is little doubt his mother was responsible for his lifetime love of serious reading, and indirectly for his having become a writer. He himself said, "My relation with her was the second closest that I have had in my life and she had a great deal of influence on my writing."

Actually, she had a powerful influence on him in every way. They were very much alike—both had penetrating intellects, strong wills and personalities; both were witty conversationalists; both were reasonable, practical, and adept at the scathing putdown; they even talked alike (crisply, with a clipped, almost English manner of pronouncing words) and listened alike (calmly and attentively, with a steady, percipient gaze of dark brown, almost black eyes) and looked alike (tall and slender, with high foreheads, strong noses and chins). Both were frugal yet generous. She claimed her son spent his money to increase capital, while she spent hers to enhance living. Yet years after her children were grown, she decided to learn to cook. She hired Alice Lee Meyers, a French-style cook, as instructor. Her first time on her own, she made a chicken dish that even pliable Howland grumbled was a little on the sweet side. "She wouldn't open a bottle of white wine," her daughter-in-law Adèle related, "so she used ginger ale to save money."

As a nephew has observed, "Priscilla and Louis had a marvelous time together, for he was her equal." A close family friend has said, "He was the apple of her eye," another that he was her favorite child. "The other three children never excited Mrs. Auchincloss the way Louis did," a lifelong friend observes, and even his brother Howland concedes that Louis had a bond with his mother that the other children did not share. Louis says he and his mother established a "deep congeniality that was to last to the end, a mutual sympathy and compatibility that made communication a wonderfully simple affair. We noticed the same things and laughed at the same things. We had similar habits of mind and the same ways of leaping to conclusions." When a critic asked Louis how he was able to write about women so believably, he answered:

> It goes all the way back to my childhood. I've never been conscious of temperamental and mental differences between men and women. I was always closer to my mother than I was to my father. I was close to him, too, but it wasn't the same deep intimacy that I had with my mother. I think it goes back very much to her. When an intimacy as solid as that is created, it makes for a bond beyond sexual differences that lasts for a lifetime.

Priscilla Auchincloss was a strict parent, for she saw that as her duty, and as her sister-in-law says, "She was always a great one for doing her duty at all costs." To her, duty encompassed regulating every move of her children. When, in 1928, Louis brought home *The Well of Loneliness*, a novel about lesbianism, she read it, and then it disappeared before Louis could read it. She banned movies, too. Louis went to precious few, though he learned about those he missed from classmates with more permissive parents. "If I wanted to go to a movie, I had to be very, very careful, backward and forward, and bother and bother." She even opened her children's mail and could not understand why they resented this invasion of privacy.

Priscilla Auchincloss's highly developed sense of duty was carried to neurotic extremes when it came to keeping her children safe. She never allowed them to take part in any sport with the least danger, such as skiing and sailing, though these were the favored activities among the young people in their communities. She ruined a summer trip to a ranch in Jackson Hole, Wyoming— taken so the boys could learn to ride horses—by refusing to let them sign up for even one of the overnight pack trips that every other child there regularly went on, confining them instead to the tame, bedraggled horses that no longer had the stamina to stray far from the ranch. "The unknown, the woods, the wilderness, the sea were for her full of images of sudden death for her offspring," according to Louis. Preventing her children from taking even the ordinary risks of life forced them sometimes to withdraw from other children their age, but their mother never acknowledged the damage she might have done to their psyches. "Behind the impressive barricade of her personality lurked a constant state of fear," her son explains. "It was a deep, inner fear that she, Priscilla, might somehow not do her duty in the eyes of undescribed, murky gods and that the lives of her husband and children would be the forfeits. It was, of course, a neurosis . . . but it was so strong that I often marveled it did not wreck her health." Why did Howland not step in and demand more freedom for the children? Partly, he dreaded her irrational fits of anxiety and partly he played the passive role in the marriage. Priscilla was the dominant force in the family.

As obsessed as Priscilla Auchincloss was with her children's safety, she was never one of those mothers who boringly talk of nothing else but children. Like her husband, she was sincerely interested in other people, but, unlike him, she asked searching questions, which sometimes could be intimidating. Even her grandchildren were somewhat frightened by what they came to call "grandma questions," interrogations about what they had learned in school, where they had been, whom they had seen. But she did draw people out. As her nephew has observed, "She would listen carefully and sympathetically; she was good company." Because both Priscilla and Howland were good company, he charming and she brilliant, they enjoyed a pleasant if not very exciting social life, centered on the family, the law partners, and friends from the world of old brownstone New York. When they entertained, it was usually at a dinner party for twelve at home, but sometimes they gave large cocktail parties. In the 1930s, however, their friendship with the four daughters of Walter Damrosch (whose family almost singlehandedly created a taste for classical music in this country) changed the texture of their socializing for the better. They were woven into a much larger New York made up of musicians, actors, producers, writers, artists of all kinds, and, according to their son, "that did more for their social life—Father always admitted that— than anything else." By no means bohemian or radical, the Damrosches were actually moderately conservative in politics and style, but above all, they were attractive, dynamic, very much alive, and through them the Auchinclosses became friendly with Walter Lippmann, a future legal client of their son and model for the protagonist of his novel *The House of the Prophet*.

Not surprisingly, Priscilla Auchincloss had "very firm opinions about people," her sister-in-law has said, "and she could speak sharply if she thought someone was doing the wrong thing," but there was no self-righteousness or complacency about her. According to her family, she judged herself sharply. And she was kind. "She had an uncanny sense of the kernel in every human problem," Louis writes, "and would cut straight through it with sympathy, with wit. She was . . . shrewd, humane, deep." This was why she could give realistic advice. If you were not her child, her nephew says, "She didn't care whether you took her advice or not. If you understood this, she was great fun. I felt free to go to her with my romantic problems." Above all, Priscilla Auchincloss was decisive, brisk, articulate, and alert.

Although Priscilla Auchincloss was a product of old brownstone New York, she exhibited few of the common forms of bigotry prevalent in that milieu in the 1920s. She never cared that Maggie, the children's Irish Catholic nurse, often took young Priscilla and Louis into Catholic churches so she could light a candle and say a prayer. Nor did Priscilla pay heed to the pervasive and stifling anti-

Semitic sentiment that characterized her New York, sending her first two sons to the Bovee School instead of to Buckley or St. Bernard's or Allen-Stevenson. Although Bovee was, according to the *Handbook of the Best Private Schools*, "a school of social standing," it admitted Jewish boys and sons of actors. Louis's contemporaries such as Tommy Craven, son of actor and playwright Frank Craven; Roger Straus, whom Louis remembers as sly and funny; Melcher Ferrer, who dropped the *cher* after he became a famous actor; and Efrem Zimbalist, Jr., son of the famous violinist and future actor, would not have been welcome at other private boys' schools. Bovee had a wonderful New York mix of the children of the great Jewish families with Astors, Auchinclosses, and the children of performing artists. In the 1920s, private schools were proprietary in that they were owned by the headmaster or headmistress, who ran them according to their own lights, with no interference from a board of trustees. Miss Kate Bovee was a woman of enormous personality and strength. She had no intention of being cramped by the inhibitions of brownstone New York. Nor did Priscilla Auchincloss, whose brothers had also attended Bovee.

Although Louis looked on Bovee as a saving grace because it helped him get away from the atrophied, terrible type of anti-Semitism that was predominant in the world his parents lived in, he could not escape that world altogether. He knew, for example, his Jewish friends could not be members of the country club his parents belonged to, but because he loathed country clubs, he rationalized that his friends did not care, either. He also remembers explaining to cousins at his grandparents' Christmas party that his father had sold the Lawrence house because the area had become too Jewish, showing that Howland was by no means free of prevailing prejudice. Yet as a Yale undergraduate, Howland had gotten a Jewish classmate accepted by a non-Jewish fraternity.

Miss Kate Bovee was not only advanced for her time, she ran a good academic program and created a relaxed, pleasant atmosphere. No hazing was permitted among the boys, though hair pulling as a means of discipline by male teachers was allowed. The female teachers did not pull hair. The school, housed in a brownstone on Fifth Avenue just south of Sixty-Fifth Street, faced the arsenal and the Central Park Zoo, so athletics took place in Central Park. The boys played soccer, which bored Louis, but he was allowed to sit on a bench and daydream. Nor did Louis like the exercises devised by Major Smith, a director of the Knickerbocker Grays, who made the boys stand absolutely still without moving a muscle for minutes at a time. Worse, his mother, who had been on the board of the Knickerbocker Grays, enrolled Louis when he was eleven in the private drill class. Every Tuesday and Friday, decked out in the all-gray drill uniform that he had worn to school, Louis joined two hundred other boys to learn close-order drill in the Seventh Regiment Armory at Park Avenue and Sixty-sixth Street. Louis felt painfully conspicuous as he walked in uniform to the armory, especially since his mother insisted on his being accompanied by a nurse. Nor did he much like the drill evolutions and exercises the cadets were instructed in, but fortunately for him, his military interlude was short-lived, as he was soon to be sent to boarding school.

Despite the hated but required sports, the Knickerbocker Grays, and Mrs. Hubbel's dancing class that met every Thursday afternoon in the Colony Club ballroom, these years at Bovee were happy for Louis. For the first time, he was exposed to and entertained opinions about people and life in general that were different from his family's, and this made him feel very grown-up. One of his confidants, Tommy Curtis, had a chauffeured Rolls-Royce that Louis loved to be seen in, and, as he writes in *A Writer's Capital*, he "developed a tiny clique of close, gossipy friends" who "happily made scathing remarks about the more popular boys and teachers." He liked the school enough to fight strenuously against an attempt by his mother to transfer him to St. Bernard's.

Kate Bovee died in 1924 at the end of Louis's first grade year. Her sister Eleanor, whom Louis recalls as "a goose," presided over five years of accelerating decline—exactly Louis's years there— that ceased only when she sold the school in 1929 to a developer. During Eleanor Bovee's five years as headmistress, even the school's pronunciation was changed from Bovee to Bovay to emphasize the Bovee family's French background. "She had a lofty soul and high esthetic ideals," according to Louis, "and the crudity of boys was a source of constant disillusionment to her." To encourage idealism and aestheticism, she offered a Noble Life Prize to the boy who led the noblest life each year. In fact, as Auchincloss recalls in *A Writer's Capital:*

> Miss Eleanor's faith in badges threatened to turn the school into a mint. For a year of perfect attendance and punctuality one received a gold medal. For a year of such perfection marred only by illness, one received a silver medal. For a year marred only by illness or lateness of arrival on Monday mornings caused by the drive into town against the traffic after a country weekend, one received a bronze medal. Three years of a gold medal culminated in a gold watch; three years of a baser metal in a watch of that metal. Two years of gold and one of silver were rewarded with a gold watch with silver trimmings; two of gold and one of bronze—but there was no end of it. It is small wonder that my mother, to my great indignation, kept me home arbitrarily for one day at the beginning of each school year to disqualify me at the outset for either the medal or watch.

Mrs. Auchincloss grew increasingly alarmed by the practices of the Bovee School, and she was justified, for Louis was definitely not prepared for Groton when he arrived in the fall of 1929. She tried to take her son out of Bovee, "protesting that the school was obviously going to pieces," but Louis resisted her so tenaciously that she gave up the idea.

To have let the young Louis have his way when his choice was so decidedly not in his best interest was unusual for Priscilla Auchincloss. An imposing matriarch who constantly worried about duty—and surely her duty included seeing her children well educated—she also felt a strong obligation to family. She taught her children that a sense of family loyalty was self-sustaining and that she and they would be sustained by it. Unquestionably, a sense of belonging to a family, even to a larger group, a tribe, as it were, does support the individual, but even as a young boy, Louis noted the discrepancy between his mother's idealization of the tribe— "Mother tried to see the Dixon family as the ultimate in loyalty and love, Father's partners as idealistic priests of the law, the Morgan bankers as revered symbols of financial wisdom and integrity"—and his perception of the inaccuracy of her evaluations.

> The difficulty was that we lived so uninterruptedly and in such close quarters with the social fabric to which she attached these admirable qualities that I could not help but observe how much more often than not those were lacking. Had my parents sent me to a public school, or even to some private boarding institution in the South or Middle West, had they elected to spend at least their summers away from their own social world, I might have been able to ignore the accuracy or inaccuracy of mother's classifications. But as it was, I was kept with my nose at all times pressed to the pane through which I observed with her the same environment. The family routine of winters in Manhattan and summers at fashionable watering places was never varied while I was little. Nor was the daily club life at Bar Harbor ever interrupted by a camp or camping trip or sailing cruise or even a summer job.

Herein was born the future novelist's strong sense of irony that permeates everything he writes and accounts for his simultaneous insider-outsider view of the world he grew up in and never left. In contrasting the "silly side" of fashionable life (its scandals, the all-too-apparent material blessings of so many inhabitants, the gossip of the social scene) with his parents' view that the "silly social types" were "utterly ridiculous" and "the worthy people in Maine and Long Island so worthy," Louis found the glitz and glamour far more interesting than "innate decency" and "high moral standards." From his observations, he developed a sense that whatever he enjoyed was judged bad and what he hated, especially sports, was good. All his life, his brother John remembered Louis's protesting over and over when their mother promoted some activity she deemed good for him, "But do I have to enjoy it?"

Weekends and early summer weeks at the spacious white frame Lawrence beach house were pure enjoyment for the young Louis. Life there was simple and unstructured. He and his sister could entertain themselves as they chose. Most days, they went to the Lawrence Beach Club to play in the breakers, which they liked. But during the first week of 1927, his parents moved to Locust Valley and the only home they built. Louis did not like the move to the North Shore. Locust Valley was a richer and more social town than Lawrence, and Louis found it a good deal less friendly, as well. Worse, he had to attend a boys' athletic class there. His mother was elated: "Oh, how wonderful! Something for Louis to do in the daytime." So every morning from nine to twelve, he played baseball or practiced calisthenics, all very mild he remembers today, but he hated it and prayed for rain so class would be canceled. When a well-meaning woman from Oyster Bay who had a gymnasium on her property offered it to the boys on rainy days, even that occasional liberation disappeared. Locust Valley provided little escape from the structure of sports, but the social scene intrigued Louis, to his parents' horror.

> I observed that often the only interesting thing about some of the families near whom we lived was their wealth. I saw perfectly that their big houses, their shining cars, and their glittering yachts were designed to impress just such onlookers as myself. And I began to see that there was diversion and interest in the rivalries of the social game. When I bubbled over at the family board with snobbish observations and gossip about our wealthy neighbors, Mother and Father were genuinely astounded and depressed.

Similar social diversions were as readily available at Bar Harbor, a place Louis found more congenial than Locust Valley, for here were no athletic classes (only tennis, which he enjoyed) and lots of friends. "Our living wasn't anything like the scale going on around us," Howland junior observes, "but Louis was interested in the wealthy people, and he'd talk amusingly about them." Sister Priscilla recalls Louis's love of the stylish cars their neighbors drove. "He knew all their makes and their cost, a lot more than the Buicks we drove. He'd keep after Mother to get a job so we could have a Rolls or a Hispano-Suiza." Fascinated by the social game, Louis admits he sought "all the drama I could find in the wealth and greed that surrounded us."

Yet Louis understood that this delicious drama was not for consumption outside the family—even though ironically his mother told him the best stories, as "she could see every stain and wart"—nor was it to be emulated. His life must be an earnest one that began with boarding school and culminated in professional life. He intuited this fate from his parents, and he did not look forward to it. He remembers, for example, going to the Cedarhurst Railroad Station with his mother to meet his father's New York train early every summer evening when they still owned the Lawrence house. He felt his father "was coming back to us a poor driven man, a hostage from the inexorable city that made a dull misery of the lives of men. And clinging to him, loving him, I felt that this would be my fate, too, and that it was a bond between us." And he writes of the first time his father showed him his office:

> He meant it to be fun. He got quite excited pointing out the buildings. There was Morgan's, there was the stock exchange, there was Wall Street itself. Never shall I forget the horror that was inspired in me by those dark narrow streets and those tall sooty towers and by Trinity Church blocking the horizon with its black spire—a grim phallic symbol.

Granted, Auchincloss the man is writing about childhood impressions from the vantage point of maturity, but that makes them no less real. Louis looked on his mother's lot as far happier than his father's. His mother stayed home all day, telephoning friends and reading great books; his father spent all day downtown doing "dull, soul-breaking things" to support his family.

> I shuddered at the future my parents seemed to offer. The happiness of life, according to them, or according to my perverse interpretation of their philosophy, would consist in undergoing the strain and boredom of an overworked existence in order to provide funds for the large noisy family whose function in turn was to provide solace and consolation to the father who was giving up his life for it.

The contrast between a life Louis judged to be exciting and happy, dim though the specifics of this life were, and the life he was expected to pursue gave birth to tensions and ambivalences that were not resolved until he went through psychoanalysis in the 1950s.

On April 22, 1929, Howland Auchincloss submitted Louis's application to the Reverend Endicott Peabody, headmaster of Groton School. Five short months later, Louis went to Groton to begin "to learn the dusty task of being a man."

CHAPTER 3

Boarding School

I spent six years in a New England church boarding school considered one of the finest in the land (the same attended by President Franklin Roosevelt a generation earlier) and learned a great deal about the arrogance and insularity of the business and banking class that before the New Deal dominated the commerce of the nation.

LOUIS AUCHINCLOSS

T he Groton Louis had so dreaded turned out to be worse than he had imagined. From the moment the frightened eleven-year-old kissed his mother good-bye, on the stairway in the headmaster's house, he was unhappy. He was not much comforted by the presence of his brother John—kindly, solicitous, but as a sixth former, a remote figure to a raw first former such as Louis. Louis had a cousin, Gordon Auchincloss, who was also a first former, but Gordon proved no comrade-in-arms. He had come to Groton from Buckley, a more prestigious school than Bovee and one that sent so many students to Groton, Priscilla Auchincloss was moved to asked Dr. Peabody whether it might "become necessary in the future to limit the number of candidates accepted from any one school." Right from the start, the boys from Buckley stuck together, snubbing the two boys from Bovee, Louis and Rivington Pyne (who did not last long at Groton). Nor was being ignored by the Buckley boys the worst, for they soon turned overtly antagonistic. From the day his cousin introduced himself to

Louis and then promptly pushed him into the mud, Louis became the victim of what he later called "this stuffy little group of snooty, cruel boys." When he made the fatal error of snitching on two classmates, he earned the contempt of the whole form.

Soon after school began, as he and the two form mates walked the two miles to Groton village, which they were allowed to do once a week to buy candy and ice cream with their weekly twenty-five-cent allowance, they threw stones at a passing train and inadvertently broke a window. The engineer called the Rector, as headmaster Endicott Peabody was called, to accuse Groton boys of the crime, whereupon Dr. Peabody quizzed the school. Right away, Louis admitted guilt.

"I did it, sir."

"You did?" the Rector asked, surprised that a Groton boy had committed such an act. "Were there any other boys with you?"

"Yes, sir. Biddle and Bigelow were with me," Louis volunteered with a swift and spontaneous honesty that would characterize him throughout his life. "It no more occurred to me to withhold those names," he explained much later, "than it would occur to a resurrected body to equivocate with Jehovah on the Day of Judgment."

From that moment, Louis was singled out for persecution that did not let up all year. Reviled as a tattletale, he was sneered at, his books were flung in the mud, his face shoved in the snow, and he was hit on the head, his hat knocked off and thrown in a puddle. For his fastidiousness, he was called "Louise" and "Rebecca," which was sometimes shortened to "Becky." So incessant was the daily hazing that Louis later likened getting around the Groton campus then to walking down a New York street at night now: "You have one eye out for a mugger." Only once did he cry. At a party in his dormitory one night, he was pelted with ice cream, and in trying to protect himself, he lost his bite plate and burst into tears. Gurnee Gallien, the dormitory master, sent the boys to bed and got down on his hands and knees to look for the bite plate, which he found. Incredibly, Louis did not complain about his treatment, not even in the required weekly letters home, because he accepted Groton as the test he had to take and pass to reach manhood.

* * *

The Reverend Endicott Peabody founded Groton as a church school in 1884, shortly after his ordination as an Episcopal priest. Its Gothic-style chapel, where compulsory daily and Sunday services were conducted, dominated the ninety-acre campus and its redbrick buildings—a dormitory known as Hundred House (because it could sleep one hundred boys), a classroom building called Brooks House (after Bishop Phillips Brooks, who had influenced the young Peabody to give up business and enter the Episcopal Theological Seminary in Cambridge, Massachusetts), and a gymnasium—arranged around a circle shaded by great elms on a wide ridge overlooking the Nashua River and hills and mountains beyond.

Groton and Endicott Peabody seemed synonymous to most people; he made the school in his image by virtue of his dominant nature and purposefulness. Even Theodore Roosevelt called him the most powerful personality he had ever encountered, and Franklin Roosevelt claimed that apart from his mother, Peabody was the strongest influence in his life. None of the other headmasters, and this was the era of great headmasters—Samuel Drury of St. Paul's, William Greenough Thayer of St. Mark's, Frank Boyden of Deerfield—ever attained the fame of Endicott Peabody of Groton. He utterly dominated the school, the many strong men who served on his faculty, his board of trustees, all powerful men themselves, and, of course, the students. "I don't think I ever met a man who radiated such absolute authority," Auchincloss has said. Moreover, he was physically large, a handsome six-footer with piercing gray eyes, a fine, narrow nose, and rugged square jaw—in short, a commanding figure who could be very dramatic when the occasion called for it. When Auchincloss delivered Groton's centennial address in 1984, he gave a personal illustration of how in awe of the Rector even his father's generation had been.

My father and brother, John, and I, all graduates of the school [discussed] at John's wedding reception, which of us should have the delicate task of offering the Rector an emolument for performing the ceremony. None of us knew how to do this; could one *tip* the Rector? I argued that John, as the groom, was the obvious choice. He retorted that it was clearly a "job" for the best man. Then we joined forces to gang up on Father who, we insisted, as senior graduate, must rank us both. Poor Father approached the Rector in fear and trembling only to be put instantly at ease when he felt the firm hand take the check from the clenched fist and heard the deep voice mutter: "That's all right, Howland. I always put it in the chapel fund."

Unquestionably, the Rector had great charm and was likable, some said lovable, but only to those who agreed with him, though not in any narrow sense. The eminent sculptor George Rickey, who was a history master part of the time Louis was at Groton, told the story of his initial interview with Dr. Peabody.

"Rickey, do you believe in God?" the Rector asked. The young Rickey, penniless at the time, needed the job badly, but he answered, "No, sir, I do not."

"Would you feel obliged to tell the boys that?" the Rector continued.

"No, sir, I should not."

He got the job.

Like a benevolent dictator, the Rector managed every detail of his school his way for more than half a century, even to decreeing its colors—red, black, and white—the same that had flown from his ancestors' ships in Salem harbor. He would have made a top corporate chief executive officer, for he handled masses of paperwork with dispatch, making rapid decisions and keeping his desk clean. He thought nothing of changing his mind when he felt he was wrong. As Auchincloss, quoting another graduate, George Martin, has said, "He never spent any time or effort proving he was right yesterday; he simply went on to the next thing. He never tried to get even with anybody or bore a grudge. Thus he saved so much time that his life appeared almost leisurely." Yet he was always occupied. He had a wife (his first cousin) and six children, he taught, he administered, and he preached, not especially well, the daily chapel service, hammering away at the same themes: obligation of service, sacredness of family life, love of God, love of one's fellowman, and ideals of purity. Although his sermons were predictable and poorly organized, the way he continually sawed the air with his hand, saying, "You see, boys," kept the students awake.

Intent upon preparing his boys for life and not just for college, the Rector insisted on having his charges a minimum of five years, although most came for six. In that time, he hoped to foster numerous vocations to the Episcopal priesthood, but in this he was disappointed, which is not surprising given the composition of his student body. The school drew primarily from prominent old Boston and New York families—Morgans (J. P. Morgan had helped finance Groton), Whitneys, Gardners, Roosevelts, Livingstons, Harrimans, Webbs, McCormicks, Crockers, Stillmans, Higginsons, Coolidges, and their sons and grandsons. The influence the families exerted on their sons and that they, in turn, exercised in the banks and boardrooms of the nation made the school good training for business, but not, certainly, a breeding ground for the religious life. As David Halberstam wrote in his 1973 bestseller, *The Best and the Brightest,* "The overt teaching was that the finest life is service to God, your family and your state, but the covert teaching, far more subtle and insidious, was somewhat different: ultimately, strength is more important; there is a ruling clique; there is a thing called privilege and you might as well use it. That is the real world and it is going to remain that way, so you might as well get used to it." Parents sent their sons to Groton to make friends with the right people, for these connections served well later on Wall Street and in Washington. No one sent a boy to Groton to become a priest.

As early as 1938, a mere three years after graduation, Louis showed in an unpublished novel he wrote at Yale that he understood "the central problem of all New England Protestant church schools of [Peabody's] day was the conflict between the piety and idealism of their inspirers and the crass materialism of the families from which they drew not only their students but their endowments. I found some evidence that Dr. Peabody, in retirement, had come to a troubled awareness of this dichotomy; but during the bulk of his entire life I am sure that, beyond a mild disappointment that so few of his graduates went into the church and so many into the stock market, he was happily unconscious of how far his reach had exceeded his grasp." This realization, in fact, was the inspiration for one of Auchincloss's finest novels, *The Rector of Justin*.

Endicott Peabody also regretted that so few of his boys entered public service. Again, this is not surprising, since the United States, unlike Great Britain, lacked an upper-class tradition of public service. Rich men in the United States tended to look with suspicion upon young men of intelligence and training who turned to public life. Groton provided a good illustration of this tendency. By the time Louis graduated, only ten out of the one thousand graduates of the fifty-year-old school had ever served in government; the notable exception, Franklin Roosevelt, was hated by the predominantly Republican businessmen who sent their sons to Groton. The fictional Rector of Justin partly blames Peabody for their attitude. "A man who considers that Theodore Roosevelt was America's greatest statesman and *In Memoriam* England's finest poem is [only] equipped to train young men for the steam room of the Racquet Club." When a young master points to FDR to undercut the clergyman's criticism, the Rector "roared with laughter," certain that "ninety percent of the Grotties" wish he had ended up in the steam room, "and evaporated there!" Although the Rector's assessment of the school's politics is fictional, it is entirely accurate. In a 1939 memoir of Groton for *Harper's Magazine*, George Biddle told of attending a dinner for Dr. Peabody at the Union Club in New York. At the end of an hour-long address that had been liberally punctuated with laughter and applause, the Rector made this statement.

> Something has troubled me a good deal lately. Personally I don't pretend to know much about politics or economics. But in national crises like the present one, we get pretty excited and perhaps we give vent to expressions that later on we are sorry for. I believe Franklin Roosevelt to be a gallant and courageous gentleman. I am happy to count him as my friend.

His tribute to one of his "boys" was met with complete silence. Even Louis admits in his own memoir of his school days that spotting FDR's cortege during the 1936 campaign, he waved a Landon sunflower as the presidential Packard sped by. In revealing his anti-Roosevelt sentiment, he reflects the prevailing politics of Groton in the 1930s. A history of his form prepared for the 1935 yearbook provides evidence of this. "The 1932 presidential campaign was in full swing. Blair's speeches [William McCormick Blair, cousin of Colonel Robert McCormick, publisher of the *Chicago Tribune*] carried most of the school on a wave of Hoover enthusiasm. Hoover was on every tongue, and a poor thing indeed was a coat lapel of those days which did not display a dozen or two Hoover buttons, made in Chicago."

Not only was the student body more secular than spiritual and more mercantile than political, it was inbred, and this, inadvertently, was the Rector's doing. Because Endicott Peabody wanted his school to be a family, he never admitted more than 180 students. When Louis entered Groton in 1929, the school was forty-five years old and fully two-thirds of its students were sons of graduates. Louis was the eighth Auchincloss to attend. Worse, most of the boys came from New York and Boston, and many, having attended the same primary schools, had known one another before boarding school. The Rector's persistence in keeping the school familylike and thus small, coupled with this goal of attracting graduates' sons and grandsons, resulted in a student body that came from the same narrow social circle. Moreover, most Grotties, as they came to be called, were Episcopalians, at least in name, some were Presbyterians, but none were Roman Catholics or Jews.

From the time Dr. Peabody met the first formers in sacred

studies, to their daily afternoon tea in his house as sixth formers, he got to know everything about his boys and their families, and he never forgot, following them throughout their lives and careers by sending annual birthday wishes, appropriate congratulations and condolences, and sometimes even criticisms, by marrying them, and by christening their children. This cozy brotherhood is what made Groton different from other boarding schools and what prompted outsiders to call it the most exclusive in the country. Certainly Groton was the smallest of the best New England preparatory schools. Andover and Exeter were five times Groton's size and therefore better able to diversify their student bodies. At St. Paul's, the oldest and largest of the Episcopal schools, Drury, unlike Peabody, kept apart from the students; and at Kent and Deerfield, boys made their own beds and waited on tables. St. Mark's, Groton's great football rival, was closest in size and spirit to Peabody's school, probably because the great man had taught there for a short time. During Louis's years at the school, Groton was much written about, owing to the presidency of Franklin Roosevelt, class of 1900. Noting Roosevelt's patrician manner, but ignoring his obvious egalitarianism, the press tagged Groton a school for snobs. While it is true the "best" New York and Boston families sent their sons to Groton, it is questionable whether the school or the families deserved the reputation. Writing to Priscilla Auchincloss about Groton's public image, Endicott Peabody said he thought most outsiders misunderstood

> our view in regard to social eligibility. As a matter of fact, up to the time that we began to prefer sons of graduates, we received boys as they were placed on our register. We did not consider the social position of their parents in any way. Now that we are preferring the graduates' sons, the boys are supposedly in the same class with their parents. In our competitive examination, there has never been the slightest attention paid to society. Friends may write to us commending their friends and other friends' sons, but we pay attention only to the views expressed of their characters.

The fictional Rector of Justin, however, declares categorically that the private schools are riddled with snobbishness, "a cancer in America because we pretend it's not there and let it grow until it's inoperable. In England it's less dangerous because it's out in the open. In fact, they glory in it."

Cotty Peabody, as his contemporaries called him, was not a snob, though his own background included wealth and social prominence: He came from the prominent mercantile Peabodys of Salem and was named for his distinguished ancestor John Endicott, an early governor of the Massachusetts Bay Colony. Dr. Peabody cared most for integrity, and he believed he could best instill this quality in his boys in a small school, which is why, although he created Groton in the image of Eton, Harrow, and his own alma mater, Cheltenham, he steadfastly resisted increasing his student body to match their much larger sizes. In this way, no Groton boy escaped his watchful eye or authoritarian and moralistic influence.

*　　*　　*

Once a boy arrived at the beginning of a term, he was there to stay until the end. Groton issued no weekend passes. Even the boys from Boston, just thirty miles to the east, escaped only for a few hours on Thanksgiving Day. This little isolated community did everything as a group: They worked together, they played together, they prayed together, and they ate together. Meals were served in Hundred House. The Rector and Mrs. Peabody presided over the raised head table, which was usually set for twelve. The rest of the school ate at long tables seating nine or ten on a side, with a master or a prefect (one of a handful of sixth formers singled out by the Rector to help keep discipline) at each end. If a master was married, his wife sat next to him. Once a week, each boy moved one place but kept the same boys on either side of him. Only the face across the table changed.

From the time the boys rose in the early morning for their daily cold shower before breakfast until they bid the Rector good night, they were never alone. No students could enter the dormitories except when getting ready for meals—stiff white collars and black patent leather pumps were required for dinner—or going to bed, times when everyone else was there. Even the toilets, which were partitioned off from one another, had no doors. As Oliver LaFarge wrote in *Raw Material,* his 1945 memoir of life at Groton, "one could get fragments of a sense of being alone by sticking one's head inside his desk or locker, but only for a moment."

Not only were the boys never alone, they followed a daily regimen not unlike cloistered monks. Bells started at 6:50 A.M., which was rising hour, and continued off and on all day, including Saturday, until the older boys' bed hour at 10:00 P.M. Each boy slept in a six-by-nine cubicle sparely furnished with a narrow, hard bed, a bureau, a chair, and six hooks for the mandatory classroom attire of coats and ties. In the lavatory, he had a small space reserved for him in front of a black soapstone watering trough lined with cold-water taps, his own tin basin, and three more hooks. Hot water had to be awkwardly drawn from a bathtub. Following breakfast, the boys went to chapel, then to classes. There were five classes a day except on Wednesdays and Saturdays, when there were only four. All the boys did daily calisthenics and had to participate in sports.

Football was king. "I am convinced," the Rector wrote in 1909, "that football is of profound importance for the moral even more than the physical development of the boys. In these days of exceeding comfort the boys need an opportunity to endure hardness and, it may be, suffering." It was a matter of school pride that a one-armed student willingly played the game. Football, not to mention baseball, rowing, basketball, boxing, wrestling, fencing, fives (an English form of handball), even the daily calisthenics, made Louis suffer. Not only was he a clumsy and awkward participant, he disliked sports, at least those available at Groton. Boys did not have to excel in sports to be popular, but at least they had to like them. Louis's form mates considered his noninterest, of which he made no secret, effeminate, and they taunted him mercilessly for it. Nevertheless, there was no escaping football in the fall—until sixth form, that is—and baseball or rowing in the spring, or the daily calisthenics, or any of the other prescribed group activities that made up a Groton boy's day. (Louis got out of football fifth-form year because he had had typhoid fever the preceding summer, though he had to keep producing certificates explaining his absence from practice. When the Rector confronted him by saying, "You must be over that typhoid by now," Louis produced yet another excuse. "I found a nice, old doctor in Bar Harbor who'd give me anything I wanted.")

"Fun was defined in terms of group activities such as football or singing or even praying," Louis wrote more than three decades later, describing the fictional Justin Martyr; "the devil lay in wait for the boy alone, or worse, for two boys alone. The headmaster believed that adolescence should be passed in an organized crowd, that authority should never avert its eyes unless the boys were engaged in fighting or hazing or some other activity savage enough to be classified as 'manly.' "

This relentless group living made Louis long for solitude; he wondered why some people complained of loneliness, when all he wanted was to be alone. Only after lights out, when he was safely in his cubicle, was he free from his schoolmates' ridicule, for no boy was allowed to enter another's cubicle. Although there was only a curtain across the doorway, and the surrounding walls reached only seven feet, leaving vacant space to the ceiling, he was alone. "Then, bit by bit, the whole being can relax from the constant tension of the day," Oliver LaFarge wrote about his own release from schoolboy taunts. "Bed and sleep acquired a new preciousness, for here was surcease and escape."

Louis found other escapes, too. Whenever he could, he hid away for an hour or two on Sundays in the school library, reading old *Punch* magazines, looking at cartoons, or reading novels about the French Revolution. Recurrent colds sent him scurrying to the infirmary, a sanctuary so appealing that he was not above touching his thermometer to a light bulb to keep his temperature safely above 98 degrees. But his big escape in first form was to New York to have his tonsils removed. Tonsillitis sent him home twice—in early April with swollen glands and a few weeks later for a full month, during which he was tutored every afternoon in his parents' Park Avenue penthouse apartment by a former Bovee master. His tonsils were removed in mid-May to allow him plenty of time to recover before the family's trip in July to a Wyoming ranch. But before the summer holiday, Louis had to return to Groton and his tormentors, which he did without complaint.

His mother suspected all was not well at school and talked to her son about going elsewhere. He was, he wrote later, "scandalized and actually frightened at the prospect of such defeat." He refused to admit to her how bad his situation was, because he had intuited from the way she handled her own life that suffering Groton was what was expected of him. After all, he reasoned, his mother's brilliance and strong personality should never have been confined to family and friends, but they were because Priscilla Auchincloss saw such behavior as her duty, her fate. Just as she had to act in certain ways because she was a woman, so too he must do certain things to become a man. So he accepted what was done to him at Groton because it was the system. As he explains today, his mother was a "fellow prisoner. We were in the same kind of trap. . . . She was trying to show me that this is the only way to live. She was on my side, telling me how to deal with the world of Groton. 'Darling, we're going to have to live in this world. Let me show you, this is the way to do it.' " Not until ten years after graduation from Groton did he acknowledge these feelings in a letter to his mother.

> I never turned over much to you because I felt that Groton was
> something one *had* to get through, that it was part of the cruel
> fabric of life on which you, sympathetic but helpless, were
> similarly impaled. . . . I never thought I could be taken out of
> Groton; to fail there was to fail in life. And when I one time
> broke down and drank mercurochrome (spelling!) to make my-
> self sick so I wouldn't have to go back and you saw red on my
> tongue, I told you I had been sucking on my tie (which was
> red). I could never admit the shame of what seemed the equiv-
> alent of suicide.

After a family summer holiday in Locust Valley, Wyoming, and Bar Harbor, John Auchincloss entered Yale as a freshman and Louis returned to Groton as a second former, feeling a little more grown-up, having finally and permanently relinquished knickers for "longs." He returned full of determination to make his life there better, but life for him got much, much worse.

Because Bovee had inadequately prepared him for the academic rigor of boarding school, he had done poorly in first form. Then, after missing more than a month of classes, he had fallen further behind. He might have survived second form anyway, had he not been placed in Fritz De Veau's A-level Latin class. Every day, Louis got a zero, "which made [his] line in Mr. De Veau's grade book appear, as he mockingly put it, 'like a chain across the page.' " Louis dreaded Latin class, waiting "in dumb misery" for the inevitable, invariable dry comment " 'another goose egg, Auchincloss.' " That such humiliation happened in Latin was more significant than if it had occurred in a science class, for example. The Groton curriculum, close to Thomas Arnold's Rugby model, was heavily weighted toward the classics (Latin and Greek) and modern languages (German and French). There were classes in mathematics, science, history, and sacred studies, but they were secondary to Latin. If Louis did not improve, he would have to drop back a form. The thought of an extra year at Groton galvanized him into action. Now he did confide in his mother, begging her to intercede for him with the Rector to allow him to take the B-level Latin class. Although the Rector was opposed to moving Louis, Priscilla Auchincloss convinced him that it was better "to try it Louis's way" than to put him back a form. So Louis went to B-level Latin, and he did well. By the end of the second form, having catapulted from the bottom of his class in September to fifth place in June, Louis realized that he had "a key at last that fitted the Groton lock, the key of marks."

For the next four years, Louis turned himself into a grade grind, determined to make a more dignified mark on his form than as "Becky." "Louis demanded respect," a classmate remembers. "He made everyone in the form take admiring notice, and he did this by conforming not to the Groton model but to his own." During most of third form, he vied academically with William Bundy (the future assistant secretary of defense under Kennedy and assistant secretary of state under Johnson) for first place, which he achieved in May and June. By fourth form, he was first all year, but in fifth form, he fell back behind Bundy, finishing in second place. In his last year, Marshal Hornblower, who had been third all along, now jumped ahead of Bundy to first place, leaving Louis in third place. Even so, Louis won the English essay and French prizes, and he graduated magna cum laude.

Not only did he better his grades, he started taking part in extracurricular activities. He joined the Civics Club, Missionary Society, choir, library volunteer staff, debating team (on which he won a book on English usage donated by alumnus Franklin Roosevelt), and the Dramatic Association, becoming its president in his last year. His performances in *The Pickwick Papers* and *The Would-be Gentleman* were highly praised in the Groton yearbook. Only his membership on the editorial board of *The Grotonian*, the school's literary magazine, engendered any lasting enthusiasm. Between his fourth- and sixth-form years, Louis published eleven stories, eight editorials, and four book reviews. He served on the magazine's editorial board, and was editor-in-chief as a sixth former. He had also written two stories that were published during his third-form year. "At Groton," Louis told an interviewer, "I wrote a story on the French Revolution (I was 14) for a thing called *The Third Form Weekly*. It was published in the boy's magazine and my interest in writing has never completely dissipated since."

Louis had started writing about the French Revolution and its causes and effects even before he entered Groton, when he composed a play in two acts about Louis XV's mistress, Countess du Barry. Groton, which seemed to him very like Louis XIV's Versailles, "with students and teachers bowing to the headmaster: a close community with a strong central figure," rekindled his interest in French history. The France of the Bourbons inspired two stories ("The Futility of Prophesy" and "Versailles"), one editorial (in which he used contrasting experiences of French Revolutionary figures to illustrate how to enjoy periods of "titanic transition"), and one book review (about Marie Antoinette). This fascination with France has lasted throughout his life. In 1973, Auchincloss published an account of Richelieu's life; in 1981, he wrote a fictional rendering of Saint-Simon's life at Versailles, as well as two essays about the second Duc de Saint-Simon, which appeared in *Reflections of a Jacobite* in 1961 and in *Life, Law and Letters* in 1979. Nothing else from Louis's Groton publications carried over to his mature writing. The stories, replete with suns that "frown," swallows that "dart hither and thither," and sparrows that "flutter about," are, by his own admission, undistinguished. On the other hand, his book reviews demonstrate informed and attentive reading. "It seems impossible that anyone could write an original life of Marie Antoinette, the subject of so much dissent, but to a large extent Stefan Zweig has succeeded in doing this. . . . Throughout the book he insists that she was an average woman, cast by fate into a role with which she could not cope, but which she at least managed to handle with redeeming dignity during the terrible revolutionary years." So, too, the editorials, discounting an occasional pompous tone, are, for the most part, sensible, encouraging students to scrutinize the reproductions of great art that adorned the halls so that when they found themselves at the Louvre or the National Gallery, as Louis had the summer before the editorial, they could savor the delight of recognition.

Despite his academic and literary accomplishments, Louis never achieved the same status as an athlete. The students respected grades to a degree, but certainly not articles in *The Grotonian*. Neither the athletes nor the Rector read the literary magazine. Dr. Peabody had little interest in or use for any of the arts, believing it was better for a man to be part of his times than an observer of them. Louis Auchincloss remained an eccentric in the eyes of his form mates. He had a funny, almost English way of speaking, they thought. Ten years out of Groton, Louis related a story to his mother that shows he was aware of how different he sounded to his schoolmates. When his World War II troop transport was in California for repairs, two naval captains came aboard to inspect his ship. As they were leaving, one asked, "Groton?" and the other, "Yale?" "Both!" Louis answered in astonishment. "My 'accent' is what the world thinks of as Groton, whereas at Groton I was much kidded for it." Even his dress—double-breasted suits from De Pinna's rather than the more fashionable single-breasted Brooks Brothers or Rogers Peet style—and his gait—"he didn't stride the way boys usually do, but he walked with a swinging motion"— made him conspicuous. "Louis has style," a former history master has said; "he was slightly an aesthete but awfully likable and bright." The teacher's remark suggests even fifty years later the attitude that made Groton so difficult for Louis. Nevertheless, by unyielding enterprise (aided by his innate gregariousness and developing sense of the ridiculous), he achieved a certain respectability, but at a considerable price.

Ten years after Louis's graduation, Oliver LaFarge wrote a memoir that incorporated *his* experiences at Groton. Priscilla Auchincloss sent the book to Louis, who was at the time the commanding officer of an LST in the Pacific. The book bowled him over, and he wrote LaFarge to explain why.

I feel I must write you because I think one must write an author to whom one is indebted. Your chapter, "The Dream," in *Raw Material* has altered my entire concept of my childhood, and I am quite sure that this was not a healthy concept. You say you were 38 before you were freed of Groton; perhaps you have freed me at 28. But I was in a worse state; I didn't even *know* that the little school had bitten me so deep. When I read your dream I sat bolt upright. I have experienced that and know that it's as bad as anything in war, the terrible sense of being back amid the varnished walls surrounded by boys who are waiting to kill the smallest aspiration. And the mask! That is what I want to thank you for. I think I would have paid a psychologist a large sum for your paragraph on page 20 about the mask. The sense of being a fraud that worried me. . . . — Why, of course, it's *Groton's* heritage! I was bitterly unpopular for three years there. I had no friends; I was a hopeless athlete;

my marks were abysmal. Yet I never thought of leaving. . . .
Father had been to Groton; so had my brother, John. I had to
work it out. I turned myself into a grind and slaved until in my
fourth year I led not only my form (in marks) but the school. I
made a cult of despising the despisers. I even sneered at athletes. Later I became the Editor of the Grotonian and President of the Dramat. The family shouted that "I had found
myself," that Groton had taught me the battle of life. I believed it myself for awhile. But, oh, how clear my [tormentors]
(I had two who were dedicated to my destruction) made it that
this sort of success did not make me a "real" person. I knew I
was the same person and they reminded me of it. And the
mask persisted. You may have helped me to remove it altogether.

You see, I thought I liked Groton. I see now that it filled
me with a reactionary intellectual snobbishness (my only answer to the Groton clique). . . . But I returned several times
to Groton. I adored Dr. Peabody; I used to write to him; at
school I became an Episcopalian because it was his church. I
used to go to his study and talk to him about prayer (you see
why I was so loved by my form!). Now, until your book no one
has ever (to my knowledge) written about school without writing about him. . . . If I could only have my pictures of the
Rector without the picture of the school—well, maybe I can.
The world thinks of them in the same breath—but the world
is always wrong. I believe now that the Rector was a saint and
the school his smallest achievement. . . . He created a robot
that perhaps got out of hand. The "Groton" boy was never
what he wanted. It was a strange distortion of his vision of the
spiritual life. Teddy Roosevelt and not Peabody was the father
of the Groton the world knows.

Yet Endicott Peabody had so admired Theodore Roosevelt
that he had asked him to be one of the founding masters of Groton.
Roosevelt refused, saying he preferred to go west. Theodore Roosevelt sent his sons to Groton, though, and as the twenty-sixth

President, he delivered the prize-day address to the form of 1904, the year of Howland Auchincloss's graduation. When Roosevelt said, "I believe with all my heart in athletics," he was only echoing the Rector's own strong conviction. Roosevelt had also influenced his cousin Franklin to go to Groton, which he did as a member of the form of 1900. FDR, in turn, sent his four sons to Groton (two were there at the same time as Louis). And when *he* was President, he delivered the fiftieth anniversary prize-day address in 1934, Louis's fifth-form year. Louis was enormously impressed by the arrival of a President of the United States at the school. "He was the first of our chiefs of state to travel in the imperial style, as is done today, and he arrived with a long motorcade and much blowing of horns, as the whole school turned out on the Circle to greet him. 'Ah,' I cried to myself. '*That* is how *I* want to come back to Groton.' " But such dreams of grandeur were far from his thoughts after reading LaFarge's Groton reminiscences. After thanking LaFarge for "lifting his mask," he wrote his mother.

> I don't know when I've read anything that has had a more profound effect on me. I feel as if after a decade of illusion the scales had dropped from my eyes, and now I see Groton as the stifling institution it inherently is. . . . All my strivings to get to the top of the school, editor of *The Grotonian*, etc., was the most elementary type of psychological revenge. . . . I know other schools may share the guilt, but the peculiar smallness and tightness of Groton makes it far worse. We had no business there. Poor John bore it all meekly, but do you think it had nothing to do with his austerity? Those five years of steady lack of appreciation? And Howlie who was always sneered at? [Louis's younger brother, Howland junior arrived at Groton as a first former when Louis was a fifth.] It didn't help, I suppose, that you and Father ranged yourselves so solidly behind the system. *Every* time you came up I remember so distinctly the *constant* repetitions on your part: "It *is* a wonderful school, isn't it?" And "The Rector *is* a great man." Of course, that was only your own distrust and old desire for reassurance. . . . Deep

down we *knew* it was odd to go to schools like Groton. But have I ever dared to face this?

And the vanity of our tiny group! We tell each other all this is essential to a child's sense of independence. He must learn to stand on his own feet! It's like teaching a child to walk by knocking him down. . . . But if one at last sees it clearly, it's all right. I sincerely believe that Groton was bad for me; it extended my ego by constant smashing at it. . . . As a family our atmosphere was faulty by a persistent effort, led by the parents, to see our environment in its finest light. We learned to see financiers in the light of their "responsibilities" rather than their materialism, and it was with business that we were surrounded. And even in Dr. Peabody I can now see harshness and intolerance. For they were in him.

Louis's ambivalence toward the Rector ten years out of Groton—on the one hand, writing LaFarge that Peabody was a saint, and on the other, telling his mother the Rector could be harsh and intolerant—might have surprised the young man who graduated in 1935. At that time, he wrote a letter thanking Dr. Peabody for his communion lectures—"helpful and a real source of inspiration"—and for creating his school—"a perfect whole in itself with neither too much nor too little of anything. . . . When I think of the school I think of you and Mrs. Peabody. It is impossible to disassociate the two ideas. I owe you more than I can possibly know myself."

Yet even in that 1935 letter Louis gave way to reservations, indicting the compulsory football and the awful hazing to which he had been subjected—a boy "may be impertinent as a result of not being beaten up, but it's ever so much better to be an objectionable boy than a miserable boy." In time, he came to view the headmaster's single-minded emphases on discipline, athletics, religion, and school spirit as an impediment to creativity. Granted, during Louis's own school days, Dr. Peabody allowed Robert Tilney to build and fly a glider, Cornelius Roosevelt to restore and drive a Stanley Steamer, and Quentin Roosevelt to rig and operate a ham radio, and granted, one of Groton's cofounders, William.

Amory Gardner (who died during Louis's first form), built a small building behind Hundred House that he called a Treasure Dome, to which he invited boys for "google," a kind of fruit drink. But while these out-of-the-ordinary pursuits were occasionally condoned, "sensitive young men like Louis, who did not fill the Rector's criteria and thus got *no encouragement*, were bound to feel stifled," according to Gordon Auchincloss.

Louis, in fact, came to look on Groton as an unenlightened school chiefly because the Rector was unconscious of the "infinite variety of human beings, the different manifestations. He didn't have any sympathy with different manifestations; he liked particular patterns." Still, Louis left Groton convinced that Endicott Peabody was a godly person. "His character and personality were sustained by a vibrant religious faith that, so far as I know, was never clouded by doubt." Years later, Auchincloss said that he "had complete faith and trust in him, but talking to him was a little like talking to God." He regards the Rector as "this huge, magnificent old man," who was "simple, straightforward, literal, and always sincere," a man with unshaken faith in his particular God and in his preoccupation with keeping his boys physically fit, sexually clean, and morally honest—in every sense of the word a gentleman. Most Grotties concur with Auchincloss's judgment.

The Rector may have been the dominant figure in Louis's memories of Groton, but another man had an impact on his life that was perhaps even greater. Quite possibly, Louis Auchincloss might never have pursued his literary interests had he not fallen under the influence of Malcolm Strachan, who inspired him more than any other teacher. Strachan, who came to Groton in Louis's fourth-form year, taught English. He was an enormously attractive, sensitive, open, generous, and gentle man who won the respect and affection of nearly all his students, even those who cared little about literature. Moreover, he sometimes stuttered, was painfully shy, and called the boys by their first names, unlike any of the other masters, who used surnames only, but his sincerity and goodwill were so evident that he touched everyone, even the Rector, whom he admired intensely. Louis has often said that Strachan came into his life at just the right time, "when I was reaching out for something and there he was."

Part of the something was Strachan's passion for literature, electrifying in a place that seemed not to value great writing as highly as Louis did. Another part was Strachan's intense efforts to convey the importance of literature in a way that had nothing to do with marks. He was a breath of fresh air in the highly charged competitive atmosphere of Groton, and he saw all too clearly that Louis read and wrote for distinction, not for pleasure. The Rector's public announcement of monthly average grades, beginning with the lowest and ending with the highest, had become intoxicating for unathletic and unconventional Louis, especially when he received grades of 90 percent or higher, the norm in his last three years, because the students applauded any average over 90. This recognition assuaged the pain of his early ill-treatment, but though Louis had no intention of abandoning his "grade grubbing," as he called it, he saw that Strachan

> presented a model of a different life, and I was not so benighted that I failed to perceive the high quality of it. I was wise enough to attach myself as closely as one could to a master. . . . Malcolm cared nothing for marks, nothing for worldly distinctions. To break through our schoolboy preconceptions he would hand out to his class mimeographed copies of poems, without date or name of author, and invite an open discussion of them. One did not know if one were reading the verse of Tennyson or that of Ella Wheeler Wilcox. At first I felt vaguely outraged by what seemed to be a rather Bolshevik procedure, but in time I began to be intrigued by a new sense of being alone with a poem, free of other judgments or prejudices, and free, above all, of "marks."

Strachan taught by moving slowly around his point. He approached a story or a poem or a play by singling out an anecdote or line or scene; any one led to a work's central meaning. Howland,

Louis's brother, who followed him to Groton, remembered how Strachan always asked why an author had used a certain word, why he had positioned a particular line where he had, and so on, thereby leading students to a work's theme, whereas Gurnee Gallien carefully explicated the writer's intent. "I thought at first we were learning more from Mr. Gallien," Howland has explained, "but what do I remember today? Malcolm's course, and that was the point."

On occasion, Auchincloss has dramatized first-rate schoolroom practice in his fiction, nowhere more effectively than in *The Rector of Justin*. Here, the fictional Rector presents a lesson on the role of Richelieu in the Thirty Years' War in sacred studies class, and in so doing illustrates Strachan's methodology.

"Do you know . . . what the Pope is supposed to have said when Cardinal Richelieu died?" [the fictional Rector asks a fifth former].

"No, sir. . . ."

"The Pope is supposed to have said: 'If there be a God, the cardinal will have much to answer for. If not . . . he led a successful life.' Have you any comment on that . . . ?"

"Well, of course, *I* believe in God, sir. It seems strange that a pope should say a thing like that."

"Popes in the seventeenth century were in some ways very broad-minded. As to what things popes were allowed to say. Then you would agree that the cardinal had much to answer for?"

"I suppose he did his best, sir."

"For mankind? Or for France?"

"Oh, for France, sir. That was his duty, wasn't it? To his king?". . .

"Evidently *he* thought so. Do you know what he said on his deathbed?"

"No, sir. . . ."

"He was asked if he had forgiven his enemies. 'I have

none,' came the reply, 'but those of France.' The man who has been called the architect of modern Europe was evidently satisfied with his handiwork. Think of that . . . !"

"Shouldn't he have been, sir?". . .

"What *was* Richelieu's policy in the Thirty Years' War?" [the Rector asked.]

"To support the Protestant cause, sir."

"You astound me. . . . I had thought he was a prince of the Roman Church."

"He was, sir. That's why he had to do it secretly. Sometimes he helped the Catholics, too. He had to keep the civil war going in Germany as long as he could."

"*Had* to . . . ?"

"Yes, sir. To weaken the power of the Hapsburg Alliance."

"Do you think that was ethical . . . ?"

"It worked, sir!"

[The Rector] laughed cheerfully now. "What a pragmatist we have in our midst! Does it mean nothing to you . . . that millions may have died to effectuate that policy?"

"But not millions of Frenchmen, sir. Richelieu made France the first power in Europe. It wasn't *his* fault if people in other countries were stupid enough to fight about religion.". . .

"Let me put you one more question. As you look abroad at a Europe in flames, created by just such policies as Richelieu's, does it not occur to you that the cardinal's inspiration may have been something less than divine?"

"Perhaps, sir. Yes, sir."

"Thank you. . . . I guess I made it sufficiently clear what answer I wanted."

To this day, Auchincloss can visualize Malcolm Strachan reading Wordsworth, almost "an act of religious devotion," inspiring the novelist-to-be to read the great lake poet himself. Once Louis told Malcolm, calling the teacher by his first name outside class, to the astonishment of his form mates, that he was enjoying the *Rubáiyát of Omar Khayyám*. "Oh, I remember when I liked the *Rubáiyát*," Strachan replied. "At Cambridge, we'd walk the quadrangles at night and recite some of those stanzas." In retrospect, Louis realized Strachan was amused at his liking such sentimentality while at the same time he was encouraging Louis to read anything he wanted.

After Louis's graduation, Strachan took Holy Orders, after which he resumed teaching at Groton. He and the Rector, a saint in the young priest's eyes, became intimates, giving rise to his plan to write a book about Peabody, but somehow, maybe because he "was so intense in his efforts to convey the emotional quality of great poetry to the student before him," he never wrote the biography. "I don't think he had the heat or energy left over to publish a word," Auchincloss told an alumni audience, and unfortunately Strachan died just before the publication of his student's fictional biography, *The Rector of Justin*. His reward for consecration to teaching was the nearly universal love Grotties felt for him. "He was the dearest, sweetest man in the world," Auchincloss has said, "and, as a consequence, many people wanted to take him under their wing." In addition to his friendship, Malcolm Strachan gave the future writer the astonishing perception that literature was something very, very powerful. The beloved teacher often visited the Auchinclosses in Southampton during summer vacations, and right away Priscilla Auchincloss recognized the man's worth. Still, Auchincloss understood that although his "mother was an intellectual . . . she always, always stressed that the biggest thing in life was family, not literature." For her, literature was diversion; for her son, it became life itself.

Despite his strong attachment to Malcolm Strachan, his very real admiration for the Rector, and his recognition of Groton's high academic standards, Louis has never been able to decide "whether my own education has done me more harm than good." What is perfectly clear, however, is the indelible mark the school made on his psyche. He himself has admitted his imagination, which was at its most impressionable, "was utterly engrossed by [the] school."

This is borne out by the reality that he has been writing about Groton in one way or another since graduation.

At Yale, he wrote a short story and a novel (reworked and published in 1990 as *The Lady of Situations*) that focused on the boredom with boarding school life of a young master's wife. In his first published novel, the 1947 *The Indifferent Children*, the protagonist attends a "Massachusetts church school modeled on the religious and social lines of Dr. Arnold's Rugby." During the 1950s, Groton appears under various names in four novels and four short stories. *The Rector of Justin*, which appeared in 1964, is the book most people associate with Groton, though Justin Martyr is not Groton, with three times as many students, nor is the Reverend Frances Prescott the same as Endicott Peabody; Prescott is a far more complex man than the Groton headmaster and his family is nothing like Peabody's. *The Embezzler*, which came out in 1966, is a fictional account of Groton graduate Richard Whitney, who while president of the New York Stock Exchange in 1934 was caught stealing and was sent to Sing Sing Penitentiary, where he was visited by Dr. Peabody. Groton not only figures prominently in Auchincloss's fiction but takes up one-sixth of his 1974 memoir, *A Writer's Capital*. President Truman's secretary of state, Dean Acheson, a Groton alumnus, turns up in the 1980 novel, *The House of the Prophet*. Its Walter Lippmann–like protagonist blames Dean's anti-Communist belligerence on Groton. "I suspect that if there be a danger in schools like Groton . . . it is pugnacity. The violent games, the football, the intense team spirit, the sense of Christian gentlemen standing together against the Barbarians—I wonder if it doesn't all tend to make their graduates too aggressive, too belligerent. As if America were one team and the Soviet Union another, pitted against one another, in a new kind of world series." Groton figures in two more novels of the 1980s and in three short stories.

Finally, in the second story of the 1992 collection, *False Gods*, cousins Gurdon and Horace Aspinwall (a character with some traits of Groton graduate Howland Auchincloss, Sr.) are both former Grotties. As Auchincloss had written Oliver LaFarge in 1945, Groton had bitten him deeply indeed. While there, he accepted its values; later, he questioned them.

> I don't have any individual pout against the school. It probably was good for me to get a grip on myself and pull myself to-gether. To go from the bottom of the class to the top was an exhilarating experience, too exhilarating. But in the first two or three years I was too low, too depressed, and had no self-confidence at all. I don't think Groton or any of those schools were very good during my time. They concentrated on making life uncomfortable for the boys deliberately because they thought that was good for them.

Auchincloss readily admits, however, that Groton did not seem as severe to others as it did to him, and he candidly points to the successes in his own form in support of its system. In his form of twenty-nine, there was a secretary of the army, an assistant secretary of state, presidents of the First National City Bank, the Mellon Bank, and the Celanese Corporation, ambassadors to the Philippines, Australia, and Indonesia, a novelist, a Benedictine monk, several eminent doctors and lawyers, and not one failure. What their careers might have been had they matriculated elsewhere cannot be reckoned, but what seems irrefutable, as Louis observed in 1982, is that "a case can be made that the time from age 12 to 18 is when a human being becomes what he is going to be. It appears to me that all my own classmates are very much what they were in 1935, except, of course, for mileage."

The Reverend Endicott Peabody had had them during their most impressionable years.

CHAPTER 4

University

You couldn't go through any place as amiably philistine as Yale in my day without realizing that what Gore Vidal calls "the real world" has nothing to do with the world of letters.

It wasn't till Virginia that I ever relaxed and enjoyed myself.

LOUIS AUCHINCLOSS

L ouis graduated from Groton in 1935, during the middle of the Depression. Congress, urged on by Franklin Roosevelt, had recently approved the Works Progress Administration, the Social Security Act, and the National Labor Relations Act. Millions all over the United States were out of work, but Louis's family was little affected. During the Depression's worst years, 1929 to 1934, they lived in a penthouse at 1185 Park Avenue that cost ten thousand dollars a year, a high rent for the period. When their lease expired, the Auchinclosses moved to 66 East Seventy-ninth Street, an apartment notable for its handsome Frederic King–designed Jacobean living room and its bargain-basement Depression purchase price of $150! Here they remained until Howland died in 1968. The senior Auchinclosses were careful with money, for, unlike many of their background, they lived on Howland's earnings, and liberal as these were for the 1930s, they had to be stretched to maintain three residences (the inexpensive apartment on Seventy-ninth Street had high maintenance costs), to educate four children at the best private schools and colleges, and to travel. During the Depression years, they went to France and England in 1934, to England and Ireland in 1937, and in 1935, they sent John and Louis on an Odyssey Cruise to the Greek Islands. Upon their return, the brothers drove together to New Haven, John for his second year in the law school and Louis to start college.

Groton graduates had acquired the habit of making Harvard or Yale their college choice, and the sixth form of 1935 was no exception. Twelve young Grotties entered Harvard's class of 1939 and thirteen Yale's. (Of the remaining members of the form, two chose Princeton, one Cambridge, and one the University of Hawaii.) When asked why he had picked Yale over Harvard, Louis replied, "My father went to Yale, my older brother went to Yale, my great-grandfather Stanton and my two grandfathers went to Yale, not to mention several uncles and cousins—everybody went to Yale. What would I be doing at Harvard?" His father had offered to send him to any college he chose, so Louis pressed for the University of Grenoble, chiefly because his friend William Mc-Cormick Blair, one of a handful of boys at Groton not from the Northeast, said he might go there, and because, not yet having read American writers, Louis associated Europe with literature. Suggesting that his son needed more rather than less of America, Howland Auchincloss circumscribed the original offer by limiting Louis's choices to institutions in the United States. So it happened that Louis Auchincloss (and 853 others culled from 1,400 applicants) registered for classes on a warm September 23, 1935, Yale's 235th year. Ruby Keeler and Dick Powell in *Shipmates Forever* and Madeleine Carroll and Robert Donat in Alfred Hitchcock's *The Thirty-Nine Steps* were playing in the New Haven theaters.

Louis still remembers going to the movies his first night there and the heady sense of freedom this simple act gave him. In his six years at Groton, he had seen only a handful of movies, and these were censored by the projectionist's hand being suddenly slapped over the projector lens during any potentially erotic scene. But Yale was different from Groton; here he did as he pleased, which translated at first into a "paradise of permitted films." Looking back, he wonders why he went so often to "sit through those interminable double features." Partly it was to wallow in the "happy escapism in the larger-than-life images" of Garbo and Gable, Lombard and Harlow, and, above all, Joan Crawford, "the star who dominated my freshman year," but also it was to evade the "rumbling approach of 'life.' "

Nor were movies Louis's only frivolity. By his own admission, he attended an "extraordinary" number of debutante parties. The families who staged these affairs mocked the Depression with feats of conspicuous consumption. At such coming-out balls, a thousand guests might dance all night to the beat of Meyer Davis's orchestra in ballrooms at the Plaza or Pierre hotels in New York City or under big marquees at country estates on Long Island's North Shore, in Connecticut, or New Jersey. Bars that dispensed limitless drinks, tables set for the continuous breakfasts that usually appeared around 2:00 A.M., and thematic decors that transformed an ordinary ballroom into a Petit Trianon, perhaps, or a Ringling Brothers circus, contributed to the staggering cost of these events. One of Louis's classmates had to resign from college to help his father pay for his sister's debut. After the war, such extravagant parties gave way to more modest ones. Louis recalled the women who came out in his years as "the last of the serious debs." He went, he said, for the "spectacle"; he "collected" parties. The social spectacle fascinated him because, as he writes in his memoir, *A Writer's Capital*, "I was perfectly clear from the beginning that I was interested in the story of money: how it was made, inherited, lost, spent. It never occurred to me that society people would be any more interesting than other people or that I would hear unusually stimulating talk at dinner parties. That was not what I went for."

His roommate and fellow Grottie Marshall Green corroborates Louis's memory. "When Louis went to the coming-out parties on Long Island, he was more interested in the parents than in the debutante. How did they live? Was their money old or new? Was their life that good or interesting, or were they having problems?

Curious about the kind of mementos the family cherished, he could be counted on to say sometime during the party, 'let's go upstairs,' and we'd roam the halls and bedrooms of the second story. I was always scared we'd run into a family member."

Louis said he went to observe, and as he gadded about, finely measuring social behavior that he stored away for later use in his fiction, he also enjoyed himself. As a witty and trenchant spectator, he regularly regaled friends with comic renderings of the parties he attended. A scene from a fictional sketch of another Yale roommate in his 1989 story collection, *Fellow Passengers*, suggests his own skill as a mimic. In the story, a Long Island debutante sits with friends on Piping Rock's beach, hashing over the previous night's festivities. When she complains about the newspaper coverage of her party, deploring its emphasis on her family's ancestry, the protagonist bursts out laughing.

"Well, if that isn't the most ungrateful thing I ever heard! When your poor mama must have labored an hour on the telephone with some bonehead reporter to get it all straight." Here he sat up and pretended to lift a receiver to his lips to ape remarkably the voice of Mrs. Gray, with whom he couldn't have exchanged more than three words the night before. "Hello, is this the society desk of the *Herald Tribune*? I want to make a correction to the draft I sent you of the notice of my daughter's dance. Yes, and I might just add that I'm a friend of your editor, dear Helen Reid. I'm afraid my secretary described my daughter's paternal grandmother as simply Mrs. Albert V. Gray. No, of course it's not right. It should read Mrs. Albert *Van Rensselaer* Gray. What? Why, certainly it must be changed. And what? You don't want to run that bit about Mr. Gray's being a cotillion leader in the Bachelors Ball of 1899? I'm sorry, I must insist. Do you want me to call Mrs. Reid? No? What? You can't spell Van Rensselaer? And you call yourself a society editor? Really, you people should take courses in American history. All right, I'll spell it for you. V as in Vanderbilt, A as in Astor, N as in nobility—"

Despite his determined partygoing, Louis did well in his studies, winning literary prizes and getting elected to Phi Beta Kappa. But then, he only took those courses that interested him (with the exception of physics)—namely, literature and history classes. He studied French history with John Allison; Elizabethan and Jacobean drama with Samuel Hemingway, who invited students to read Shakespeare with him in the basement of the master's house at Berkeley College on Sunday evenings; and eighteenth- and nineteenth-century English poetry with Chauncey Tinker, a ham who regularly wept when describing the deaths of Keats and Shelley. The course that stayed with him longest was Joseph Seronde's class in French literature. Long after college, he wrote about its effect.

> I was fascinated to learn how passionately the French public sided for or against the new trends of the century: romanticism, naturalism, realism. It was my first glimpse of a society where literature was the concern of someone besides teachers and students. I had been brought up to view the world as a more serious affair. I could not imagine my own father or the fathers of my friends donning red vests at the opening of *Hernani*. My mother used even to ridicule a college education that consisted so largely of reading novels. It is not that she disapproved of novels—she was . . . a voracious reader of them—but she believed that they were intended to provide diversion rather than education. She thought that courses for young men who would have to live in a troubled world should be in science or philosophy or economics. I could and still can understand her point of view. . . . But the fact remains that the reading taste established by Joseph Seronde was the most concrete thing I bore away from Yale and that it has given me more lasting pleasure than I can possibly imagine that I would have received from any course in economics. Yale and French nineteenth-century literature will always be bracketed in my mind.

Seronde's course heightened his love of everything French. He steeped himself in the culture and became proficient in the language—years later, he ate lunch once a week with a Berlitz instructor to test his skill in conversing about current subjects such as Watergate—so he could read the novels in the original French. His favorite vacation was a two-week barge trip in Burgundy.

"I was drunk with literature" is the way he has described his undergraduate years, and by literature, he does not mean only French. He tried to crowd as many English literature courses as he could into his schedule, and when he could not fit in Tinker's The Age of Johnson, he asked to audit the course, though that meant Saturday lectures. Apparently miffed that Louis had not chosen his course for credit, the great man said no, disillusioning his admiring student. Louis also continued to read widely outside of class. Although he never took the one American literature course offered by the English department, it was at Yale that he read American writers—James, Wharton, Dreiser, Fitzgerald, Hemingway, Lewis, Wolfe—for the first time and was exhilarated. He often called on Wilmarth Lewis (later fictionalized as Guy Hallowell in *Fellow Passengers*), the great Horace Walpole scholar who happened to be married to Annie Burr Auchincloss, his father's first cousin, and he became a devoted theater and opera aficionado, making multiple trips to Manhattan, often to accompany an old friend of his parents and of his maternal grandmother ("Aunt Marie" in *A Writer's Capital*) who had seen fifty-five performances of *Tristan* at the Metropolitan. His mother was appalled that in the disintegrating world of the 1930s, he should be so exclusively preoccupied with the arts. Everything he did reflected his literary interests (in three years at Yale, he attended only two football games), including college-sponsored extracurricular activity.

Although Louis understood that power and prestige at Yale resided in the *Yale Daily News*, the Political Union, and in the fraternities, he opted for the Dramatic Association, the Elizabethan Club, and the *Literary Magazine*. A few years later, he claimed to have posed as "arty" and "individualistic," fearing rejection by

Yale's elite organizations (his own grandfather, father, and father-in-law had belonged to the exclusive Scroll & Key), yet his "arty" collegiate avocations turned into lifetime pursuits. He joined Dramat, a thirty-six-year-old organization that boasted of luminaries such as Monty Woolley, Cole Porter, and Stewart and Joseph Alsop, and was rewarded by three big roles. He played in *Journey's End*, a play that takes place in the trenches of World War I, in *Whispering Gallery*, a murder-mystery melodrama, and in *The Servant of Two Masters* by Goldoni, a comedy of mistaken identity with commedia dell'arte borrowings. If the local critics are to be believed, his best performance was as the disguised Beatrice in *The Servant of Two Masters*. According to the *New Haven Register*, he was "the only convincing female in the play"; the *Yale Daily News* thought he approached "a zenith in his suave and sophisticated interpretation." Even so, it was his last Dramat performance. Ever since Howland Auchincloss had watched his son play Frances Arnott in *Whispering Gallery*, he had been urging Louis to resign from the drama club. "Father came backstage just when some wag friend sent me a lot of flowers," Louis remembers, and this plus the female impersonation alarmed Howland. He argued that Dramat had a reputation as a haven for homosexuals and thus "wasn't good for my image." Louis tried to get male parts, once playing a cowardly man, but in the Goldini play, he once again got the female lead. After its run in the fall of 1936, he quit Dramat. He thinks his father had a point. "All the others who took women's parts turned out to be homosexuals"; for him to have continued playing women, he implies, might have meant he, too, would have been taken for a homosexual.

The Elizabethan Club, composed of undergraduates interested in literature, took up the slack. The club scheduled no regular meetings but served tea every afternoon in its attractive white clubhouse on College Street, noteworthy for its massive safe that secures a fine collection of Elizabethan folios. Louis went often to have tea with old Dr. Harvey Cushing, Massachusetts General Hospital's renowned neurosurgeon, whose three beautiful daughters married so publicly and so well: Minnie to Vincent Astor, then to James Fosburgh; Betsey to FDR's son James, then to John Hay Whitney; Babe to Stanley Mortimer, then to William Paley. "I didn't foresee," Louis said later, "that his daughters would be queens of just the kind of world that I later described in some of my books." Not surprisingly, Louis wrote for the *Literary Magazine*, the nation's oldest student-run monthly. His eight stories were better than those he wrote at Groton, but only barely; he called them "exercises," an accurate description. After *Lit* had published his fifth story in the fall of junior year, he was elected to join the editorial board, which he did. His roommate and closest friend, Jack Woods, was already a board member.

Louis Auchincloss and Jack Woods had gotten to know each other during freshman year, when Louis was rooming with Marshall Green. In a class that produced William Scranton, Stanley Resor, William Bundy, Richard Ellmann, Cyrus Vance, and Louis Auchincloss, Jack Woods had a reputation among his classmates as the most brilliant. Although he never appeared to study, preferring to go to the movies or play bridge (he won the university bridge championship in junior year), he became a member of the *Literary Magazine* in sophomore year (six months before Louis), won election to Phi Beta Kappa and received the Edward Tompkins McLaughlin Prize for excellence in English in his junior year, and graduated with honors. His bad complexion was mitigated by dark, penetrating eyes and thick, wavy black hair. He came from Orange, New Jersey, an only child of divorced and unaffluent parents. Although he had graduated from Lawrenceville, New Jersey's finest preparatory school, his background provided him no entrée to the New York debutante parties he wanted to attend, but he saw Louis as a way to get invited. Louis had no objection to taking him to a few, and thanks to Jack's wit and gregariousness, he was soon receiving invitations on his own. Louis understood he had been used, as he shows in a fictional story about Woods. "It was as if he had winked and said: 'Take me where I want to go and I'll make it worth your while.' "

With his passion to impress, Jack Woods did make it worth Louis's while. He was wonderful company, congenial, quick, affectionate, occasionally emotional, with an uncanny and sometimes disturbing insight into people's thoughts. As his roommate, Louis was sometimes subjected to his quick changes of mood and cruel wisecracks, but Jack's passionate interest in literature more than compensated for any erratic behavior. Jack was, in fact, Louis's first intellectual friend. His mother and brother John shared his love of letters, but they were family. Jack kindled in Louis a lifetime enthusiasm for Henry James and Edith Wharton, but his probing acumen and mordant judgment of what made for good writing caused Louis to distrust his own stories. When Jack read and criticized them, Louis both feared and valued his opinion. "I was terribly pleased if he liked something I'd written and rather devastated if he didn't. I remember his saying to me about a story —'You're something you've never been before—dull.' And I was dazzled by his saying I'd never been dull before, and then terribly disappointed that I was dull now. That's the way Jack was. He'd always lead you both ways."

"But the great thing he did for me was to shake (at least temporarily) my inhibition about becoming a writer."

Louis had often dreamed of a future as a writer, yet he always felt somehow that a lifetime of commercial pursuit was inevitable. Going downtown "was a thing that happened to men, like shaving," a character says in *Portrait in Brownstone*. This assumption came partly from his father's natural fear of the precariousness of an arts career and of Louis's boxing himself into such a course too soon, partly from his mother's abhorrence of second-rate art, and partly from the consequence of his early realization that the "real world" of power brokers paid no attention to the arts. The arts were for dilettantes and women, he deduced. Jack, however, saw nothing precious or effeminate about the writer's profession, nor to him was it any less prestigious than law or finance. Maybe so, Louis mused, but how would the fledgling writer support himself? Teach, Woods suggested.

For the first time, Louis seriously pondered a life of letters. By the end of sophomore year, he was spending afternoons in the Linonia Brothers Reading Room in Sterling Library working on a novel, which he completed early in his junior year. Although the words tumbled out of him, and he never felt happier than when writing, he kept his project secret until he showed his 424-page manuscript, called "A World of Profit," to his parents. They were horrified by his intention to seek publication. His father objected on the grounds that the book would do him no good on Wall Street, where he hoped his son was headed, and his mother reacted against "the vulgarity of the society parts." Crushed by their reaction, he submitted his work to Scribner's, anyway.

"A World of Profit" develops some of the themes from his Groton and Yale stories and is, in a way, a fictional autobiography. "I learned then and there," Louis has said, "that all a novelist's characters are himself. There may be a character who is the author dressed up to look like John Jones or Mary Smith, but it is still basically the author." In "A World of Profit," both people and places were drawn from Louis's personal history. Chapin, his mother's and sister's school, appeared as Miss Waterman's School, Groton as Chelton, and its headmaster, Endicott Peabody, as Lowell Minturn. The characters' dilemmas and ambivalences are Louis's own. A young man named Stephen Hill, for example, experiences conflict similar to Louis's: Should he acquiesce to his father's desire to have him become a banker or should he please his artistic self? He returns to teach at Chelton, his alma mater. There he is seduced by Audrey Emerson, marries her after she gets a divorce from another Chelton teacher, becomes a banker, loses his old ideals, and commits suicide. The protagonist, Audrey Emerson, also reflects the turmoil that was in Louis. She repudiates her roots and by so doing creates a terrible mess. From a nondescript social background, she is introduced into what she judges to be the glamorous world of the Sabatière family. Yet with an implausible sense of irony, befitting her creator more than her fictional persona, she tells Barclay Sabatière, "Buckley, Chelton, Yale—and then the bank. You're not a person; you're a class," after which, she declines his offer of marriage. In a fit of disappointment at giving up the world she covets, she marries her college beau. Soon bored by him and by Chelton, where he teaches, she turns to Stephen Hill. At the end of the novel, she retreats to teach at her old college, which is Middlebury, where Louis and his sister, Priscilla, took French during the summer of 1936.

The lessons are all too obvious: By challenging the values of their respective worlds, Stephen ends a suicide and Audrey a battered survivor of two disastrous marriages. This half-baked variation on the *Madame Bovary* theme, as Louis later called his first novel, showed narrative skill, always his strong point, but lacked his later stylistic elegance. It was marred by puerile expressions that cropped up from time to time: "hands fluttered," ivy stems "clung around buildings like bony fingers"; by stilted dialogue: "Isn't it a lovely day?" "Is it? Well supposing it is; aren't we a little too old to be discussing the weather?"; and by overwrought description: "Rows of brownstone houses, cut by occasional gray fronts, sparkled in the glare; horns rasped in the general hum; impatience at the standstill of affairs hung oppressively over the city."

Still, Louis had possessed the discipline and persistence to write the novel, and he demonstrated, to himself most of all, that he could sustain a story for 424 pages. It was surprising, then, that when he received a letter of rejection from a Scribner editor, despite his offer to read a subsequent effort, Louis accepted it as the final judgment on his fitness for a writer's life.

> I was not indignant at Scribner's. I was not even surprised. I actually agreed with their decision now. What caused my acute distress was my sense that the letter was really a message from Jove to warn me that I had been making a fool of myself. What in the name of all that was holy did the likes of me think I was up to, dabbling in literature, rushing to every play on Broadway, dreaming of teaching, and worst of all, writing a novel, when all the while I knew that my real destiny, my serious destiny, my destiny as a man, was to become a lawyer and submit to the same yoke to which my poor father had so long and patiently submitted?

He determined to leave Yale at the end of junior year and enter a law school that would take degreeless applicants. He found such a school at the University of Virginia. No one, except his mother, who was delighted, could understand why he was suddenly in such a rush to go to law school. His father prevailed upon him to finish college, insisting that Louis would spend the rest of his life explaining why he had not graduated, but probably because Louis had chosen the law, Howland finally acquiesced. Many years later, a friend said that in retrospect he could see that what Louis did was completely in character. Once he decides on a course of action—in this case, to pursue law rather than literature—he acts quickly.

Not until after he had left Yale did Louis show the manuscript to Jack Woods, who read it straight through. Then he wept, angrily accusing Louis of modeling the mercenary Audrey on him. "I know why you're leaving Yale; because I'm Yale to you and you hate me." Louis denied this, but later he admitted he was afraid of Woods. "I was afraid that I could not live with the image of myself that I saw reflected in the limpid pool of Jack's mind." Asked to explain his remark, he points to Jack's shattering criticisms. "He would put his finger on your weakest spots in no time at all. He was a very uncomfortable person to have as a friend, because you couldn't get away with anything. He always made me feel superficial, and so I thought I must be." Even though Louis fully realized that Jack was "terribly egocentric, easily hurt, fragile really, and extremely unstable," he accepted his friend's unspoken judgment that he was too superficial for the artist's vocation.

With grim determination, therefore, he set off for law school in the fall. To his happy surprise, he found Charlottesville and its "romantic university, where youth and beauty seemed to gambol before the white paint, red brick and shimmering greens of Mr. Jefferson's inspired vision," enchanting. Thomas Jefferson soon became Louis's favorite architect. The white columns and serpentined redbrick walls of the lawn, the rotunda, and the arcades make this school one of the most beautiful in the country. He (and his mother, who had driven down from New York in her son's new Pontiac to see for herself the famed beauty of the Albemarle County countryside) found an off-campus apartment just before classes started.

Even more surprising, he found in the law literary qualities that solaced him for having given up literature. In Hardy Dillard's contracts class, for example, he read Benjamin Cardozo's 1917 *Wood* v. *Duff-Gordon* opinion, the first five sentences of which he quotes in his memoir, *A Writer's Capital.*

> The defendant styles herself "a creator of fashions." Her favor helps a sale. Manufacturers of dresses, millinery and like articles are glad to pay for a certificate of her approval. The things which she designs, fabrics, parasols, and what not, have a new value in the public mind when issued in her name. She employed the plaintiff to help turn this vogue into money.

"Like every author of fiction," Louis observed, Cardozo "started with a donnée, which he then had to dramatize, interpret, make striking and interesting." Many judges besides Cardozo, he was to discover, resemble literary artists in the close attention they pay to their choice of words, as well as in their fondness for metaphors and similes.

For torts, he had Leslie Buckler, "the most imaginative of the faculty, a tall, charming, cynical, handsome man, very much the tweeded Virginia gentleman," and a most romantic figure who delivered stimulating lectures on the philosophy of the law. Louis suspected he was a writer manqué like himself. Dillard and Buckler stimulated Louis's interest in the history of English jurisprudence and the growth of common law. The cases he studied in contracts, torts, and criminal law in which judges decided how to fit a given situation to previous ideas as to what the law was, or should be, were the ones he liked. He likened the judge who had to depict a plaintiff's or defendant's behavior in a case so plausibly as to justify his opinion to a novelist who must describe his character with an air of verisimilitude. Not surprisingly, he did not care for statute law, the rules and regulations passed by Congress and state legislatures. There was no drama in this law, nor even the possibility of literary style. "Legislatures . . . are drowned in the small print of their endless enactments," Louis has written. Given the inevitable growth of statute law corresponding to the growth and ever-widening diversity of the United States, it is unlikely Louis Auchincloss could have found solace in the law today. It was the larger picture Louis responded to, which was why he appreciated courses taught by men such as Noel Dowling, a visiting professor of constitutional law who examined the entire political scene —the backgrounds, biases, and briefs of the nine Supreme Court justices—as a way of interpreting constitutional law and the judicial process. His was a class not only in law but in philosophy, psychology, and sociology, as well as literature.

Louis's literary bent, which he purported to have jettisoned, was unmistakable. Professor Buckler recognized it right away. So, too, did Princess Pierre Troubetzkoy (in her time, the well-known novelist and poet Amélie Rives), who met Louis during his first semester at Virginia. A friend of Louis's father had urged him to call on the writer, since she lived near Charlottesville. He did not drive out to Castle Hill, her manor house, until November, so determined had he been to put aside literary matters. Though she was seventy-seven at the time, the two struck up a friendship immediately. He was fascinated that she had known Henry James, and that Oscar Wilde had introduced her to her second husband. Writing to thank Louis for his Christmas present, she showed that she sensed the turmoil he subjected himself to in trying to reconcile his desire to be a novelist with his perceived duty to be a lawyer.

I saw my dear friend Leslie Buckler about two weeks ago, and he stayed with me nearly three hours talking of the things that interested us both most of all. We talked of *you*, and he said some things that will show you how keenly observant he is though he does not seem so.

I asked him how he thought you were getting on with the

study of law, and this is what he replied: "Very well indeed—excellently. But there's something. I find him an unusual boy. Keen and sensitive in the best meaning of that word. But the 'something' I mentioned is this: I feel that his will and brain are concentrated on his study of law, but his whole *heart* isn't in it."

I didn't say anything for a few seconds, then I asked, "Do you think that will interfere with his coming out on top?"

"No," said Leslie. "He will come out all right. It's only that one's heart must be in it to devote one's whole life to the law."

Then (I hope you will forgive me, dear Louis, but we were talking confidentially and I thought it best there shouldn't be any mystery about it)—then I said: "The truth is, Leslie, that the chief thing in his heart is to be a writer. *I* think, though he has never even hinted anything of the kind to me, that he is devoted to his father and is studying law to please him. I know when I asked to see some of his manuscripts he replied that he had locked them all away in New York when he decided to come to the University of Virginia and study law. So you see, though his "heart" mayn't be in it his will and mind and determination *are* in it.

"Good," said Leslie. "He will come out—I'm quite sure."

The manuscript Louis had locked away was one-half of a second novel that he had written during the summer before law school began—he had allowed himself to write for "fun" only during vacations—and that he finished during the summer after this first year. It was so bad, he thought, he threw it away without letting anyone read it. He was not tempted to write another, for in December of his second year, he and nine other top scholars of the class of 1941 were chosen to be on Virginia's *Law Review*. For the rest of the school year, he contributed legal "Notes" and "Decisions" to the review. "Notes" were full-fledged essays on legal topics. A "Decision" was as analytic and precise as a sonnet. Summarize the case, give the origin of the principle involved and its historic variations, and end with an evaluation.

Six months after his election to the editorial board, he moved to the board of managing editors of the *Law Review*. His all too evident literariness was responsible, no doubt, for his assignment to the book-review section. He would have preferred being Decisions editor or Notes editor to being Book Review editor, since book reviews were not the important part of the *Law Review*, but it gave him the opportunity to review the kind of legal subjects he preferred, those of a general nature, such as autobiographies of legal stars, correspondence of great jurists, and treatises on legal sociology. In one review, of *The Struggle for Judicial Supremacy*, he shows himself as a political conservative. "I've gone left all my life," he says today, "but I started so far right, I haven't gone very far." Criticizing the author's New Deal bias by looking carefully at his language, he also demonstrates a keen sensitivity to the nuances of words.

> The book speaks to the reader with the suppressed excitement of the raconteur in the "March of Time" films. Emphasis is laid on the dramatic. In the early part of the book the phraseology is burdened with such terms as "storm signal " and "first ominous rumble," as the author sets the stage for the battle of Titans. A "dynamic" people led by a "great" president are on the march to burst the fetters of a clutching past. In their way stand nine old men in black, champions of the old régime, who stage a bitter last fight in their desperate effort to enshrine the crumbling doctrine of laissez-faire in constitutional raiment. So [the author] sees it. It is all quite clear to him. Galahad Government on one side with a "mandate" from the people, and on the other a gang of "coupon-clippers" and "tricky knaves" invariably represented by "a brilliant array of long-coated counsel."

Louis assigned to others more technical books, such as *The Federal Income Tax* and *Cases and Materials on the Law of Evidence*.

"I loved being on the *Law Review*," he told an interviewer. "It was actually read by people outside the university. I felt part of the system, which was very exciting. I felt like a man. Law was a man's world, and I succeeded. I had always known that high marks and reading novels and poetry were nothing in the real world," which was why no one at Yale read the *Literary Magazine*. "It was a joke, absolutely nothing, and even disappeared," he has said in comparing it to the *Law Review*. In Charlottesville, Louis felt he was in the center of things and not on the fringes, as he had been in New Haven. "I wasn't in the circle that was running Yale, [but] I was a member to be reckoned with in my law school class." Years later, he said he had been "very happy at the University of Virginia and have always looked upon it as more my alma mater than Yale."

Besides the *Law Review*, he was invited to join the Raven Society, a group (named for Edgar Allan Poe's poem "The Raven," for no discernible reason except that Poe had been a student at the university in 1826) that endeavored "to bring together the more outstanding men in the various departments of the university that they may derive the benefits of mutual acquaintance," and the Order of the Coif, an honor given for high grades. He was also popular, not only with his fellow *Law Review* editors, among whom existed a camaraderie and esprit de corps that made working as a group enjoyable, but with his classmates in general. Social life at Virginia, Louis said, was far more sophisticated and enjoyable than at Yale, and he partook of it enthusiastically. Two or three afternoons a week, he rode horseback with other students, faculty members, or neighbors. On Saturday nights, he was apt to have dinner with one or another of the married law students— most often with department-store heir Marshall Field, Jr., and his wife, Joanne—who lived in cottages out by the Farmington Country Club. Surprisingly, a place where he was happy and at peace for the first time appeared infrequently in his fiction. The protagonist of his first published novel spends a year in the law school, riding, dining, and drinking but reading little law, a scene is set on the lawn in his second novel, and Amélie Rives's house and the "serene dome," the "noble lawn," the "graceful pavilions," and "multitudinous columns" of the university show up in the first story of his 1992 *False Gods*. In between, the school is mentioned in passing every once in a while. Two of his three sons, however, followed him to Virginia, and a collection of his manuscripts is kept in the Alterman Library.

Louis's status in his class is reflected in his having been selected in the summer before his last year of law school as one of four "summer boarders" at the prestigious firm of Sullivan & Cromwell. This was his first summer employment. He was assigned to the trusts and estates group, probably because he was known to both partners in the department, Pearce Browning and Curtis Pierce, the grandson of Cromwell's first partner after Sullivan's death, the son of another partner, and the brother of a classmate of Louis at Groton and Yale. At times, Louis felt he had been "shoved" into this department, but for a future novelist who said he had always been interested in the story of money, to work with the well-off and their monetary problems—planning their wills and estates, setting up their trusts, handling their marital separations and divorces—was eminently appropriate. Besides, it was the trusts and estates departments of the great law firms that preserved the fortunes Louis would write about so knowingly.

Louis Auchincloss's fascination with the nuances of influence and position was agreeably stimulated by the powerful yet venerably old-line Sullivan & Cromwell. Thus, when the firm offered him a permanent job after graduation, he was honored.

> It was at once clear to me that such institutions were completely dependent on the legal aptitudes of their partners and clerks. For no client will long leave his affairs in incompetent hands because of a social or political connection. The firm's whole inventory must consist of brains and character. I was proud to be starting in a job where social qualifications counted for so little and which I had obtained by my own aptitude in a profession not originally selected by inclination.

His family's social qualifications probably accounted, at least in part, for his having been put in the trusts and estates department, for many of Sullivan & Cromwell's clients were their friends and acquaintances, but social position without more important endowments was useless to a law firm, especially this firm. In 1940, Sullivan & Cromwell was the only important Wall Street law firm to have Jewish partners. Alfred Jaretzki, hired in 1881, was one of the four first-generation partners. His cousin, Edward Green, his son, Alfred Jaretzi, Jr., and his son-in-law, Eustace Seligman, were made partners in 1915. Sullivan & Cromwell anticipated by decades the meritocracy that eventually characterized all Wall Street firms. (The reason for Sullivan & Cromwell's liberal stance in this respect had as much to do with its having been founded by poor Anglo-Saxon Protestants as with lack of prejudice. In 1870, William Nelson Cromwell was a bookkeeper in Algernon Sullivan's newly founded firm of Sullivan, Kobbe & Fowler. His employer, impressed by his talent, sent him to Columbia Law School in the last class to accept students with no undergraduate degree. In 1879, the two men, Sullivan, fifty-three, and Cromwell, twenty-five, started Sullivan & Cromwell.)

After graduation in 1941, Louis returned to New York to study for the bar examination. In mid-June, he was an usher in a Yale classmate's wedding. So, too, was Jack Woods, who stayed with Louis in his parents' Seventy-ninth Street apartment. The former roommates had seen each other off and on during the past three years, as Jack had taken a job as a reporter at the *Herald Tribune* and lived in New York. In March, he had been inducted in the army as a private and was stationed at Fort Hancock, New Jersey. After the wedding, the two friends had gone to different parties. When Louis got back to the apartment, he found that Jack had left a terrible mess, so he left him a note on the hall table, reprimanding him for being such an inconsiderate guest. Jack had returned to the apartment after Louis had gone to bed, saw his note, wrote a reply, and went out again. The next morning, a telephone call awakened Louis; he learned that Jack had fallen out of a sixth-floor window to his death. According to his obituary, he had been perched on the windowsill of an open front window of a friend's apartment on Fifty-seventh Street, swinging his feet, when suddenly he had lost his balance and fell. His death appeared to be an accident, but it was a suicide. Under Louis's note in the hall was the note Jack had left only hours before. "He had the exquisite consideration to understand that I might have worried about the effect of my 'silly' note," Louis writes, so he gave his reasons for not wanting to live.

Although Jack Woods's emotional ups and downs had been common knowledge to his friends, not many besides Louis knew about his father's suicide a few years earlier. These psychological factors notwithstanding, it was puzzling why a young man with so much promise had wanted to end his life. Nor did his note, at first, make his reasons clear. In a scarcely fictional portrait of Woods, Louis tells how his friend alluded in his note to an A. E. Housman poem—the forty-fourth poem of *A Shropshire Lad*—the two had supposedly discussed at Yale. Louis, who had no recollection of the poem or the discussion of it, discovered in it why Jack had committed suicide. In the first stanza, the poet congratulates a young suicide who chose to die rather than to yield to his repressed homosexual inclinations. Woods appeared to have been bisexual, for prior to his death, he had simultaneously formed a strong attachment to a young man and woman. Apparently unable to come to terms with his bisexuality, he had jumped to his death after having imbibed steadily for hours at the apartment of a fellow reporter, one of the objects of his amorous obsession. A young woman Louis had known all his life had made the phone call that brought the unwelcome news. Louis burned the suicide note in the presence of Jack's uncle, who wanted his sister to think the death was accidental, so she could arrange for a proper Catholic funeral for her son. After the shock wore off, Louis realized "how deeply [Jack's] personality is imbedded in my mind and how often I miss him." That such extraordinary talent went unrealized, "quite aside from the sadness of losing one's closest friend," never quite left him. Not until his 1974 memoir did he write about Jack. In 1989, he fictionalized him as Leonard Armster in *Fellow Passengers*.

In July, Louis was best man in John Auchincloss's wedding to Audrey Maynard and went to work for Sullivan & Cromwell.

CHAPTER 5

War

There had always lurked in the back of my mind an uneasy sense that over and above the tests of manhood that school and Wall Street were bound to provide, there might lie in wait an even rougher and more elementary one: that of war.

LOUIS AUCHINCLOSS

Sullivan & Cromwell is best known today as the firm of the Dulles brothers—John Foster, who became secretary of state under Dwight Eisenhower, and Allen, who directed the CIA during the same period—but in 1941, it was William Nelson Cromwell, one of the two founding partners, who was the more famous; some would say notorious. Cromwell had masterminded the international intrigue that led to the bloodless Panamanian revolution in 1903 and the construction of the Panama Canal, all for a French client. The Paris-based New Panama Canal Company had hired Cromwell to sell the assets of its projected but failed Panama undertaking, which consisted of an excavated 19 million cubic yards, plus rotting houses, hospitals, and roads that had been built for the thousands of Frenchmen who had moved to Panama to work on the canal. Cromwell spent four years persuading Congress to abandon its plan to build a canal in Nicaragua, a site favored by southern senators, owing to its proximity to the ports of Biloxi, New Orleans, and Galveston. In the end, he got a paltry fee, and even for this he had to go to court, but was confident that the future business to his firm would repay his efforts.

With remarkable prescience, he saw that Washington, D.C., would become a lobbyist's nirvana, a place where contacts helped clients, and in his work for the canal, he developed the most powerful contacts of any lawyer in America. Moreover, he had the field to himself for decades to come. As just one result of Cromwell's vision, Sullivan & Cromwell lawyers played a major role in drafting much of the New Deal's securities legislation.

When Louis Auchincloss joined the firm as an associate in the summer of 1941, the most lucrative work Sullivan & Cromwell was involved in was the drafting of indenture agreements under which financial institutions advance millions of dollars to corporations and foreign governments. John Foster Dulles, the managing partner, was primarily interested in foreign governments. Between 1929 and 1941, he had supervised the handling of nearly $2 billion in foreign loans, primarily to Germany. The German business was so heavy, Sullivan & Cromwell opened a Berlin office in 1929 to produce prospectuses for bonds. In 1933, when Hitler came to power, the cables from this office bore the government-required salutation, "Heil Hitler," shocking the partners at home, especially the Jewish ones. Not until 1934 did they force Dulles to close the Berlin office, but he continued to do business with the Nazi-run cartels of Europe. As late as 1939, he publicly defended Hitler in his book *War, Peace and Change*, insisting the Führer wanted peace. When Hitler's blitzkrieg overran Poland on September 1, which started World War II, Dulles substituted his long-held defense of Hitler with the rationalization that the Nazis' aggression resulted from the unjust terms of the Treaty of Versailles that followed World War I. His dealings with the Axis powers finally halted with Pearl Harbor.

Louis was one of nine new associates hired just months before the entry of the United States into the war. As the only graduate of the University of Virginia, he was teased for having come from a country club. He himself admitted that "Virginia encouraged superficiality and indolence," and in his first published novel, he writes of the protagonist that he "evaded the sordid grind and competition of northern law schools by selecting the University of

Virginia." Still, Auchincloss had distinguished himself enough at Virginia to join what was one in a handful of the best law firms in the country. As he later advised his cousin and future federal judge Louis Stanton, "if you're going to be at the top of the class at UVA, you'll be as good as the top anywhere. If you're in the middle, forget UVA." Auchincloss had returned to his slot in the trust and estates department, which he knew was somewhat removed, in the firm's view, from the mainstream of law. Not that this mattered much, for with each passing day it seemed unlikely that Louis's group of new associates would practice much law. By mid-1941, Great Britain, the only country in Western Europe still holding out against Hitler, had been subjected to nine straight months of massive bombing raids by the full force of the Luftwaffe. The dogged determination and stoicism of the English helped to turn American public opinion from isolationalism to advocacy of hemispheric defense. The first U.S. peacetime military draft had been instituted in late 1940, and in the fall of 1941, Louis was certain to be called. To avoid this, and by implication the dreaded basic training, he applied for a commission in naval intelligence, not anticipating the negative reactions of his friends, who equated the desk job that intelligence work implied with draft dodging. Incredibly, so, too, did his mother, who could never be taken for granted. "Although an ardent isolationist, desperately apprehensive of the approach of a war which threatened to make hash of all her efforts to keep her sons from physical danger," Auchincloss explains, "she could still recognize that physical dangers were not the only kind. What was more dangerous than the scorn of the tribe for a youth who did not aspire to be brave?"

Auchincloss let his application stand, at least until late October, when it became clear that U.S. entry into the war was imminent. Only then did he try to change his application for a commission as an ensign IVS (Intelligence Volunteer Special) to DVG (Deck Volunteer General), so as to be able to serve on a fighting ship and not from a stateside desk. To do this, he applied for midshipmen's training on the USS *Prairie State*, for which he needed trigonometry. He and Yale classmate Jack Pierrepont signed up for a six-week course that was given at the dental college at New York University in a building that stank of formaldehyde. For the next several weeks, Auchincloss had a night class to add to his nine-to-six day at Sullivan & Cromwell.

"New York in the autumn of 1941 was an unsettled town," Auchincloss writes. "It was a city of rumors, of draft stories, of applications for commissions, of a gaiety that seemed the fruit of an almost deliberate effort to cash in on a 'what the heck' war fever, of a sense of doom so strong to us in retrospect that in some anomalous fashion it has become part of the time before the event occurred." The event occurred when the Japanese bombed Pearl Harbor on December 7. Although Louis had completed four of the six weeks of his math course, he was ordered to report for duty immediately at the Naval Intelligence Office at 50 Church Street, obliging him to abandon trigonometry and hope of any *Prairie State* schooling. For the next two months, he checked applications like his own until his commission came through.

Ensign Louis Auchincloss went on active duty on February 9, 1942. His parents saw him off at Pennsylvania Station three days later, "and after that," Louis writes, "it was all a confused blur of Norfolk, of long grey passageways on a Navy transport, of ringing annunciators, of strange and unsympathetic faces at the mess table, and finally one hot, clear morning, the long, green, mountainous coast of Panama." Thus began a military career the future writer described as closer to Gilbert and Sullivan than to *The Red Badge of Courage*.

Auchincloss did not care much for Panama. "All life centers around that narrow strip of water which Mr. Cromwell refers to as 'my canal,' " he wrote home. Panama City, the capital of Panama, and Balboa, the capital of the Canal Zone, where he lived in the bachelor officers' quarters, adjoined each other. "It's impossible," Louis wrote, "to drum up much affection for either place. The zone, a strip of America 53 miles long and 10 wide, is a community entirely made up of officials—army, navy, marines, or canal employees—a bureaucrat's heaven and a capitalist's hell." Panama, "an opera bouffe community," he admitted had a few attractions, the Cathedral Square, the *presidencia,* and the long, narrow streets nearby, but overall, it was a sprawling, dirty city with only occasional splashes of color. The Caribbean, by contrast, was a striking blue, with bright-colored reefs and sudden rain squalls. Once, flying to Honduras through one, the word-minded Auchincloss was reminded of Tennyson. " 'When through scudding drifts the rainy Hyades *vexed* the dim sea.' Pathetic fallacy or not," he wrote his mother, "I was struck at what a perfect word 'vexed' is to describe the reaction of a great body of water to sudden fits of rain."

He liked the Panamanians better than the "flat-footed American Zonites (those dowdy engineers who live down here sometimes as long as 30 years without learning one word of Spanish or moving one step beyond their own little circle)," but complained they were "too emotional" and "thoroughly dishonest," like the president's sister, who became wealthy from real estate in the red-light district, and the city's leading socialite, who made her money from slot-machine rackets. He saw little difference, though, between his "inevitable disillusionment" with everything Panamanian and his discovery of "the shameful and discreditable role played by William Nelson Cromwell" in the building of the Panama Canal. "How we romanticize men like Cromwell!" he wrote his mother. " 'Empire builders,' 'men of vision,' or even lovingly 'pirates.' And if one examines a single transaction carefully, what is Cromwell but a crook? I am ashamed, not of him for he is old and passé but of the admiration shown him and his career by Sullivan & Cromwell."

Louis liked his work no better than he liked Panama. Naval Intelligence, or Naval Information for the District, as it was called locally, had nothing to do with communications or with operational intelligence but, rather, with information about Panama and its neighbors that might affect the navy. Basically, the office kept the navy informed of political changes (which it learned from the daily paper) and of Canal traffic. Although not much more than a wartime clipping bureau, the office employed thirty officers and as many enlisted men. Administering the office—interviewing recruits, typing personnel reports, ordering equipment, writing public-relations releases, sorting and distributing official mail—squandered the services of four additional officers and fifteen enlisted men and civilian secretaries. Ensign Auchincloss was assigned to this clerical detail, which he described in letters home as "fussy," "dull," "a bureaucracy gone mad." Once his immediate supervisor ordered all copies of a fifty-page report to be destroyed and retyped because it had been done on the wrong-sized paper. One of his jobs was to compile a Who's Who in Panama City, which he was sure no one looked at. His information came from Naval District officers who had been in civilian jobs before the war. For all this silliness, Auchincloss wrote home, "They keep wanting more officers down here. It's quite extraordinary to me. And discouraging. The war effort is needlessly extravagant."

Part of the trouble was the unimportance of the navy in Balboa. The governor of the Canal Zone was an army general, and the canal had been built by army engineers, so any important work was done by the army. The navy was so incidental to the district and Louis's work so inconsequential, he learned "to be thankful for the days when the intelligence office accomplished nothing, as opposed to those when it actively (if microscopically) impeded the war effort." He was dumbstruck when officers investigated canal-bound airline passengers to see whether they had ever employed a Japanese servant; when a lieutenant who claimed to have clairvoyance was consulted by the admiral to help him locate German submarines; and when he was ordered to spend a week spying on the commander of a patrol boat (whose job Auchincloss's superior officer wanted) to find out whether the commander had had a woman in his cabin overnight.

Small wonder that more than half the two hundred pages of letters Auchincloss mailed home during his ten months in Balboa detail his frantic attempts to escape his ignominious job. "I'm opening up that old Prairie State problem again"; "I have written to Lieutenant Commander Thomas about V-7"; "the Captain will never endorse [my application for sea duty], but he has to let it go through"; "no word from Washington"; "I'm beginning to hope that Chief of Staff Captain Stone might help me get to sea"; "my drive for a change of duty will continue unabated"; "I do hope I get out of here before bitterness makes too nasty and permanent a dent in my character." All his efforts were frustrated, however. "The district intelligence officer," he wrote many years later, "faithful to his trade of bureaucrat, wished to swell, rather than diminish, his useless staff. His position in the hierarchy depended on the number of his lackeys."

His parents were alternately sympathetic and critical. "It's a little sickening," Louis wrote in reply to one of their letters, "to have one's family assume that one is suffering from an immature Alsopian craze for combat instead of concentrating on the job at hand." Even their sympathy annoyed him.

> Don't, please, use the words 'useful' and 'valuable' to me again. Such roseate optimism as to the role I am playing is not in any way justified by the facts. At least credit me with the intelligence to evaluate my own activity. I don't so much mind being in an office. The word 'desk job' has no terrors for me. That's what you simply will not understand. It's what I'm doing and the intensely bitter way I feel about how it's being done that's hurting me so. Father suggests that I resign myself. Not while I have a spark of life.

At the end of 1942, Louis Auchincloss got the long-sought-after transfer to sea duty. In a letter announcing his good news, he summed up his Balboa experience as a waste of time. "For an active mind it has surely been a barren stretch." Yet during Louis's "barren stretch," he had signed up for and completed two navigation classes, had taken a correspondence course in navy regulations, and had studied military law in order to serve as defense counsel in several court-martial cases. "I don't enjoy it terribly because I feel sorry for the defendants (enlisted men usually about Howlie's age), and the courts are severe with them," he wrote his mother. "But it's a chance to see the law again, and that means a lot." It also provided material for the best scene in his first published novel, the protagonist's defense of a mustang skipper (an ex-petty chief from the regular navy) accused of having had a woman in his quarters overnight. At first, he had been homesick— "the most trivial incident of New York life seems just carpeted with glamour from down here"—but a membership in the Union Club, "Panama's spiffiest organization," tea dances at the Officer's Club, stag dinners given by the American Society for the President of Panama and Cabinet, a continuous flow of friends passing through the Canal on their way to the Pacific theater of operations, old friends who worked at the American embassy, and new friends kept his mind off of New York. "Some of the new arrivals in the Navy down here are nice," he wrote home. "Jack Laughlin, one of the Jones & L. tribe, a friend of Lefty [Wilmarth] Lewis and all the Yale middle '20 boys, and a very nice and intelligent Professor McDaniels from Dartmouth. Socially the Navy down here has the army ranked."

Despite the heat, he played tennis, and he swam, the only way to cool off in the steamy Central American climate. "The Tropics can beat the resistance out of anyone," he complained in a letter home. "Why people ever live in places like this in peace time is beyond the scope of my imagination. One feels tired all the time, and sweats and sweats." Still, he claimed that life was so dull, he had to fill his time with movies, and still found time for a good deal of reading—Henry James, Evelyn Waugh, James Boswell, Samuel Johnson, Virginia Woolf, Henry Adams, John Dos Passos, and lesser talents. He discussed them, as usual, with his mother. "I disagree with you about Virginia Woolf. Her subtlety was not unhealthy, and her suicide was the result of a periodic insanity that was not connected (so far as I know) with the fine spun quality of her mental processes." "I have suddenly decided that Trollope is too low-brow for continued reading (this after some seven of his longest novels!) and turned (as a complete antidote) to a perusal of James' *Golden Bowl*." "Henry Adams is entertaining, never, I think, dull, but what he is not is profound. His tendency to generalize at the drop of a hat leads him to every extremity." For the first time, he regretted the lost last year of Yale for the reading he had missed. "Oh how wrong you were at deploring the time given to English," he wrote his mother. "Where would I be without books and the background to fit them (roughly) into the history of thought?"

By the start of 1943, Auchincloss had finally joined the navy afloat. If Balboa was Gilbert and Sullivan, his next phase of wartime service was the Marx Brothers. True, he had gotten to sea, but it was still the Caribbean. He was assigned to a converted private yacht that operated as a very ineffective submarine chaser, but since only an occasional German boat inadvertently slipped into the area, her inefficiency, due mainly to continual engine trouble, was not life-threatening. As he wrote in a novel much later, "It was dull duty, punctured by a very occasional submarine attack, for all the Germans were more occupied with the supply route to England than with stopping the shipment of cigarettes and magazines to the armed forces in the Canal Zone." Still, the USS *Moonstone* gave Auchincloss the opportunity to practice the navigation he had learned in his classes in Balboa.

In mid-February, the yacht sailed to Guayaquil to train Ecuadorian midshipmen as part of the State Department's Good Neighbor policy. "I enclose a street photo of me when I was on shore patrol one night," Auchincloss wrote from Ecuador. "I look like just what I am, a rather prissy person in the company of some tough looking sailors. The man in khaki squatting down is the chief Boatswain's Mate (senior enlisted man on board) who is my main prop. He is very good at handling men but also very stupid so he has great respect for my ideas. Very nice combination. I do like this ship and all on board very much." Even so, he added, he preferred "something more combatant."

Because the State Department decided to give the *Moonstone* to Ecuador, the ship was sent to the Charleston Navy Yard for a complete engine overhaul. The crew was given home leave, but Auchincloss, as much as he wanted to see his family and New York, wangled a place in a class at the navy's Submarine Chasing Training Center in Miami. By luck, his uncle Lee Stanton was also there, so they shared a room in the crowded Liberty, a small hotel for navy people. The Miami of 1943 was a simple little town with a main street, surrounded by small islands and a pleasant beach club that navy people could use for eating and swimming. Few had time. Auchincloss's class of 160 men met eight hours a day for two months. The school and the dreadful summer heat, worse than Panama he complained, were difficult, but he was determined to get a transfer to "a more fighting vessel" than a converted yacht. After graduation, he almost made it to the "real" war, but "the long remorseless arm of the Fifteenth Naval District plucked" him back to the *Moonstone*. The repairs finished, the crew returned to Balboa, a place Auchincloss had hoped never to see again, where the Ecuadorian navy examined and refused the ship. The now-harborless and -homeless *Moonstone* sailed from port to port looking for anchorage. Key West scorned its offer to serve as a sound school; Charleston declined its proposal to operate as a patrol boat; finally, the naval base at Cape May, New Jersey, gave the *Moonstone* a home. On its first patrol at Cape May, during a week that Auchincloss was temporarily detached to acquire new sounding gear, it collided with a destroyer and sank.

Thus was Ensign Auchincloss freed from the Fifteenth Naval District. He applied for amphibious training, which was instantly granted, for, as he later wrote, "The idea spread quickly throughout the Navy that selection to amphibious meant that one was not only incompetent but expendable, and no amount of popularization programs, and there were many, could ever quite clear it of this vaguely scrofulous atmosphere." Auchincloss learned to handle the LST, or landing ship tank, a 330-foot, four-ton landing craft in Chesapeake Bay, practicing navigation and landings. His fellow officers were largely ex-enlisted men or recent midshipmen and "not the cream of the class," he wrote home. At the end of February, Auchincloss, as executive officer and thus second in command, the captain, an ex–quarter master of the regular navy who both despised and feared his college-educated officers, and a crew went to Boston for their newly commissioned LST 980, which they took back to Camp Bradford, Virginia, for another few weeks to practice beaching the ship. As executive officer, Auchincloss became a "two-striper," as the servicemen called the full lieutenants. He was in charge of setting the watch for the 120-member crew, which worked in eight-hour shifts, except under fire, when the men were on duty four hours and off four hours. The young lieutenant got to know and was liked by most of the enlisted men on the ship, who, unable to pronounce Auchincloss, called him Mr. A.

An episode that occurred during the vessel's shakedown cruise before sailing for England made it clear what second-class citizens the amphibious men were in the eyes of the regular navy. The battleship *New York*, blocked by a group of LSTs in maneuvers, signaled to the group commanders, "Get your trash out of my way." But after D-day, just a few weeks in the future, the LST, as the solution to the age-old military problem of landing men and equipment on enemy shores, rose in stature. General Eisenhower called the LST "one of the greatest factors in the defeat of Germany."

LST 980 left for Plymouth in April. After a series of exercises in the channel, she anchored near Tilbury Docks in London. Despite bomb craters everywhere and entire streets that had been wiped out, the city was lively, full of Allied troops marking time for they knew not what. But the American LST officers and the Allied Supreme Commanders knew why London was so crowded. As Louis wrote:

> With what still seems to me incredible folly the navy believed that every officer of an amphibious vessel had to be apprised of every detail of the operation, instead of being told simply to 'follow the leader,' as the similar British units were. After one of our flotilla conferences in Tilbury, an old janitor at the base came hobbling after the departing officers with some papers which had been left on the table. They contained the entire plan for the Normandy landings! How this was kept secret from German intelligence agents must remain one of the mysteries of the war. I imagine that it never occurred to the spies that they could find what they wanted simply by hanging around the docks. They may have been too subtle for their job.

On June 6, the Allied fleet headed toward Normandy. Louis Auchincloss stood on the bridge of LST 980, which gave him a marvelous view of the incredible undertaking. Seven thousand vessels of all types crossed the Channel, carrying 131,517 men to land on the beaches code-named Utah, Omaha, Juno, Gold, and Sword. LST 980 landed at Gold, one of the English beaches, far less dangerous than Utah, Omaha, and Juno, where the greatest casualties occurred. The flotilla to which LST 980 belonged experienced no loss of life during the invasion, despite low-flying German planes, one of which dropped three bombs on LST 980. Two passed through the bulkheads to the water; the third came to rest in an ammunition truck. A British demolition expert who happened to be aboard the 980 offered to defuse the bomb.

"It's your bomb," he acknowledged, "but if it goes, we all go."

"Defuse it, by all means," executive officer Auchincloss readily responded. The terrified captain hid in the safety of his cabin while the demolition man removed the bomb with exacting dexterity and slowly lowered it into the sea. In a letter home, Auchincloss brushed aside the real terror he and his men had felt, admitting to "some tight moments" mitigated by "some absolutely God-sent luck." Forty years later, he described the episode in *Honorable Men*, his 1985 Vietnam novel.

LST 980 had been under fire on other occasions, as well. On one trip around the Brittany peninsula to bring ammunition for the siege of Brest, the ship, routed too close to the island of Guernsey, which still had German garrisons, was fired on from coastal artillery batteries. The 980, in a convoy of three LSTs, was loaded with explosives, yet when the Germans started lobbing flak, it took fully thirty minutes to get the slow-moving LSTs out of their range and "safely" into mined waters. On this occasion, Auchincloss said he felt "a moment of terrible, terrible panic. I almost wished we had been hit and can understand how sometimes pilots try to bail out of their planes because a certain death was preferable to the sickening fear." Unlike the fictional LST captain of *False Gods*, whose terror provoked him to walk off the bridge, leaving his battle station "without even transferring the 'conn' to the exec," executive officer Auchincloss remained at his watch. On another mission to the Straits of Dover, the 980 came under fire from the "Long Toms" of Calais. Worse were the robot-bomb attacks the 980 endured in the London docks. On June 13, Hitler sent the first flying bombs, more commonly called guided missiles today, over London. The Germans called their new secret weapon the V-1; the British called it the buzz bomb. "They make a horrible stalling sound as they come overhead," Auchincloss wrote his parents, "and then they are suddenly quiet: everybody gets under the nearest thing, and then—bang! And several more houses gone. It's a peculiar and unique feeling of terror that seizes one when the noise stops. Yet between the explosions one doesn't think too much about them," he wrote, despite extensive damage to London. "The city is beginning to look awfully messy," he commented, "but a great deal of sang froid is displayed." Only two LSTs in the 980's flotilla were disabled, despite the continuous bombardment by V-1s and the later and even more powerful V-2s.

For the next six months, LST 980 operated a shuttle across the Channel between various ports in England—Southampton, Falmouth, Portland, and London—and the Normandy coast, picking up troops, medical supplies, and, when the front moved away from the beaches, entertainers, and bringing back wounded Allied soldiers and German prisoners. At the end of August, Auchincloss described one such trip in a letter home. "The bells are ringing, they say today, in St. Paul's for the liberation of Paris, and I am ready to weep for joy. The 980's big doors are open, and hundreds of prisoners are filing off to England. As I watch them go, I feel the exhilaration of revenge, and what a discreditable sensation it is. But I've been watching the women prisoners, the army nurses with their flaxen hair, wide cheeks, and huge derrieres, and I can't repress a sentiment of satisfaction."

Lieutenant Auchincloss found the shuttle service interminably dull, despite his nearly having to take charge of the ship. The captain, unpopular, insecure, vain, lazy, and boorishly proud of his venereal record, cared only about the cleanliness of 980, relinquishing his ship-handling duties to his executive officer. "My life is a continuous bicker with the Captain as to how clean a ship has to be to be clean," Auchincloss complained. "He has no standards on anything except this, but he has a fetish against dirt." But because the 980 was at sea so infrequently—most of her time was occupied in loading and unloading—the executive officer had too much free time. He played bridge, read, and started work on a novel about Panama, which he regarded "as the only war experience I've had which has any literary possibilities," and he and his closest friend on the ship, Chauncey Medberry, the communications officer and future chief executive officer of the Bank of America, read Shakespeare's plays aloud. They read anywhere, on the bridge, in the wardroom, in their cabins. "At first I was a bit self-conscious when other officers or passengers would peer over our shoulders to find out what the hell we were up to," Auchincloss wrote, "but Chauncey never was. He had purchased a third Shakespeare in Southampton, and he would simply hand it, open at the correct page, to anyone who lingered beyond a few minutes, asking him to join in." They managed to read all of Shakespeare's plays, all of Christopher Marlowe, and much of Beaumont and Fletcher. Three decades later, Auchincloss wrote, "Despite the Battle of the Bulge and the buzz bombs, the cold, foggy winter of 1944–1945 still echoes in my mind with iambic pentameter."

LST 980 must have been the most literary ship in the navy. Besides his immersion in Elizabethan drama, Medberry organized literary discussion groups with the crew, and Auchincloss took volunteers to cultural landmarks such as Salisbury and Winchester cathedrals, Stonehenge, and Thomas Hardy country. On his own, Auchincloss got to the theater when he could, raving to his brother John about John Gielgud in Congreve's *Love for Love*. Through a friend, he gained entry to the House of Commons to hear Churchill, whose slow, sure manner reminded him of Endicott Peabody, and Lady Astor, who "was at her most typical, hopping up and down and shouting, but so well dressed, smart, and with such pearls." He visited Cliveden, then a military hospital, "where the

Sargent portrait of Lady Astor is breathtaking." He frequented London's used bookstores for first editions, which he had started collecting; and he often met friends at the Ritz for drinks and dinner. All this was suddenly disrupted when LST 980 made a faulty landing on a rocky beach at Le Havre late in the year, damaging her hull. Instead of taking part in the invasion of southern France, the 980 headed for Norfolk for repairs.

The convoy commodore, a naval commander, rode LST 980 for the rough winter crossing from Plymouth to Virginia. Since Auchincloss was assigned to be his navigator, Louis gained a partial independence from his hated captain and revenge for a year of his persecution, settling accounts in an unexpected way. During a storm one night, when Auchincloss went to the bridge to check the convoy's course, he sensed something was wrong. Realizing the gyrocompass had failed, and that as a result the 980 was headed straight into the second ship of the convoy, he relieved the officer of the deck and ordered an immediate and hard right. The sudden lurch in the tumultuous seas threw the ship's crockery to the deck and flung the captain out of his berth. In a fury, the captain forbade Auchincloss ever again to relieve an officer of the deck. Long after the captain had forgotten his irrational and unjust command, Auchincloss was on the bridge, watching for the first sea buoy at Norfolk. Once again, he realized the officer of the deck was not compensating for conditions properly and as a result was going to hit the buoy. Auchincloss called out for a course change, but, having been disempowered by the captain, he was ignored. He kept calling out charges, which were also disregarded, and insisted they be recorded in the log. By the time the officer realized his mistake, it was too late. LST 980 not only hit the buoy, scraping its bottom and making a horrible noise, it led the whole convoy over it. The commander nearly annihilated the captain for this humiliation, while Auchincloss felt victorious, vindicated, and a little ashamed. "That buoy might easily have damaged the screws of the ships that passed over it. And I had had the gall to criticize the fools in the Panama Canal Zone for impeding the war effort!"

The incident became a short story, "Loyalty Up and Loyalty Down," which appeared first in *The New Yorker* and later in a collection of stories, *The Romantic Egoists*.

After a short home leave that included a visit with Marshall and Joanne Field in Chicago, Auchincloss headed to the Pacific to take command of his own LST, once again preferring a war zone to the proffered shore duty. Once in Hawaii, he set out to find his ship, covering thousands of miles by sea and air. "I still haven't found my ship, the LST 130," he wrote home early in May, "but I am hopeful of being on the right track and believe that a couple of more weeks may do the trick." Three days after this letter was written, he flew into Ulithi, impressed by his first glimpse of the Pacific navy, and found his ship. "We plowed our way through the crowded anchorage," he wrote in "The Fall of a Sparrow," a very funny short story about an incident that occurred on LST 130, "past battleships and cruisers, past naval auxiliaries and transports, through endless rows of liberty ships and tankers, but it was forty minutes before we came in sight of the LSTs, looking like fat sea cows, riding placidly and securely at anchor near a small coral island with three palm trees."

The episode he related in "The Fall of a Sparrow" concerned his worst fear in becoming a skipper: having to moor his ship alongside a dock or another ship. Confident in his skills in navigating, beaching, and all manner of managing the ship and the men, he dreaded the day of his first mooring. When it came, his most ghastly presentiments were realized. The group commander ordered him to pull alongside an auxiliary vessel to take on water. With his crew watching from the deck, he made two approaches, the second time hitting the auxiliary ship. Finally, he turned to his navigator for help, and the mooring was successfully completed on the third approach. Unlike the fictional captain who abdicated his command as a result of his public humiliation, Lieutenant Auchincloss turned his embarrassment into an asset: He thanked his officers for helping him and set about preserving life aboard LST 130 as it had been before his arrival.

Not long after taking command, he returned to the United

States with the 130 for repairs and refurbishing. While Auchincloss was in Stockton, California, the war ended. To this day he remembers an irreverent headline announcing V-J day: *Second Bomb Knocks Nagasaki Wacky*. Ordered back to the Pacific in September, this time with a new crew of eager seventeen- and eighteen-year-olds, the 130 sailed to Hawaii for supplies intended for Sasebo, the great Japanese naval base. While anchored at Sasebo, he went to Nagasaki. "We really are living in a world that's as different from our old one as is the Land of Oz," he wrote home. "Nagasaki is not the devastation that I saw in England and France at all; not only are the buildings gone, but there's little rubble. The very material of construction has crumbled into small fragments! . . . I know it's natural to say that the use of the bomb ended the war and saved lives, but the man who can contemplate the hospital, large as Bellevue . . . gutted from one end to the other, in a single moment, and say: 'it's all for the best' must have a giant faith in the victory formula of the Anglo-Saxon world."

With the exception of this emotionally wrenching excursion, life aboard LST 130 was both pleasant and dull. As usual, Auchincloss read a great deal, declaring at one point that Proust was "the most significant novelist of our century," and he turned this time in earnest to his Panama novel, finishing a first draft before November 19, 1945, when he got his orders home. In a last letter home, sounding more like a homesick schoolboy than the mature, self-confident naval lieutenant who had endured the frustrations of Panama, the rigors of military life, and the dangers of combat, and who had commanded his own ship at twenty-seven, he expressed his eagerness to pick up life on Seventy-ninth Street exactly as he had left it in 1941. "I have no intention of taking 'a little apartment' (paid for by you) or living with a friend or anything. I shall stay with you and father until I'm married and probably after that."

Asked if he felt the war had changed him, he replies he supposes so but that exactly how is hard to say. "I was awfully glad to have been in it once it was over." Years after the war, he wrote that he had hated the very idea of it "not only because I feared to be killed or maimed, but because military life seemed of all lives

LOUIS AUCHINCLOSS

the most incompatible. I felt incapable of giving orders and averse
to receiving them. I was hopeless with machinery . . . and I abom-
inated the close community living . . . which I associated with the
least happy of my Groton years." He had survived unscathed, for
which he felt oddly guilty yet grateful; he had demonstrated to
himself as well as to his men that he could exercise authority and
maintain respect and approval; he had showed himself he was able
to navigate by successfully piloting an LST from California to Oki-
nawa without loran; and despite the close living quarters he had
dreaded, he had filled his letters home with comments about how
he liked the *Moonstone*, the 980, and the 130 for the people on
board. "I continue to reflect how unusually lucky I am to have
such pleasant companions" become a refrain throughout more than
four hundred pages of letters home. What he did not remark upon
was that for the first time in his life he had been in daily close
contact with people from backgrounds different from his own,
which had the effect (demonstrated in the letters) of lessening and
even expunging certain arrogant presumptions of his class. For
instance, he wrote his mother, "I remember Robin [Brewster, Yale
classmate] and I at the Savoy in London saying how much we'd
got out of boarding school, how necessary it was for boys, and
Medberry clearing the air by saying that 99 99/100% of American
boys must then be in a parlous state for they had never been
educated away from home!"

One last naval duty awaited Lieutenant Auchincloss in Portland, Oregon: He was made the commanding officer of a troop
train that carried three thousand sailors to New York City. Since
the war was over, the men looked on themselves as civilians,
making discipline impossible. Although liquor was forbidden,
drunkenness was rampant. At first, Auchincloss tried to keep
order, but when a group of chief petty officers suggested they run
the train to avoid certain mutiny, Auchincloss agreed. When they
got to New York, every man who had boarded at Portland was
accounted for, making theirs the only intact troop train. Louis was
asked how had he accomplished so remarkable a feat. All he could
say was, "They were too drunk to get off."

Louis Auchincloss had brooded on the long train trip across the country. His war experience had been so easy, he told himself, that he felt he had not yet seen war. He compared himself unfavorably to the paratroopers and airmen whose bravery in the face of almost-certain death left him feeling uncomfortable—"how do they do what they do?" he asked his mother. He realized at last, he told his old law professor Leslie Buckler, what he had "meant by the unforgettable intensity and pitch of war which renders the rest of life anticlimactic. Not in myself or anyone amphibious, for our role is pedestrian to an extreme, but in those boys who are dropped from the air into such unbelievable hazards. So many have told me that readjustment to civilian life was going to be hard for them, and I believe it, just as I know it will be easy and delightful for me."

Instead, Louis Auchincloss was to discover readjustment to civilian life difficult and unsettling.

CHAPTER 6

Law Apprenticeship

I can't help thinking . . . how always a strange sort of fate seems to be guarding
me from contact with . . . "the real thing,"when I get shoved into the book
review department of the Law Review or the trust and estate department of
Sullivan & Cromwell, or Balboa, or [sea duty on a converted yacht]. I've never
been "really" sick or "really" in love or "really" so many things, and I'm about
the same age Father was when he was married.

LOUIS AUCHINCLOSS

L ouis Auchincloss made no rush to Wall Street. Finishing
and polishing his war novel took precedence over the law.
His parents were genuinely alarmed. After all, not only
had Sullivan & Cromwell not guaranteed jobs to associates returning from the war, their son's reluctance to practice law, in contrast
to the postwar scramble for jobs, could hardly please his former
employer. "If S&C won't hold the job, that's too bad" was his
expressed attitude. "I'm not too crazy about them anyway." When
he finished his novel early in 1946, he delayed his return still longer
by taking a month to drive south with a Yale classmate and visit
friends in South Carolina and Virginia.

In early spring, he was ready to return to the law, having been
rehired by Sullivan & Cromwell. At first, he felt ill at ease, having
forgotten much of what he had learned at Virginia, so he attended
the Practicing Law Institute at night and before long felt at home
in the firm. He liked the associates in his department, Charles

Watts, Ken Jolly, and John Bruten. Thanks to Bruten's savvy advice to buy stock in Merck, Sharpe and Dohme, his ten-thousand-dollar navy severance pay became a small fortune over the next four decades. Another, Ken Jolly, asked him to be best man in his wedding. Auchincloss not only arranged for the famous Dr. Albert Parker Fitch of the Madison Avenue Presbyterian Church (his family's congregation) to perform the ceremony, he gave the reception in his parents' Seventy-ninth Street apartment, prompting the bride, who became a lifelong friend, to comment, "I tell you, the worst food is eaten by the American upper classes." Ken and Louis were exact opposites, Jolly's widow says today. An avid tennis and basketball player with no interest in the arts, a much-decorated wartime pilot from a small town in upstate New York, Jolly was fascinated by the aristocratic and urban Auchincloss, who, on Amagansett weekends at fellow associate John Raben's, sat on the porch, scribbling stories on his long, yellow legal pads while other guests played tennis or golf.

Jolly and Auchincloss often worked together. Once, they accompanied a partner in the estates section to John Foster Dulles's house on Ninety-first Street to witness his signing a new will. (The Auchinclosses had lived in the five-story house directly across the street from Dulles from 1923 until 1928. At that time, young Louis had known the great man only as the "naked man." One morning, when the children's nurse was talking to Priscilla Auchincloss, Louis burst into the room, shouting, "Hurry up, Maggie. The naked man's shaving now." The poor, frustrated woman, Auchincloss told Jolly laughingly, was humiliated to be so exposed before her mistress.) After Dulles signed the will, the estates partner countersigned and then blotted their signatures with the wrong side of the blotter pad, smearing the still-wet ink. So fearful was he of Dulles, he exclaimed, "Jolly, what have you done?"

Aloof in personal relations and always the stern moralist with little or no humor, Dulles made many of his lawyers nervous. It was he who had promulgated the deeply resented position about not promising to hire returning veterans, despite the fact that thirty-five associates had served overseas. Even though all who wanted to be were rehired after the war, the 1941 memo was not forgotten and most certainly was a major reason for Dulles' defeat as the 1950 Republican candidate for the Senate. To the associates, he was a man of formidable reserve, utterly insensitive to others' concerns. Once, Auchincloss was in a partner's office when the partner phoned Dulles to ask whether three associates could take their fiancées to the obligatory (and somewhat dreaded) annual New Year's Day party at the Colony Club, where the partners and wives met all the associates and wives. Dulles hesitated, then replied, "No. Fiancées are not wives." "A man like that," Auchincloss later said, "should never have been in charge of the State Department."

Sullivan & Cromwell's biggest case in the immediate postwar years was *U.S.* v. *Morgan*, a huge antitrust case. Because the firm represented five of seventeen defendants, eighteen new associates were hired in 1946 just to work on this case, which Sullivan & Cromwell won. By the end of 1948, there were more lawyers than desks. The excess sat in the library, which got so crowded, associates started doing their research at the New York County Lawyers' Association near the office. Having a single office, no matter how small, was a luxury for an associate. A new recruit asked Auchincloss, who had his own office, whether he worked much at night. Auchincloss, whose tiny window looked out on a dark air shaft, laughed and said, "I don't know." Sullivan & Cromwell occupied six floors at 48 Wall Street, necessitating much riding up and down on the firm's inside elevator to travel between the spartan quarters of the associates and the luxuriously paneled and furnished offices of the partners.

Auchincloss liked the firm, "the hierarchical structure, which struck [him] as a necessity to assure fairness, continuity, and efficiency in an organization so large," and, most of all, the friendships he made among the associates. "The nine of us who came into the firm in the fall of 1941 were fairly close," says retired partner Richard Powell today, "and Sullivan & Cromwell had several outings for us." On Saturday nights, they and their wives got together and did a lot of drinking and talking, generally staying up all night.

"I liked that," Auchincloss told an interviewer, "because I wanted to belong. I felt very much a sense of being part of the Sullivan & Cromwell family." He made friends among the partners, too. He went often for weekends to Hope Farm, Eustace Seligman's estate in Greenwich, Connecticut, even though Seligman was one of the major partners in the firm. "I loved going there," he says today, "because you were given instructions: Be on the tennis court at 3:00 P.M., dinner at 7:15, whatever. In between, you were on your own. I could write and no one would bother me." He thoroughly enjoyed New York's German Jewish society, the world of "Our Crowd," which included Loebs, Lewisohns, Lehmans, as well as the Seligmans. Louis felt they had succeeded in amalgamating the arts with business, banking, and the law with an ease and naturalness he never found in the "dry and juiceless" upper reaches of Protestant society. Other associates were invited to the Seligmans, too, although not generally for weekends. Some, including Auchincloss, thought their hosts "rather scanted the cocktail hour," but since the company was exhilarating and guests felt welcome, associates were pleased to be invited. Well liked by peers and partners, Louis felt at ease in Sullivan & Cromwell's world, but the peace and contentment its congenial atmosphere fostered in him was suddenly shattered by the very thing he had expected to bring elation. *The Indifferent Children*, the Panama novel he had conceived and written during the war, was accepted for publication by Prentice-Hall.

Auchincloss had submitted *The Indifferent Children* to a friend, James Oliver Brown, Little, Brown's New York editor. Brown loved the novel, but his editorial board rejected it. Auchincloss's second submission was successful. Angry scenes at home followed upon this news. His parents were adamantly against publication; his father insisted it would damage Louis's Wall Street career, and his mother pronounced it trivial and vulgar. "Her standard was Shakespeare," Louis says with a smile today, but at the time he did not want judicious or unbiased opinion; he wanted their approval and pride in his having gotten the novel accepted by a publisher. When Louis insisted on going through with publication, his mother nagged and nagged him until he agreed to use a pseud-onym. In retaliation, he called himself Andrew Lee, the name of one of his mother's clerical ancestors, who had put a curse on any descendant who smoked or drank (which, he said with a snicker, included all of them).

That Auchincloss had submitted so readily to what he now calls his mother's reprehensible conduct reveals how deep-seated were his own doubts as to his talent. He never questioned her disinterested concern for him, and he respected her literary judg-ment. "He had a great deal to overcome," Gore Vidal has said. "He had the bad luck, for a writer, to come from a happy family, and there is no leveler as great as a family's love. Hatred of one parent or the other can make an Ivan the Terrible or a Hemingway; the protective love, however, of two devoted parents can abso-lutely destroy him. This seems to have been particularly true in the case of Louis's mother. For one thing she knew a good deal about literature (unlike every other American writer's mother) and so hoped that he would not turn out to be second-rate and wretched."

Priscilla Auchincloss may also have feared her son revealed too many of his own insecurities in the character of the protagonist. He had admitted as much in a letter from England during the war. "I enjoy tinkering with [Beverly Stregelinus, a name Jack Woods had invented to sound like and to parody Auchincloss] because . . . I find that I can clarify little points to myself by trying to work them out in fictional form." These points, specifically his own emotions at the time of writing *The Indifferent Children*, were prob-ably not noticed by his New York friends, who were mindful only of Stregelinus, whose characterization was remarkably close to a man they knew, Ken Pendar. An effete, very social man-about-town in the New York of the late 1930s and early 1940s, Pendar had been so accurately depicted, he was deeply hurt. "I learned my lesson on that one," Auchincloss now admits and he resolved then and there never again to model a fictional character so closely upon an actual person. The descriptions of Beverly Stregelinus/ Ken Pendar's feelings, however, dramatize Auchincloss's own at the time, primarily his conviction that he was more the observer of life than the participant. When a character comments on Beverly's aptitude for noticing people and he answers, "Notice people! that's all I've ever done," he is expressing Auchincloss's perception of himself in the mid-1940s.

Oftentimes when Auchincloss compared himself to his contemporaries, he found himself wanting. Nothing he accomplished at Groton compensated for his nonconformity to the school's ideal of the all-American boy who loved rough contact sports. "I couldn't ever be 'Groton,' " he had written his mother at the time he was working on his novel, "so at Yale . . . I scorned the fraternity people and fell into Jack Woods's group. It wasn't till I fled from Jack to Virginia that I ever relaxed and enjoyed myself. And even there it cropped up when the best legal fraternity (all my friends were members) asked me to join and I quixotically and rudely refused." When he went to war, he compared himself unfavorably with the paratroopers and pilots who risked their lives every time they went into combat, while he comfortably read Shakespeare, Proust, and James. "Had I once been scratched? Had I gone a single day without three meals? Had I gone a single day without shaving?" In the "real" world of law, he looked on himself as a second-class citizen as a member of trusts and estates, the department he once fictionally characterized as the morgue. Taking scant consolation in his very real achievements, not only in school but in having been hired at such a firm as Sullivan & Cromwell, and at having so capably skippered his own ship, he yearned for "real" life and "real" experience, while at the same time he wondered why he had "to assume that everything from which [he] naturally recoiled had to have a greater validity in the scheme of things than anything which attracted" him. These and similar introspections he disclosed in letters to his mother as he worked on his novel. "I got [the] two letters of yours . . . about living and experience," he answered. "Yes, of course, the quality of living is inner. My hero tries to make up for his deficiencies by a halfhearted effort to associate himself with the external pattern. Of course this only intensifies his feeling of being left out."

When Beverly Stregelinus worried that he was "to be confined forever to the restricted emancipation of the passionless," and when thinking of proposing marriage he regrets "that there wasn't in him a turbulent, frothing cataract of early nineteenth century passions to run hissing over all his doubts and half-doubts and sweep away willy-nilly in the gushing current of aliveness," Auchincloss was worrying and regretting for himself. "The day after tomorrow I'm 27," he wrote his mother in 1944, "and I mind it as much as a famous beauty dreads the border line of 40. To be 27 and to have no start in the real business of life is sickening. . . . Keats was dead at my age. Father was launched in law and marriage. Grandfather was making that proverbial $27,000 per annum at 27." His "sense of never having lived at all" is bound up with the inherited stiff-upper-lip tradition of his upper-class upbringing, and Auchinclosses, if one of Priscilla's nephews is correct, were more "bottled up" than most. It is not surprising, then, that he made the search for "real" life the theme of his first published novel. The very title, *The Indifferent Children*, from the second scene of the second act of *Hamlet* alerts the reader to Shakespeare's indifferent children, who are happy in not being "over-happy" or on the "button on Fortune's Cap/Nor the soles of her shoe"; in short, like Beverly Stregelinus, emotionally timid and not very committed to anything or anyone, hence missing "real" life.

Auchincloss made Stregelinus "the most ridiculous young man in the world," and he is just that. When the novel opens, he is thirty-one and has just lost his job at an art gallery where he had spent most of his time telephoning, taking long lunches, gossiping with middle-aged women, and planning his evening partygoing. He has vague notions of writing an epic poem, but overall he is vacillating, drifting, purposeless, until the imminence of World War II provides direction. He wangles a job in navy intelligence, and so begins his halfhearted search for real experience and life. Part of this process entangles him in two marriage proposals, which astonishes the matronly set, who believed Beverly was "afraid of girls." Beverly Stregelinus is far from the ardent suitor. Alone with one fiancée, he "held her hand in the taxi and reflected with some discomfort that he would have to kiss her before they got to the Miami Colonial," and with the other, "he felt entirely relaxed. . . . There was no uneasiness about whether or not their friendship should evolve into an affair. She gave every appearance of being satisfied with the status quo and he could enjoy himself with impunity."

Although most characters in the novel (and many readers) suspect Beverly Stregelinus's lack of interest in women indicates he is homosexual, he is, more than anything, passionless, unable to become emotionally aroused by anything or anyone. Finally, he takes action that surprises everyone, even himself, by defending a man he despises at a court-martial, because he believes the man is being unjustly treated.

> It would mean disgrace and probably transfer to some Pacific atoll; it might mean worse . . . but wasn't this the best way after all, after the commission so politically pursued, after the falseness of his hankering for sea duty and his play acting with [his fiancée], after the years of non-living in a jungle of about-to-be purchased canvases, wasn't it best—even if it did smack of false heroics . . . to jump down off the plane of the observer and do or rather be one real and unappreciated thing?

When the defendant is acquitted, Stregelinus obtains a new commission in the real war in Europe. But "in the end," Auchincloss has written, "I was to find that I could not do much with anyone as silly as Beverly so I threw a buzz bomb at him while he was on liberty from an LST in London."

Biographical considerations aside, *The Indifferent Children* shows considerable literary merit. At the very least, the novel is a tremendous leap forward from the unpublished Yale novel, at the same time sustaining its two principal characters. Much of it is fast-paced, although there are parts that lag (the novel at 424 pages is Auchincloss's longest), and the end is something of an abandonment on the part of the novelist. In an epilogue. the book's narrator acknowledges that "we'll never know if Beverly had time to picture the climax of his search for real experience. We can hope that he was conscious of nothing or else had only a moment of frozen suspense; I can even picture the novels of Henry James flitting through his consciousness: 'So it's come at last—the distinguished thing.' "

The characterization of Beverly shows impressive psychological perception. He is a precious, effeminate, tedious, silly young man (despite a few redeeming moments), in exactly the way his creator intended. Introspective and painfully shy, Sylvia Tremaine, like Beverly, is a spectator in life who seeks refuge in the novels of Henry James. Audrey Emerson, who would do a great deal to escape the smallness and tawdriness of the Panama Canal Zone, is ambitious, sometimes malicious, and not very attractive. One of the best characterizations is that of Lieutenant Commander Sheridan Gilder, a failure in civilian life who finds in military protocol and pomp the respect he had always craved. As Auchincloss admitted, the characters in *The Indifferent Children* had "a combination of sterility and irritability that makes them unsympathetic," but they are believable. In addition, the novel presents a satirical yet deadly accurate picture of the bureaucrat—petty, bickering, jealous, self-aggrandizing—a trial scene that makes the reader wonder whether Auchincloss might not have made a great litigator, and a poisonous portrait of Panama. (It prompted the reviewer for *The Panama-American* to warn, "If you part with $3 for this stinker, you are out of your mind.")

Other critics were kinder, and one, writer William McFee, wrote a review that is, a half a century and thousands of reviews later, still Auchincloss's favorite. "Here is a novelist of the caliber of the Henry James who wrote *Washington Square* and *The Portrait of a Lady* rather than the author of *The Ambassadors*. It is James alive to our times, aware of things and people James himself never even sensed, with psychological alertness and a mastery of English the master would have enjoyed indeed." How sorry Auchincloss was to have used a pseudonym.

He had never gone to extremes to hide his authorship, though he never broadcast it, either, especially at Sullivan & Cromwell, where he hid whatever he was working on under the blotter. But a second cousin who ran a bookstore called Young Books told as many people as possible in order to increase sales. When Mrs. Auchincloss realized what was happening, she ordered the cousin to stop. "A pseudonym has got to be a deep, dark secret, or nothing at all," the author later told an interviewer. "Mother was the only one trying to keep it a secret. She went around making scenes with people who wanted to expose my identity. She succeeded in ruining my pleasure in it. That was a ridiculous performance, and it still embarrasses me to think of it." By the time the "secret" appeared in Dorothy Kilgallen's and Charles Ventura's gossip columns, Louis Auchincloss had become known as a new novelist. Even John Foster Dulles had heard about *The Indifferent Children*. When accused of running a sweatshop, he is purported to have said, "On the contrary, the associates have to fill out the day writing novels."

During the summer of 1947 after the novel's publication in May, Auchincloss drove up to Yale to consult Robert French, master of his undergraduate college, Jonathan Edwards, about the possibility of entering the Ph.D. program in English. Teaching English, it seemed to him, would be more compatible with writing and less demanding than practicing law. French patiently advised him, offered to make him a fellow of the college, which would have provided room and board, and then asked, "You have trained yourself to one noble profession, and you are already cheating on it. What extraordinary compulsion makes you wish to train yourself in another in order to do the same thing?" Downcast, Auchincloss returned to New York, still vacillating about whether to commit himself to law or to writing. He did decide to move out of his parents' apartment, which he did in 1948. He and fellow Grottie Sam Shaw sublet Priscilla Auchincloss Pedersen's two-bedroom apartment after she moved to New Canaan, Connecticut. Another Grottie, McGeorge Bundy, occupied its maid's room for a short time while looking for his own apartment.

Auchincloss started writing short stories at nights, on weekends, and during the odd off-hour at Sullivan & Cromwell.

Gretchen Finletter, one of Walter Damrosch's daughters and a close friend of the Auchincloss family, spoke about them to Edward Weeks, the editor of the *Atlantic Monthly*. Weeks asked to see the stories. On reading them, he took two, "Maud" and "Finish, Good Lady." Auchincloss was in Southampton, where his parents had rented a twenty-one-room Shingle Style beach house for the summer, when Weeks invited him to lunch at the Century Association. Complimented that so eminent an editor as Weeks liked his work and determined that his first appearance in print under his own name be as perfect as possible, Auchincloss willingly interrupted his vacation to meet Weeks and then readily agreed to all revisions, which paid off in an *Atlantic* First Award for "Maud." The two *Atlantic* stories, another that was sold to *Town & Country*, plus five unpublished ones were collected in a volume entitled *The Injustice Collectors*, which was turned down by Prentice-Hall but picked up by Houghton Mifflin, which remains Auchincloss's publisher to this day.

In addition to beginning a long-standing relationship with Houghton Mifflin, Auchincloss acquired an agent. James Oliver Brown, who had left Little, Brown at the time *The Injustice Collectors* was ready for publication, started a literary agency, with Auchincloss as a client. Auchincloss remained with Brown until the latter's retirement in 1984. Over the years, Brown developed a distinguished list of authors, including Alberto Moravia, Jean Stafford, Erskine Caldwell, Ford Madox Ford, Eleanor Roosevelt, Rebecca West, A. J. Liebling, Cecil Beaton, Richard Lockridge, Jessica Mitford, Lawrence Durrell, Doris Lessing, C. P. Snow, Mary Renault, and Honor Tracy. But with Louis Auchincloss, he had a special relationship. They first met in 1938 when Brown was still practicing law. By the time Auchincloss had finished *The Indifferent Children*, Brown had left law for publishing. Besides law and literature, the two men had similar backgrounds. By his own admission, Brown has "no objectivity" about Auchincloss because he is "completely in tune with what Louis is writing." Louis phoned him every weekday morning, and, during his bachelor days, he regularly stopped by Brown's apartment for his favorite cocktail, a martini, on his way home from work, before donning a dinner jacket "to emerge into the great world," as Brown describes his client's relentless socializing.

The Injustice Collectors contains eight long stories that are unified in theme: All concern people who are their own worst enemies in their unconscious bent for unhappiness or disappointment. The title was suggested by Edward Bergler's *The Battle of Conscience*, a study of masochists. When Bergler read the collection, he praised Auchincloss for being fifty years ahead of contemporary psychiatrists in his understanding of people who are unconsciously and continuously self-destructive. Each story focuses on a neurotic such as Maud, who is so afraid of losing her ego "in the consuming fire of family admiration," she destroys every chance for happiness that comes her way, including marriage to an eminently eligible and delightful man. Each story is deceptively simple, spare, witty, wise, and elegantly written. It is not at all surprising they were uniformly praised on both sides of the Atlantic and elicited unsolicited comments from the likes of Walter Lippmann—"your apprentice days are over"—and Evelyn Waugh—"The conception of every story is stunningly mature and most skillfully achieved. It is hard to believe they are the work of a beginner."

Louis Auchincloss was beginning to believe he was a writer, after all, and this heady notion complicated his life. Sullivan & Cromwell's religion of work—the kind of pride that impelled lawyers to brag, "I haven't been home before midnight in weeks," or "I haven't taken a Sunday off in more than a year"—bothered Auchincloss, whose commitment to law conflicted with his compulsion to write. In the 1940s and early 1950s, normal working hours at Sullivan & Cromwell were nine to six and half days on Saturdays. Auchincloss put in a normal day's work but rarely a moment more. His usual practice was to rise, eat breakfast, and write for a while. On the subway to Wall Street, he read, not law but literature. At night, he wrote a little, then dressed for the many parties he attended as an eligible and socially well-connected man-about-town; when he got home from the party, he jotted down overheard conversations and observations—just as Henry James had done—and went to bed, only to start the cycle all over again the next day. By contrast, a typical day for fellow associates began early and ended late at the firm. Bob McDonald and John Raben, for example, worked day and night for eight months on one land deal that was so complicated, the closing took three days, requiring 2,200 signatures on six hundred documents. The long hours and arduous attention to detail that were demanded of these young men form part of the background to Auchincloss's 1956 novel, *The Great World and Timothy Colt*, an attempt to capture the atmosphere of what it was like to work for a great Wall Street firm in the immediate postwar years. Of course, even Auchincloss stayed late on occasion, though few trust and estates people did. Curtis Pierce, the partner for whom he worked, got to the office at nine in the morning and left by six-thirty, rarely taking work home. "If you work through the day," he told his young associate, "you don't have to work at night," and he practiced what he preached. "He'd come in," Auchincloss remembers, "and people would say, 'Curtis, did you have a nice vacation?' 'Yes,' he'd reply. 'What's up?' " By contrast, Auchincloss says, the partner with the reputation as the most industrious in the firm strolled in at ten or so, smoked and read the newspaper until eleven or eleven-thirty. "Then he'd get steamed up and work till midnight. Pierce said, 'You just start earlier.' "

Auchincloss can laugh about work habits today, but in the 1940s, looking at what appeared to him as the unstinting dedication of everyone but himself made him increasingly uneasy. Every one of the nine 1941 associates, except himself, focused considerable intellect and energy on becoming a partner. Just like the fictional associate of a later story, one actually snooped in the files of partners to compile "statistics of their states of origin, law schools, legal specialties, religions, social backgrounds" as a gauge for his own potential promotability. Auchincloss, by contrast, worried that if he became a partner, the promotion might end the possibility of a literary life. On the other hand, he did not want to be passed over.

"I *was* much disturbed by those S&C days about what I

should be doing with my life," he wrote Ruth Jolly a quarter of a century later, "but there were compensating exhilarations." He meant, of course, his colleagues, whom he liked very much, and his work. Asked by a partner to investigate the wartime activities of the French firm of Worms & Cie, a Sullivan & Cromwell client that had been wrongly accused of Nazi collaboration, he made a report that induced the author of *Our Vichy Gamble* to withdraw ("very reluctantly," says Auchincloss) his charge of collaboration, thereby reestablishing the firm's good name and strengthening its ties with Sullivan & Cromwell. He also assisted in the administration of the estate of Henry James, the nephew of the writer, who had inherited Lamb House, his uncle's residence in Rye, England, and he represented the estate of William Nelson Cromwell at a transfer of property at Columbia University, among other interesting matters. (When the school lawyer asked why Cromwell's executors, John Foster Dulles and Eustace Seligman, were not present, Auchincloss replied that he stood in their stead. The university attorney refused to go on unless Dulles or Seligman appeared. "I'll tell you what," the associate shot back. "You produce Eisenhower"—then Columbia's president—"and I'll produce Dulles and Seligman." The counselor for Columbia gave in, and the closing was completed.) Louis contented himself with his place in trusts and estates, which was not deadline work and rarely kept him late at the office, enabling him to keep writing—and by this time he was writing at the office every chance he got. Bemused and titillated by his dual pursuits, his friends "ran out to get whatever he published to see who was in it." At first, only his closest friends in the firm knew that he wrote every chance he got, but after the publication of *The Injustice Collectors*, all the partners and associates were aware of the writer in their midst. His writing was much commented on.

After the short stories were finished, he started in on a novel, which was accepted for publication in March 1951. *Sybil* is a character study of a well-to-do New Yorker who marries a handsome, wealthy young man utterly wrong for her. Without much plot— she plays the role of adoring wife; he strays; she leaves; she returns

—Auchincloss skillfully shows her growth from a shy, bookish, unsocial girl to a graceful and wise young woman in the way she deals with her unworthy, inconstant, and coarse husband. Reviewers declared the book civilized, well-crafted, psychologically perceptive, artfully ironic but somehow cold, impersonal, and, according to Orville Prescott of *The New York Times*, "dull." The criticism that Auchincloss lacked the passion and power to move a reader emotionally had been made not just of *Sybil* but of *The Injustice Collectors*, as well. Auchincloss, a born storyteller, was also, alas, "too impersonal," "too cool," "too dispassionate."

Certainly his colleagues believed his approach to his legal career was dispassionate. Little did they realize that despite the iron discipline it took to practice law, write books, and pursue an active social life, he had been agonizing since the war over whether he was slighting a promising literary career by not devoting himself to it full-time; as time passed, the tension within him grew. Sooner or later, he promised himself, he would make a decision. At one of the associates' Saturday all-night parties, he told John Raben's wife, Connie, that he might eventually give up the law to write.

"Eventually!" she exclaimed. "Hadn't you better make up your mind? You're a big boy now." He went home very upset that night, for she had struck him where he was most vulnerable. Later, he discussed his dilemma with Raben, a brilliant attorney and one whose judgment Louis trusted. A man who worked around the clock, he thought Auchincloss was going to be hopeless as a lawyer. Raben was baffled by his friend's indecision—how, he asked, could he think he might succeed in either law or literature without dedicating himself to it day and night? According to Raben's lights, Auchincloss was cheating on both.

Over a period of time, Louis had been talking to his parents about how disturbed he was over what he should be doing with his life. "I had to find out once and for all what I was," he told them. Despite their previous opposition to his literary endeavors, when they fully understood why it was essential for him to try writing full-time, "they came around," as he recalled. "Coming around" meant agreeing to support him financially, because his highest annual nonlegal earning of $1,213.69 in 1949 fell pitifully short of even bare subsistence. To Louis's relief, they backed him unstintingly. He was moved by their response.

Recalling their conversation in his memoirs, he asks, "Could love go further?" Moreover, their generosity provided a model for him when he became a father. "I'm always willing to back my children and help them, because my parents did it with me."

In September of 1951, Auchincloss announced his decision to resign from Sullivan & Cromwell. On December 31, his resignation took effect. Louis Auchincloss had unequivocally committed himself to a writer's life.

CHAPTER 7

A Writer Adrift

The nervous temperament has got to have faith, for I am increasingly convinced that life is nothing, nothing at all, "the quintessence of nothingness," until one has thrown out fear.

LOUIS AUCHINCLOSS

Louis Auchincloss was living alone by 1952—Sam Shaw having moved downtown—on one floor of a small brownstone at 24 East Eighty-fourth Street. The building opened into a dark front hall with a straight, high staircase leading to the apartment above. In Louis's first-floor apartment were what once had served as a stiff, formal parlor for entertaining guests, now a living room nicely fitted out with Auchincloss hand-me-down pieces, a Chinese rug, and fine Audubon prints, and a former dining room that now served as a bedroom. The two rooms, plus a small kitchen and bath, provided the setting for the literary life he had been so determined to pursue. His daily practice was to rise every morning around eight, then write in his pajamas and bathrobe until noon, when he went out for lunch. Back at his apartment by early afternoon, he wrote until five, read until six, and then dressed for dinner. He dined out frequently, "dinner party after dinner party," his brother-in-law remembers, "and most of them made up of people considerably older than Louis."

Although his friends thought it odd a young man in his mid-thirties chose so frequently to consort with rich old ladies and their eminent gentlemen—"he was always available to take so and so to the opera"—their attraction for the novelist was as depositories of history and as notable personages of the city. After every dinner party, he recorded his observations of the evening in a notebook, including witty snippets of conversation. He entertained his own contemporaries with stories of these dinner parties, which they loved. "As witty as his writing can be," Ruth Jolly says, "it is not nearly as alluring as his tongue. He has the gift." He continued to see his Sullivan & Cromwell friends—playing bridge with the Watts, visiting the Powells in Englewood Cliffs, New Jersey, staying the occasional weekend with the Rabens in Amagansett, eating dinner with the Jollys—as well as his old Groton and Yale schoolmates. He did not cook, so he invited people to his apartment for drinks and then ordered in dinner from the Casserole Kitchen, one of the first take-out places in the city. On more formal occasions, he gave dinner parties at his parents' apartment when they were out of the city, amusing his less formal friends with his custom of dismissing the ladies to the living room for coffee while the men remained in the dining room for port and cigars. (When novelist Jean Stafford was present, she took obvious offense at the banishment, quietly pouting until the men rejoined the women and resumed what she considered more satisfying conversation.)

As extensive as Auchincloss's social life was, for besides the nearly nightly dining out, there were numerous weekend house parties, he wanted to meet other writers. This period in New York was one of literary ferment. It seemed as if every American writer was in New York and had enormous curiosity about everyone else. (In just a few years, this concentration of writers was to be reversed by the writing programs taking hold in the universities across the country.) John Aldridge was the first serious critic to draw attention to writers such as Norman Mailer, Saul Bellow, Truman Capote, Irwin Shaw, and Vance Bourjaily, to mention a few. Aldridge had so extravagantly praised Bourjaily's *The End of My Life*, saying no book had "contained so complete a record of the loss of youth in that war," the two men met and became friends. They made a point of meeting other writers, including William Styron, James

Jones, Merle Miller, Hortense Calisher, Carson McCullers, George Plimpton, Herman Wouk, John Hersey, Ralph Ellison, and Louis Auchincloss, and before long, Aldridge and Bourjaily hatched the idea of coediting a paperback called *Discovery*, devoted to publishing these writers' best short stories, poems, and essays.

Discovery's publisher, Pocket Books, underwrote parties for these writers, which were given either at Vance and Tina Bourjaily's apartment or at a Greenwich Village bar called the White Horse Tavern, which was where Auchincloss met so many of them. Gore Vidal often attended, but Auchincloss had met him elsewhere, though he cannot remember where. Vidal remembers exactly when he first heard of his ex-stepcousin, as Auchincloss often addresses him. "Right after the war when I was told that a Louis Auchincloss had written a novel, I said: Not possible. No Auchincloss could write a book. Banking and law, power and money— that was their category." Yet Vidal and Auchincloss became friends during the 1950s. They met for lunch regularly and saw each other at literary gatherings; at least once, Auchincloss drove up to Barrytown for lunch with Vidal at Edgewater, his house on the Hudson, and Vidal went to a few of Louis's dinner parties; they correspond to this day. "I think I saw sides to Gore he doesn't show to the world," Auchincloss believes. "He has a very, very generous, amiable side."

Other than Gore Vidal and Jean Stafford, however, the New York literary coterie paid little attention to Auchincloss, though he alone of them had read everyone else's books. Norman Mailer had read at least one of his short stories, conceding, "he would not have minded having written 'The Gemlike Flame' himself." But "banking and law, power and money," in Vidal's phrase, was indeed the source material for Auchincloss's fiction, and most of the writers he met at the White Horse seemed blissfully unaware of this world and of the truth that it turns its back firmly on serious literature. Conversely, the writers looked on a representative from the great world, "a Wall Street lawyer, a registered Republican, and a social registrite . . . as a kind of duckbill platypus not to be taken seriously," Auchincloss wrote, and a real oddity. "Louis moved through those affairs with considerable charm," Vidal has said—which only proves his point, Auchincloss says with a laugh. "Isn't that sticking out?"

Auchincloss never felt part of the group at these literary gatherings, as he had with the Sullivan & Cromwell people, and one of the reasons was that he never got to know the habitués as well as they knew one another. Unwilling to spend the inordinate amount of time sitting around the White Horse that the others delighted in doing, he acknowledges, "I almost always had something else to do, and I just couldn't sit around hour after hour drinking beer. I'd leave just as everything was warming up and later I'd hear it was perfectly wonderful, but I doubt that." Auchincloss, who often came dressed for a later engagement, even looked different. "The writers teased him because he'd come to the tavern in his Brooks Brothers best," an uptown friend remembers. "He understood that they looked on him as a rich boy dabbling in literature." "Poor Louis who *knew* French and American literature, who 'kept up' with what was going on," Vidal has written, "now found himself in a literary society of illiterate young play-actors; overexcited by the publicity surrounding Hemingway and Fitzgerald, they decided to imitate these 'old masters.' At least a dozen were playing Hemingway several grizzled survivors still are. . . . So, in a way, Louis was indeed a platypus in that farmyard of imitation roosters. After all, he didn't resemble any famous writer we had ever heard of. He was simply himself, and so odd man out to the young counterfeiters." The evenhanded Auchincloss remarks that not all were counterfeiters: "Everyone I remember focusing on made their mark sooner or later in some way." Despite his lack of enthusiasm for the Greenwich Village literary circles, Auchincloss did become quite friendly with the Bourjailys. "We gave Louis safe passage below Fourteenth Street," Tina Bourjaily remembers, "and in turn he was very generous with the wonders of the upper East Side, his milieu."

The writers' regular get-togethers ceased when the Bourjailys moved to Connecticut after the birth of their first child. Auchincloss, who insisted he was too stiff and formal among the writers, was not sorry. But "to be totally fair about my experiments with literary milieus," he wrote several years later, "I should admit that I was making them, as with so many other experiments in my life, out of a false sense of duty. But happily I was learning at last to rid myself of this dismal inner companion." The source of this new self-awareness was his psychoanalysis with Dr. John Cotton.

Auchincloss had been restive for a long time, worried from the start that he had made a terrible mistake in resigning from Sullivan & Cromwell, that he did not have it in him to be a major novelist, and that he was standing still in life. Most of his friends were long married, had children, were settled in careers, and were even beginning to do well, and here he was still dependent on his parents. Before Sam Shaw had moved downtown, he had suggested Louis seek therapy. He thought it odd that Louis spent so much time with middle-aged women. "Here's a guy who's in his thirties," Shaw reasoned, "and he spends his time going to dinner with old ladies. I don't think that was well-balanced. I thought he had a hard intellect and a hard will, but there was something missing; this was not the best way to spend his life." Several of Louis's uptown friends were undergoing psychoanalysis, and they advised him to do the same. Before he resigned from Sullivan & Cromwell, he had discussed the matter with his parents, since they would have to pay for it. Although Howland Auchincloss had never been psychoanalyzed, four serious bouts of depression had sent him to psychiatrists. His mother, too, had been subject to depression and was treated by Dr. S. Weir Mitchell, renowned in the late nineteenth and early twentieth centuries for his "rest cure" as treatment of "nervous" diseases. So, too, was Louis's sister afflicted, thus both Howland and Priscilla Auchincloss had had much experience with psychiatry, though Priscilla had never felt the need of professional help for herself. Once, walking with the psychiatrist Ludwig Cast in Bar Harbor, she boasted that she had led a productive life without the aid of his profession. "Ah, but the woman you might have been," Dr. Cast replied. If her son believed he needed psychoanalysis, however, Priscilla had no objection. Howland Auchincloss once again generously agreed to provide the necessary financial aid. A friend suggested John Cotton.

Dr. Cotton was a classic Freudian analyst. He sat in a chair out of the sight of his patient, who lay on a couch, yielding himself up to free association; that is, saying everything that came to his mind. A good analyst cultivates an alert passivity, trying by skillful questioning to get the patient to discuss any troubling thoughts and feelings and to stop repressing other feelings. An analyst's interpretation should be subversive in that it should raise uncomfortable doubts about the ostensible messages the patient thinks he or she is conveying. Supposedly, this method chips away at self-deception. The entire process, which in Auchincloss's case lasted two and a half years, confirms the power of the unconscious and reveals the irrational side of the patient, which, according to Freud, will govern his or her life, so it needs to be understood. "The Senior Partner's Ghosts," a short story Auchincloss wrote ten years after psychoanalysis, dramatically embodies this hidden power of the subconscious mind. In preparation for a biography of his law firm's founder, the senior partner dredges up memories and records them on a tape recorder for two hours each morning, but he gives up his free association when untoward incidents seemingly leap out of his mouth onto the tape.

Auchincloss refuses to discuss the actual content of his own analysis except in the most general terms, and this is not because he cannot remember. He still remembers one of the first exchanges in his analysis.

"When you freely associate," Cotton told Auchincloss at the start of his sessions, "you'll find three things difficult to talk about. Sex and sexual fantasies, but you anticipated that. The second-most-difficult thing you'll talk about is money, and the most difficult is me."

"What do you mean, 'me'?" Auchincloss asked.

"My appearance," the overweight doctor replied.

"And that was," Auchincloss admits. "I'd say, 'I've blocked,' and he'd say, 'what is it?' and I'd say, 'I'm thinking how awful it is to be so fat and bald.' " And then he would add, "Oh, I can't bear it, Dr. Cotton, that I've been so rude." A fictional patient in a 1974 short story expresses this exact difficulty when she admits that "her terror of having to articulate reflections that were personally insulting to the doctor" put an end to her therapy.

Indifferent to his remarks, Cotton assured him he had heard far worse. Once Auchincloss did elicit a cry of pain, when he admitted, after "blocking," that Cotton's Christmas card was so vulgar and banal, he had thought it was some kind of test. (This incident, too, showed up in a short story.) Despite such occasional awkward moments, Auchincloss and Cotton became friends. Cotton told another friend of Auchincloss's, "Louis is a remarkable, extraordinary man, slightly driven. One can't see him putting his feet on a table and puffing a cigar and thinking." The strictest of Freudians would not have cried out as Cotton had done, nor would he have established a relationship with his patient. Still, he did his patient a great deal of good, despite his disclaimer: "We never know when our patients cure themselves or whether we had anything to do with it. Psychiatry is a vague thing."

Auchincloss looks back on the two and a half years of psychoanalysis as a very difficult time. He worried about money, "panicky from time to time, sure [he] had made a big, fat mistake," and very close-mouthed about being psychoanalyzed. Even so, his friends knew about it and speculated about the reasons for the analysis.

Most of them believed, in fact, that he had left the law primarily to undergo the therapy, although he denies it. When he first approached Cotton, the psychiatrist assumed he would need an early-morning appointment and seemed slightly shaken when his patient-to-be informed him he had already resigned from practice. Still, the words of the protagonist of *A Law for the Lion*, the novel he was writing while being analyzed, expresses a point of view that might have been the novelist's own, suggesting that the therapy was at least as important as the writing. "I'm not going to marry anyone. . . . I want to find out first what I am. I want to learn to live with myself." What he hoped to find out, whether he was a writer or a lawyer, is obvious, but what was it he had to learn? "To throw out fear," he has written time and time again, but specifically what he feared, he will not say.

Some of his friends think it was women. The Sullivan & Cromwell people noted how rarely he was seen with women his own age; some of the White Horse habitués assumed he was homosexual. Vincent Piket, a young Dutchman who wrote about how autobiographical a writer Auchincloss is, considered the prevailing opinions and concluded:

> The nonsexual friendships with middle-aged women were clearly sought by Auchincloss; being "shy with girls," he arranged his social life in such a way as to protect himself against the sexual threat. This did not mean, however, that [he] was happy about the situation. On the contrary, his lack of "dates" and friendships with younger women increasingly caused him distress.

Eleanor Elliott, a young woman he seriously courted in the mid-1950s, believed that he did indeed grow up frightened of women and that his mother frightened him. "Those women of a certain social background like my mother and Louis's mother had difficulty with sex. They maybe found sex fun but sinful, 'sex being a sweet sin.' "

While timidity with women may have been a trait Auchincloss was determined "to throw out," it is certainly only part of the story. Priscilla Auchincloss reared overprotected children unacquainted with the rough and tumble of life, and in the process, she filled her children with all sorts of fears. Although to the world she presented a self-assured, witty, urbane, even brilliant persona, to her family she was in a constant state of fear, not for herself—she was utterly stoic about her own death from cancer—but for her children, fear that they might not attain their rightful place in life and, above all, fear for their safety. She never allowed them to spend a night out-of-doors, though they had ample opportunity with country homes on Long Island and on Mount Desert Island,

and they were discouraged from sailing and flying, even as passengers. Louis's sister, Priscilla, remembers her mother forbade raw fruits and vegetables, afraid they would cause disease. The children were almost grown before they had them. She was constantly worried whenever the children were out of her sight. Louis wrote about his mother's fears about her children in a profile of her that was published in 1989 in *Family Portraits*.

> I believe that mother came to fear her responsibility for the possible death of a child more than death itself. I have no doubt that her anxiety about me when I served in the amphibious navy in World War II was substantially less than her anxiety when I was driving home in the early morning, after many drinks, from debutante parties. The war was in no way chargeable to her account. . . . Her dread of responsibility was carried to an obsessive degree. I remember her comment about a newspaper account of some children who, having been refused permission to fly and been taken to the railway station where tickets to their destination had been purchased, had awaited the departure of their parents to hop a plane which had crashed, killing them all. "Well, those parents were certainly off the hook!" she exclaimed. . . . I can remember a grotesque incident on a trip abroad, when, approaching the edge of the Moher Cliffs in Ireland, the Auchinclosses intrigued the other tourists by dropping to their hands and knees at Mother's shrill command to crawl for greater safety.

Priscilla Auchincloss's fears for her children, most likely the result of her own mother's overprotection after Priscilla's younger brother had died in infancy, leaving her an only child for ten years, kept her continuously anxious and in need of her family's solace. "But mother dear," Louis wrote in 1942, "as you know, the quality in you that never gets sympathy from me, though it gets it luckily richly from Father and John, is your constant need for reassurance. I have the same failing, and I know how silly it is, so I don't sympathize. So remember you don't need me now. . . . I could be no comfort to you, but then, after all, only God could be, because you want an absolute answer to the human question."

Many friends and relatives contend that Louis was the only one of the four children to have emerged from Priscilla Auchincloss's authoritative and autocratic influence a stronger and more assertive person, and that he had to go through psychoanalysis to achieve this. A first cousin goes further and maintains he was the sole survivor of those children. As Louis's oldest son has said, "None of my uncles or aunt had anything near the happiness my father did." One reason is they went through life deeply resenting their mother. Shortly before his death, John told Louis he had not missed their mother one minute since she had died. "I couldn't believe it—John, the ideal son," Louis's middle son said when told of his uncle's sentiments. "To me it shows that her constant, unwilting attention had a negative effect." Priscilla Auchincloss was, by all family accounts, demanding, yet she cared passionately about her family, too passionately most likely. She was "too much interested in Louis and had far too much influence on him," according to Eleanor Elliott, which, in addition to "her nutty theories about raising children," produced in him "various nervousnesses." She was also a possessive mother. "She guarded her own far too closely," Blake Auchincloss recalls, and even late in life, she manifested signs of an unbalanced need to hang on to her children. When her daughter's infirm father-in-law moved in with young Priscilla and Bill Pedersen, "she was absolutely outraged," Louis remembers, because her daughter had to care for the old man. Louis calmly pointed out how much Priscilla loved Mr. Pedersen and he her, to which his mother reacted, "I envy Mr. Pedersen." "That old, penniless man forced to live with his daughter-in-law? Why?" Louis retorted. "Because he has my daughter, and I don't," she replied. One of her daughters-in-law said, "She didn't want fusses made over her, yet she wanted the ultimate fuss. She wanted all your attention."

To her credit, when her son was being analyzed, she "helped in every way and was perfectly willing to face the most tremendous mistakes that she might have made," Louis says. "We'd talk about anything." As a result, he never resented her. "Mother was a woman of goodwill who did terrible things to her children. She was firmly convinced that the only important thing was to have children and bring them up, yet she was an inappropriate person for this." He concluded that her own familial, strongly anti-intellectual inheritance made sublimation of her extraordinary intelligence and literary talent, maybe genius, necessary; not only were the times against her, the Dixons, good-natured and kind, made rebellion unthinkable. He attributed at least part of his understanding to psychoanalysis.

The most important truth he got out of his sessions with Cotton, he believes, was learning to live with himself, accepting himself. "Was there any point," he wrote later, "in the one life that was given, for him to fuss over what he was not? Oh, how obvious these conclusions seem! And yet a man can spend his whole existence never learning the simple lesson that he has only one life and that if he fails to do what he wants with it, nobody else really cares." According to Auchincloss, if a person accepts himself, there is nothing he cannot do. "So often men are born with all the tools they need, but are blocked by the simple fear of using them." And Cotton, he says, freed him from this fear and from "all sorts of things. He widened my decisions, and he confirmed I could do anything in the world. He didn't change me; he opened doors. He worked with what I had."

With his increased self-confidence, Auchincloss not only accepted his mother's fears for what they were, largely self-created, but he also came to realize that he, too, had fabricated his own special anxieties, which became the oppressive expectation he had set for himself. The title of the last chapter of his memoir, *A Writer's Capital*, is "Compromise." In it, he tells his reader that demands that appeared to come from his family and social background were mostly demands he had created in his own mind. John Cotton made him see that a man's background is his own creation. Was it not true, Auchincloss reasoned, that what he considered important in the past was not the same as what his siblings focused on?

Louis Auchincloss at Yale.

Louis's parents, Priscilla Stanton Auchincloss and Joseph Howland Auchincloss, in 1912, about a year after their marriage.

A pony ride in Central Park for the Auchincloss children— Priscilla, Louis, and John.

Louis just before his fourth birthday in 1921.

Priscilla Stanton Auchincloss in 1941.

An Auchincloss family portrait in Bar Harbor, August 1925. The children, from left to right, are Priscilla, Howlie, Louis, and John.

The Boxee School baseball team. Louis is in the second row, fifth from left.

Groton fathers and sons assembled for the school's fiftieth anniversary in 1934. Franklin D. Roosevelt is at top center; to his left is Groton's founder and headmaster, Endicott Peabody. Louis Auchincloss, class of '35, is in the front row beneath the pillar at right center.

Behind Louis is his younger brother Howland, Jr.; behind Howland, Jr., is the boys' father, Howland, Sr.

AUCHINCLOSS PARTY
LONY CLUB   DECEMBER 26, 1937

*The Auchincloss family reunion, December 26, 1937,
at the Colony Club. A young but very recognizable Louis
gazes at the camera from just right of center.*

*Louis and his sister, Priscilla, at the wedding of one of Louis's
Yale classmates in the summer of 1941.*

*Jack Woods (at right) at the same wedding. Woods committed
suicide the same night this picture was taken.*

Louis aboard ship in World War II.

Three Auchincloss brothers in uniform--from left to right,
John, Louis, and Howland--during World War II.
On the right is their brother-in-law, Bill Pedersen.

Louis and Adèle on their wedding day, September 7, 1957. The wedding was held at Adèle's family's house in Charlotte, Vermont.

Malcolm Strachan, in clerical collar, at Louis's wedding. As an English teacher at Groton, Strachan had influenced Louis deeply.

Louis's father, Howland, in 1958.

Louis with his mother, early 1960s.

Louis and Adèle in their Park Avenue home with sons
Andrew, Blake, and John.

The Auchinclosses' house in Bedford, New York.

Louis in the living room of the Park Avenue apartment.

Adèle Auchincloss at home on Park Avenue.

Louis, with his son Andrew, aboard the Natural Resources Defense Council ship
The Observer *in Alaska. Adèle Auchincloss was a founder of the NRDC,*
and led several tours to Alaska.

Adèle fishing in Alaska.

Louis Auchincloss at his desk in the offices of Hawkins, Delafield & Wood.
(Henry Grossman, Courtesy Architectural Digest © 1984. All rights reserved.)

Drawing by James Stevenson © 1986 The New Yorker Magazine, Inc. October 6, 1986.

My parents never intended me to feel [as I did]. . . . It was *I* who unreasonably seized upon their understandable caution as a grim rule of life to which I had better submit myself as early as possible. It was I, not they, who came to think of human souls as existing in a harsh Calvinist scheme of preordained election: with salvation for a handful of geniuses, Shakespeares and Michelangelos, and for the rest of us the living death of the business community.

Auchincloss has described the process of analysis as cleaning away "the cobwebs of fears" that had obsessed him for years. He learned, as one of his characters puts it, that "there was no tyranny like his old obsession that his amusements had to be those of other people. He had digested the simple rule that the most difficult of all lives to lead was his own." Thus, analysis helped him to resolve his inner conflicts, to make peace with what his mother represented, literature, and with what his father represented, law. The result, a longtime friend believes, is "his extraordinary inner compass or center of gravity. He's extremely balanced in an unbalanced world. He doesn't get thrown to extremes as author, father, or lawyer. There's a cohesion of the roles he's fulfilled in life." He came away from therapy not the least resentful of his past but, rather, even more strongly attracted to it, though he plainly saw its flaws.

The novels Auchincloss wrote during and immediately after psychoanalysis demonstrate the force it exerted on him. Eloise Dilworth, the protagonist of *A Law for the Lion*, is a nearly perfect Freudian example of the power of the subconscious to dictate behavior. Understandably bored by her family, especially her husband, and by her environment, Eloise tries to fit in, but the harder she tries, the more she seeks release in a fantasy of being "brought out on deck, a captured princess on a pirate ship, and stripped and whipped before a leering crew." When the fantasy is realized, it becomes clear that she unconsciously set the humiliation in motion. Her first step is to invite Irene, her much-married, irresponsible, rakish, and heavy-drinking mother, to her summer home. Of course, Irene misbehaves, and George, Eloise's oafish husband, makes Irene leave. Eloise may believe her motivation was only to be hospitable to a sick mother, and she is distressed by her dismissal, but subconsciously she meant it to happen. In asking Irene out to Long Island from the city, she knows that George can be depended upon to enact the villain of the piece. Her next step is to seek the company of a boorish young writer, into whose reluctant arms she eventually casts herself with grim determination. Predictable George, goaded into jealous action, summons the jeering mob in the person of a detective who charges into the room of assignation and takes pictures. Eloise is relieved that society has at last exposed her real self.

The Great World and Timothy Colt is Auchincloss's 1956 novel about a young, brilliant, and hardworking lawyer, who, though he rises rapidly in a prominent law firm under the tutelage of the senior partner, has a compulsion not to succeed, wrecking not only his career but his marriage. In the 1958 *Venus in Sparta*, Auchincloss shows how the protagonist's sense of inadequacy and guilt (that have destroyed his life) developed, telling the story through a series of flashbacks that work like psychoanalysis, peeling away memories of actions to reveal patterns of behavior. Michael Farish's impulse to self-destruction is even worse than Timothy Colt's self-loathing. Reese Parmelee, the protagonist of Auchincloss's 1959 novel, *Pursuit of the Prodigal*, is another lawyer who almost self-destructs. He forsakes his wealth, social position, wife, two children, and the comfortable world of Parmelee Cove to find himself. He takes a job in a less respectable law firm than the one he left and meets a girl whom he marries. When his new life leads him into a crisis, he almost does not emerge. Like his creator, though, he comes to realize that "the world he resented might be of his own invention" and progresses to asking, "What can happen if I don't learn to be happy?" Unlike Timothy Colt and Michael Farish, he opts for trying to learn to be happy.

Reviews of Auchincloss's "psychological" novels were uniformly positive but not enthusiastic. John Barkham's *New York*

Times review of *A Law for the Lion* set the tone: "This is Mr. Auchincloss's fourth book and let it be said at once that it is not the major novel we have been waiting for." All the reviewers called Auchincloss's writing precise, beautifully controlled, polished, and witty, but his characters only moderately interesting. "He is a fine stylist but no puncher" sums up the majority view.

Auchincloss was not displeased by his reviews, but he worried about his lack of sales; the novels of the 1950s sold between three thousand and five thousand copies, except for *Sybil*, which crept to number fifteen on *The New York Times* best-seller list for one week, then disappeared. Late in 1953, he wrote Paul Brooks, an editor at Houghton Mifflin, about this concern.

> I did want to talk over my failure to sell dispassionately and sensibly to see what could be done. Here are a few conclusions: *A Law for the Lion* has had uniformly excellent reviews and a reader reaction such as I have never experienced before. I can see that it is liked as *Sybil* was never liked. Yet it is laying an egg—obviously. I haven't received one single request to appear, to speak, anything. You know, of course, that I don't want to but never before has there been such a void. I have discussed the matter seriously with various friends in the publishing world, writers and editors, and all agree that either (a) I am intrinsically unsellable (which is possible) or (b) I am being improperly presented. If the latter, I think it goes back to the old arguments I lost with HM Co. When *The Injustice Collectors* came out, when I begged that the social thing be dropped and that the terrible words James and Wharton not be mentioned. Because the public that wants "society" books doesn't want my sort of books. They want something more Ouida. And the others are disgusted by the tag. One person told me brutally that the literary world was unable to take me seriously because of the label and the "high life" lovers unable to find what they had been promised. . . . I know that the Cholly Knickerbocker label may be *more* my fault than HM Co's., but doesn't it make sense to change tactics in view of failure?

Auchincloss had asked Houghton Mifflin to abandon the "society" approach several times before. "Is it strictly necessary to say that I used to spend the summer in two places, i.e., Long Island and Bar Harbor? Don't you think that it looks too plush and might antagonize?" James Brown, too, had written letter after letter about his client's "aversion to publicity based on the fact that he is a member of a distinguished family and himself socially and societally important. . . . Like Louis, I feel that people read books for a variety of reasons, and the least of them is that the author went to Groton and is in the Social Register." And again, "I just hope that we will have no further mention of the Social Register, Groton, Bar Harbor, etc. . . . You are picturing him as a popular society writer and nobody can stomach such a being." Brown worried that "the name Louis Auchincloss has come to mean . . . refinement, culture, Park Avenue, Social Register." In still another letter, Brown wrote, "I am not happy with the lack of enthusiasm which has been evident on the part of Houghton Mifflin toward *A Law for the Lion* since it was not chosen as a book club selection," and he blamed Houghton Mifflin for fostering the image of Louis Auchincloss as a "teacup society" writer. Paul Brooks wrote back proclaiming their enthusiasm and enclosing a schedule of advertising that included ads in *The New York Times*, the *New York Herald Tribune*, the *Virginia Quarterly Review*, *Retail Bookseller*, *Publishers Weekly*, *McClurg's*, *Bowker Book Guides*, *Library Journal*, and *The Saturday Review*, and promised no more mention of Henry James, the *Social Register*, or Edith Wharton in blurbs about Louis Auchincloss. In a private memo, he complained that "the agent Jim Brown is constantly fussing and clucking over his most distinguished chick."

A Law for the Lion excited more discontent on the author's and agent's part than any other Auchincloss book. Auchincloss himself had had serious misgivings about the book since showing the manuscript to his mother. She told him "that she thought most of the book was as dull as anything [she had] ever read." Because he respected her critical judgment, he was "shattered, really shattered" by her pronouncement. Many years later, he admitted that "the little plot in the end, where the lawyer marries the reserved girl, is sheer muck. I find the book embarrassing. I can't look at it."

In 1953, however, he was far more upset that the quality of his work had not improved substantially as a result of having become a full-time writer than dissatisfied with *A Law for the Lion*. Moreover, he resented the financial independence he had traded for the solitude of writing, being alone in his bachelor apartment and missing "being tied up and busy all day, and with things going on all around." Once again, he debated his professional identity— was he a writer, a lawyer, or both, in sequence or tandem? By the end of 1953, after the reviews for *A Law for the Lion* were out, he had decided to return to the practice of law and write when he could. "A great step was taken," he has written, "when I ceased to think of myself as a 'lawyer' or a 'writer.' I simply was doing what I was doing when I did it."

Two factors precipitated his decision: the completion of his analysis—he joked later that when he began to suspect a bored Cotton was doing crossword puzzles while his patient droned on, it was time to quit—and the conviction that extra hours had made no difference in his writing. If he was not going to become a major writer, why, he reasoned, should he give up his life to be a minor one? "If a person really has a gift to be a novelist," he has said, "he should give it one hundred percent of his time. But you never know if you have the talent. You risk wasting your life." The conundrum did not make its way into fiction until 1989. The narrator of a collection of connected short stories, himself a writer and lawyer, is visibly moved when he learns that the man he works for understands his dual career.

> He hopes you won't give up the law again. He feels that your two disciplines are now in the harness and that it would be a mistake for you to give up either one. He told me that some of your partners think you'd be a better lawyer if you gave up the

distraction of writing. But he feels, and I agree with him, that you wouldn't give the time you saved to the law. You'd just give it to fretting over what you'd done.

Sullivan & Cromwell policy prevented his returning there, so he was unsure where to find work. He was thirty-six; he had no clients; he expected employers would presume he had "rusted in his quixotic literary interlude."

The job search did not begin propitiously. A friend of his father's, a very prominent lawyer, asked him to come to his Wall Street office, as he had "something." Auchincloss went, waited a long time for the "great" man, and then all he proffered was useless information. "The City Bar Association of New York has a list they put out of people looking for jobs, and I thought you might want to put your name on that." Irritated that he had wasted half a day for this inane advice, Auchincloss said, "I don't think I'm reduced to that quite yet." Today he dismisses the incident with characteristic humor. "That man was a dunce, but he made a great marriage." Subsequent interviews were more fruitful but frustrating, even so. "I'd get an offer that wasn't right"; "they didn't pay me enough"; "I didn't see the opening ahead of me." His courage picked up when George Leisure, the senior partner of Donovan, Leisure, offered him a job. When the other partners objected to hiring laterally on the legitimate grounds that it would wreck morale among the associates, Leisure rescinded the offer. At this point Sullivan & Cromwell's George Sharp, "on the surface a charming gentleman of reserved manner but underneath a man with a deep and wonderful heart," stepped in to help. "Why didn't you come to me in the beginning?" he asked. Because he had not worked directly for Sharp, Auchincloss replied, it seemed "more natural" to seek advice from Pearce Browning, Eustace Seligman, and Curtis Pierce. "That's where you made a mistake. Now let's see what we can do." Sharp sent him to Reeves, McGrath, and right away Auchincloss got an offer, but after discussing it with his mentor, he turned it down. "The next person he sent me to was Dexter Hawkins."

The search took five months, but he found a place at Hawkins, Delafield & Wood in the trust and estates department, which consisted of Dexter Hawkins, head, Lawrence Morris, partner, and two associates. Hawkins, Delafield & Wood dates back to the general-practice firm that Dexter Hawkins founded in 1854. In 1909, the firms of Hawkins and Delafield merged. Today, it is one of New York's and the nation's preeminent bond firms, specializing in the issuance of tax-exempt bonds by states, public authorities, municipalities, and other government bodies. When Auchincloss joined the firm, Hawkins, Delafield & Wood was not as large or prestigious as Sullivan & Cromwell, but, like Sullivan & Cromwell, it was a "white shoe" firm; that is, a Wall Street firm populated by men who had attended schools such as Auchincloss's alma maters. Although Auchincloss's department was peripheral to the specialization of the firm, he now considered this advantageous: he would have no evening or weekend work and yet would enjoy a privileged position as detached observer of the workings of a great law firm, an ideal situation for his fictional purposes. "Returning to Wall Street in the spring of 1954," he wrote much later, "I felt that I had come home."

As a result of his psychoanalysis, Louis Auchincloss had come to terms with his dual career and with himself. It is probably no coincidence that right after completing therapy he began seriously courting a beautiful New York woman. She was Eleanor (Elly) Thomas, the sister of a former associate at Sullivan & Cromwell, who happened to live in Washington, D.C., at the time, where she was serving as social secretary to Janet Dulles, whose husband, John Foster Dulles, was President Eisenhower's secretary of state. Auchincloss often went down to Washington to see her, staying with his brother John, who lived in Georgetown. "When we went out," she remembers, "we'd stay up all night talking. Louis would tell me who all his characters were based on. I'd see it right away, and we'd laugh and laugh." When she was in New York, he took her to his parents' apartment for dinner, which she likens to a scene from the Auchincloss novel *Portrait in Brownstone*. Irish maids in uniforms with white lace served a not-too-tasty dinner presided over by a courtly Mr. Auchincloss and an inquisitive Mrs. Auchincloss, who asked searching questions, as if putting a potential daughter-in-law to a test. It was clear to Elly Thomas that both Mr. and Mrs. Auchincloss, as well as her own mother, hoped that she and Louis would marry. So, too, did he. During the courtship he introduced her to his friends, including Gore Vidal. "Would it be possible for me to lunch with you on Saturday, August 7th? And bring a girl, Eleanor Thomas, a sister of Jimmie's and Mrs. J. F. Dulles' secretary and cousin? I think you ought to meet *some* Republicans. You can say anything under the sun to Elly, but you must not call Ike a 'baboon.'" Everyone the couple knew, even John Elliott, whom Elly eventually married, assumed she and Louis were serious. "It was not hot and heavy," she says today, "but he was a beau." Auchincloss did eventually propose marriage, but she refused, hoping to marry Elliott. "I always felt if I had married Louis, I could have managed because I would have had his help." Elly Thomas Elliott and Louis Auchincloss have, however, remained friends to this day. "One of the reasons I've always liked Louis," she says, "is his respect for women, which came out of his relationship with his mother. It's in his books, too. When I was going out with him, he thought what I was saying was interesting and he listened."

Not long after his aborted romance, Auchincloss met Adèle Lawrence, another New Yorker, fourteen years his junior. Adèle shared a fourth-floor walk-up on Eighty-second Street with Elizabeth Nelidov, a friend from Bryn Mawr and a great-granddaughter of Sarah and James Coats, making her a cousin of Louis Auchincloss. When another Bryn Mawr classmate, Alice Sedgwick (Edie's sister) came to New York, Adèle organized a dinner party given in her parents' apartment at One East End Avenue. The girls needed an extra man, so Liz asked Louis at the last minute. Although he was not busy, he said no, but after he had hung up the phone, he changed his mind. He called to accept, and thus met the woman he would marry nine months later.

Louis Auchincloss and Adèle Lawrence were utterly unalike in nearly everything except background, and even there, Adèle's was more distinguished than Louis's. She was closely related to Vanderbilts, Sloanes, and Burdens. Her early years, as different from Louis's as can be imagined in terms of their emphasis on self-reliance in the out-of-doors, were divided between New York City and a 360-acre gentleman's farm on Lake Champlain in Charlotte, Vermont, a village twelve miles from Burlington. It was in Vermont that she developed her love of nature. Swimming, paddling, over-night camping trips, caring for animals, and learning to live in the woods filled her idyllic childhood summers. Quite understandably, Louis, who as a boy was never allowed a single overnight outdoors, did not appreciate nature as keenly as Adèle. In fact, she used to get slightly irritated when they walked together in the woods, as he insisted on talking. "He's too social," Adèle explained, "except in Alaska, where it's okay to talk to scare off the bears." Louis was social, and no one loved a party more than he. Adèle, by contrast, was shy; she hated the debutante parties—"I can still remember the nasty little girls at Piping Rock," she said—that Louis could not get enough of. One of the first times he took her out, when they barely knew each other, he installed her as hostess of a dinner party that included Cyrus Vance and his wife, Sam and Elizabeth Shaw, and Margot Finletter and her husband, Jack Mitchell. Louis and his friends were almost forty. Adèle was in her middle twen-ties, an age difference that would have been unnerving even to a person far less shy.

Part of her education, at Milton Academy and Bryn Mawr, was quite similar in quality to Louis's at Groton and Yale. But her two years in Tucson at the Potter School, located on the edge of the desert, where shootouts were still common, and a year at the University of Florence, where she took classes in Italian, gave to her schooling a more exotic air than Louis's. Where he was rational and intellectual, she was intuitive and artistic. He was utterly word-oriented. "It's the word on the page and the sound of the voice in his head" that counted for him, his wife observed. "Adèle was not at all literary," Auchincloss says. "She read all my books, but she would not have read them had she not been married to me, because she didn't read any other fiction except the mystery novel." She loved working crossword puzzles, something Louis had ignored until he met her, when he, too, became an aficionado. Adèle was interested primarily in the visual arts. After college, she earned a master's degree in industrial design at the Parsons School and she continued art lessons off and on throughout her life.

Adèle had begun working during her college years, whereas Louis had not. (His first paid employment was as a summer boarder, as interns were called in 1940, at Sullivan & Cromwell before his last year of law school.) Through family connections, she had gotten a job one summer at the United Nations when it was at Lake Success and another position the following summer in London's south end, working with underprivileged children. A final summer job was with the Opera Guild, where she was charged with getting tickets for old ladies, who complained no matter what. As a result, she grew to hate opera, which Louis adores. The two differed in domestic matters, as well. Adèle loved to cook; Louis was indifferent to food. She cared very much how a room was put together; he never noticed; even if it needed painting, he did not care. He was frugal; she was not, throwing out his worn clothing when he was not at home.

Opposites in this case definitely attracted, for they saw each other steadily during the winter of 1957. By summer, they were engaged. "I am quite absurdly happy and pleased with myself," Auchincloss wrote Gore Vidal announcing the news. "Adèle, who though the ablest of industrial designers . . . is not shall we say a specialist in the modern novel. Determined to bone up on this field she read a few pages of dear Norman's *The Naked and the Dead*, but put it away in a sad fit of boredom. You will like her."

Most people did, although some openly expressed misgivings about the likelihood of success in such a union. Adèle's mother worried about the age difference. She had known Louis for years. Both belonged to the Thursday Evening Club, a group organized in the 1890s that met three Thursday nights each winter to introduce New York society to the faculties of Columbia and New York universities. Over the years, the original purpose and professors had been forgotten, but the club had carried on with dinners, lectures, dances, and musicales. "Thirty-nine years old!" Mrs. Lawrence exclaimed: "Is this a very good idea?" "I wasn't a good catch," Auchincloss allows. "I wasn't even a partner. My books hadn't sold." The doubts, fortunately, faded very quickly. Louis and his mother-in-law established a marvelous relationship. "We had almost no secrets from each other," he says. Adèle knew of the skeptics, and more than thirty years later, she showed how wrong they were. With characteristic understatement, she accurately described the marriage: "People think of Louis and me as being so different, yet it's worked." Their interests never coincided. She came to care passionately about the environment, in which her husband had only a passing interest. She never developed an enthusiasm for literature or for the law, "and it never made any difference," Louis says today. "It may even have been better."

The afternoon wedding on September 7, 1957, less than a month before the groom's fortieth birthday, took place in Charlotte. The tiny Episcopal church had space to accommodate family only. A local minister, assisted by the Reverend Malcolm Strachan, married the couple. The reception, which followed, was at the Lawrences' farm. The eighty out-of-town guests wandered over the great grassy lawn that stretched down to the lake, walking between the tent that had been erected for the day and the rambling white farmhouse. The bridal couple left for a wedding trip to Mexico. On their return, they settled in Auchincloss's Eighty-fourth Street apartment. On January 1, 1958, Louis Auchincloss became a partner in Hawkins, Delafield & Wood. Six months later, his first son, John Winthrop Auchincloss II, was born.

The Upper East Side's ideal extra man had finally learned to "throw out fear" and to put to rest forever the ghosts of the past. The effect on his writing was liberating.

CHAPTER 8

Writer Arrived

"But what you don't see . . . is that your world is doomed. . . ."

"What do you call my world?"

"The world of the private school. . . . The world of the gentleman and his ideals. The world of personal honor and a Protestant God."

I have told myself all along that it was brash and egocentric to expect from the reading world anything more than I have got. Yet, I have always suffered from the suspicion not so much that I write about the wrong people (look at the success of O'Hara and Marquand!), but that I write about the wrong people in the wrong way. Perhaps I tend to accept the *status quo* more than seems acceptable.

LOUIS AUCHINCLOSS

I like married life," Louis Auchincloss wrote Gore Vidal. "So much less knocking about town." "Less knocking about town" may have meant fewer evenings out, but the Auchinclosses had hardly settled down to a quiet life. Their first child, John, was born ten months after they were married. When Adèle became pregnant again a year later, they bought a spacious Park Avenue apartment, which Louis still occupies today. Then John and Blake Leay were joined by Andrew Sloane, who was born in 1963. For getting out of the city, Louis and Adèle had bought an old farmhouse that had been renovated by Cleveland Cobb, Cleveland Amory's uncle, on four and a half acres in Bedford, New York, a village close enough to New York City for weekend use. "You have to go too far out in New Jersey, such as Far Hills, or Long Island to find 'country' with deer and raccoon" is how Louis characterized their choice, though the desired wildlife wreaked havoc on any landscaping efforts. "Adèle is planting bulbs all over," Louis wrote Gore Vidal, "which should be a riot of color—but for raccoon and deer." In the summertime, Louis commuted daily to Bedford, except during July, when the family went to Charlotte, Vermont, and occupied a cottage on the Lawrences' property.

Before their Bedford purchase in 1962, Louis and Adèle passed many a pleasant weekend with her maternal grandmother, Adèle Sloane Burden Tobin, on her four-hundred-acre estate in Syosset on Long Island's North Shore. The frequent trips to Woodside Acres provided the inspiration and impetus that enabled Louis to produce *The House of Five Talents*, still his favorite novel.

Mrs. Tobin, the great-granddaughter of Commodore Cornelius Vanderbilt, came of age in the 1890s and was the recipient of all that wealth and privilege could offer in that opulent era. She and her multitude of cousins dwelt in eclectic châteaux up and down Fifth Avenue, traveled in private railroad cars to their country estates in Lenox, Massachusetts, the Adirondacks, Bar Harbor, Newport, and Asheville, North Carolina, cruised aboard their families' steam yachts in the Mediterranean, and, during the season in New York, danced until daylight with eligible young men from families as rich as their own. During the weekends he spent with her, Louis Auchincloss encouraged Mrs. Tobin to talk about this era, a time when the rich unapologetically filled their leisurely lives with world travel, house parties, extravagant balls, and, above all, lavish weddings. Adèle Sloane's 1895 wedding to Jay Burden, an heir to an upstate New York iron-foundry fortune, represented, if presents, dresses, and wedding parties are taken into account, an outlay of a million dollars. (After Mrs. Tobin died in 1960, Auchincloss discovered a diary she had kept from 1893 to 1896; he published an annotated version of it as *Maverick in Mauve* in 1983. Millicent Fenwick called it the diary "of an obviously intelligent young woman of great good will who might as well be writing about imperial Rome.")

After the marriage, Adèle's father, William Sloane (of the well-known family of rug merchants), gave her a Beaux-Arts mansion with a third-floor ballroom on Ninety-first Street, and at twenty-seven, Adèle moved in with her young husband and twenty-seven servants. In 1917, the year of Auchincloss's birth, she and Burden bought Woodside Acres, built a Georgian house, hired the famous Frederick Law Olmsted, Jr., to design formal gardens, stocked its extensive meadowlands with a herd of Black Angus, and gave fabulous parties. In 1924, the Burdens lent their Syosset estate to the Prince of Wales for his first visit to the United States.

Anyone would have been fascinated by stories of such a life, but for Louis Auchincloss, they provided incomparable material for a sweeping chronicle of America's great robber baron era and its effect on the contemporary mores of the very rich, and he was ripe for it.

For years, he had been brooding about critics' assumptions that he wrote about the effect of environment on people in the sense that money determined, or at least shaped, character, usually for the worse. Even his erudite and astute older brother made this presumption at least once. John Auchincloss failed to understand why a certain character had to end up the way he did just because he was from a particular New York circle. But Louis saw the problems of his characters as psychological, and their background, chosen because of his familiarity with it, as just that—background. In his next novel, *The House of Five Talents*, he chose to take an opposite tack from what he had done before with regard to his characters' background. A 1963 letter to a *New York Times* book critic elaborates his view of the matter.

When I wrote *Venus in Sparta*, *Pursuit of the Prodigal* and *A Law for the Lion*, I was concentrating in each case on a specific psychological problem that was by no means confined to the background of the characters or even necessarily relevant to it. The lack of sexual confidence that dominated and destroyed Michael Farish had nothing to do with the Social Register. Reese Parmelee's rebellion was a rebellion against the mores of New York—not simply of New York Society. And Eloise Dilworth's discovery of her own true powers is a kind of self-analysis that might be practiced in any walk of life. However, my public, such as it is, always insisted that the problems must have grown out of the background. It was finally with a kind of defiance that I addressed myself squarely to the background of privilege and wrote *The House of Five Talents*, basing the book on a careful study of New York's 19th century millionaire families, with particular emphasis on the Vanderbilts.

Stimulated by Adèle Tobin's "vivid and colorful sense of the past," Auchincloss set himself the task of showing what five generations of financier Julius Millinder's descendants did with the $100 million he had accumulated by his death in 1886 and what the money did to them, and in doing so, he brought a class and an era to life. In preparation, he read about the robber baron families, discovering they had certain "figures that kept repeating—the daughter who married a duke, the son who became a crook, the grandson who became a Communist." He wrote much of the first draft, following his usual method—in longhand, in pencil, on long, yellow legal pads—on weekends at Woodside Acres. He had it typed triple-spaced and carried it around in a briefcase in order to work on it anywhere—on subways, in the office when he had a few minutes to spare, in the evenings at home. "You have to be fresh for the first draft," Auchincloss believed, "but I find that once I get to work on the second or third draft, it's like knitting." Auchincloss always writes quickly, partly because he carefully outlines his plot in advance and partly because he has extraordinary powers of concentration. *The House of Five Talents* was produced in a matter of months; he began the book in November of 1958 and finished it by September 1959. "I never wrote a book that came faster, because I knew the beginning, middle, and end as I never knew them before," he says, "and the result was the book most closely achieved what I set out to do."

His self-imposed mission was to limit himself to the point of view of the woman who tells the story, a person less perspicacious than her creator. This was his seventh novel, but the first to jettison the third-person narrator. Although he had used the first-person narrator in short stories, this was his first use of the device for a novel, no small feat, since the Millinder family, according to his own assessment, was "all such poor stuff, such very small people." Yet he believed *The House of Five Talents* was his best novel because "the background had a much more vital function in the story than in the others. I set my other books against the background that I could draw most easily." But the Millinders *had* to be set against opulence, as he intended to show that their money was more important than they were. The novel is a real breakthrough, for by using his own social milieu as a source of thematic as well as background material enabled him to exercise more fully his literary gifts.

The House of Five Talents is a novel in the form of a memoir written by Augusta (Gussie) Millinder, the granddaughter of the family's great accumulator. She is not so much interested in the tycoon himself and the making of his fortune as she is in his legacy and what the possession of his money did to his descendants over seven decades. It made Gussie suspicious of outsiders' attitudes toward that money, seeing the world as divided between the trusted familiars and the clutching masses who were after the money. Afraid that her assured inheritance amounted to her principal attraction, she has remained an old maid. Never mind that her parents had never discussed their wills—"it was one of the rare delicacies of a rather vulgar era and a constant bafflement to Europeans who could see in [such reticence] only the grossest hypocrisy"—she knows she is very rich. Her mother, whose fixed principle "that every human being was fundamentally motivated by a financial goal and that those who would not recognize this were either fools or hypocrites," asks her squeamish daughter,

"What's the good of your father's money but to give you a good position?" Even into early middle age, Gussie resolved to be loved for herself.

"What is yourself?" a sister-in-law asks. "We're all bits and pieces of our background, our tastes, our inheritances, even our clothes. It's only natural for people to be curious because you're a Millinder and live in a big house. It's up to you to turn that curiosity into something better!"

"It was the simplest idea in the world," Gussie reflects, "yet it changed my life." But Gussie is in her middle forties by this time. Julius Millinder's twelve living grandchildren, who owned estates spread out all over the globe requiring "no less than a thousand human souls to wait on the old pirate's progeny," have disseminated family fame. Their very houses are tourist attractions. On a nostalgic trip to Newport in the 1930s, Gussie pays a dollar for a guided tour through the house where she had spent the summers of her youth. "In this room Mrs. Millinder had tea every afternoon at five," the guide tells the group, who listen with unabashed reverence. "In that corner you will see a marble figure of a poodle that belonged to the Princess de Conti. The painting over the mantel depicts Julius Millinder receiving President Arthur on board the Western Star."

Julius Millinder had none of the social ambitions his children unleashed as soon as he died and that put the Millinder name on the social map. The unequal bequests made to the two sons (Fred's business acumen laid claim to twice the amount settled on Cyrus, Gussie's father) incites a hilarious social rivalry between their wives. Eliza, who is Gussie's mother, and Daisy, Fred's wife, compete in giving dinner parties, in collecting art, in attracting the best foreign aristocrats as spouses for their daughters, even in designing their Newport houses.

Aunt Daisy's was rigidly conventional. She and Uncle Fred had commissioned Richard Morris Hunt to build them a late Gothic French château of dull, featureless limestone. It sat up on a high point, a big, bold placid product of the Beaux Arts, absurdly dominating four small acres of lawn and ocean which it should never have crossed. Mamma, on the advice of Stanford White, built more indigenously of shingle. Her great rambling house seemed to climb out of the very sea and rocks to a tumble of different levels with a sweeping view from every room.

Forty years later, after Eliza and Daisy are dead, Gussie returns to Newport to take a final look. From a point on the Cliff Walk from which she can see both her mother's and Aunt Daisy's Ocean Drive houses, she contemplates "their vast woebegone, peeling facades," wondering "for one last time what it was that Mamma had found so different about hers. For time had stripped them both of everything except what they had in common, and what was that except swagger?"

Eliza's indifference to anything but the social game (until late in life when she gives herself to collecting art) and her struggle for precedence, which she sees in heroic dimensions, give the novel an exuberance unseen before in Auchincloss's writing. No scene better illustrates this than Mrs. Bell's luncheon party to introduce her son Lancey to Eliza's beautiful daughter Cora, a party given despite Mrs. Bell's condescension toward the upstart Millinders. Gussie, as Cora's younger sister, is invited and seated next to Mrs. Bell, who tells her young guest stories of her Newport childhood. "It really had charm then. . . . My family lived in a dear old stucco, bracketed thing designed by Upjohn that the Herron woman has just pulled down to make way for her monstrosity." Sixteen-year-old Gussie reflects that "no one ever talked to me this way at home, and I was delighted. What did I care that the 'Herron woman' was my Aunt Polly?" After a glass of wine, Gussie "felt disposed to be confidential."

> "Of course you don't like Mamma," I said.
> "We all know that. And she's terribly cross about it."
> "My dear child, I don't even know your mamma!"

"I know. But you will." I nodded twice to emphasize this. "She says you'll have to."

"Why in heavens name will *I have to*?"

"Because we're the coming thing."

Mrs. Bell burst into a hearty laugh. "Bless me child, you make your family sound like the yellow peril. Must we all band together to resist you?"

"I think you'd better!"

At this point we both became quite hilarious. I decided that I was a great social success.

The entire novel is made up of a series of scenes such as this, scenes that aptly define characters and, taken together, the era. Although the story shifts its focus from one place and family member to another, it is always told through Augusta's eyes. So skillfully does Auchincloss confine himself to Gussie's experience and nature, that, like Ibsen with Hedda Gabler, his scrutiny of mores melts into a novel of character from which emerges not only a crystal-clear portrait of a frustrated, confused, insecure, meddlesome, sometimes witty, usually generous, and always likable narrator-protagonist but lifelike secondary characters as well. Despite an ever-widening complexity of characters, Auchincloss never loses his control over the large scene nor over his sure sense of the periods, showing the shift in values between 1886 and 1948, the time covered by the novel. When Gussie looks back to the 1890s at one of her aunt's dinner parties—"We must have been fifty at table, seated in great carved, gilded Venetian chairs before the splendor of a full gold service"—and when she comments on a sister-in-law's 1940s apartment—"It is the fashion now for wealth to be inconspicuous, and even my sister-in-law, Julia, conceals her grandeur in a duplex apartment high over Park Avenue"—she reveals a sea change in attitudes of the rich toward their money.

Because of Gussie's training in art history, her comments on works of art are credible and do not sound out of place, as they sometimes do in the mouths of businessmen or socialites in other Auchincloss novels. Her lively descriptions of the houses, gardens, pictures, and clothes, displaying the author's knowledge and love of the arts, count in making a telling picture. Finely observed details of setting, character, and behavior make this a large, inclusive novel, a sensuous, fully realized evocation of bygone times. *The House of Five Talents* is sociology, history, and literature of the highest order, and it is a delight to read. No wonder it became Auchincloss's first best-seller. Sales of almost 25,000 hardcovers pushed in onto the best-seller list, where it remained for several weeks.

"I worked very hard on that novel," Auchincloss told an interviewer, "and I still think it's unique in that I don't know of another work of fiction that suggests what those families were like. A great deal has been written about the earning of nineteenth-century fortunes, but very little about how they were preserved and sent down through the different branches. I like that novel." He also liked, he discovered, being the kind of novelist critics had supposed he already was; namely, an inside reporter of one segment of American social history.

Although his next novel, *Portrait in Brownstone*, focuses on that same facet of the social scene and on roughly the same period (1903 to 1951), the fictional Denisons are not like the Millinders. Closely modeled on the Dixons, Auchincloss's own maternal grandmother's family, the Denisons are merely prosperous, not superrich, having no patriarch such as Julius Millinder. Moreover, they are content to live among themselves in Denison Alley, the enclave of family homes on Fifty-third Street, never aspiring to the eminence Eliza and Daisy Millinder sought. Originally from Brooklyn, they cross the East River to Manhattan one by one in the 1890s, following the lead of the oldest Denison sibling. They are a tightly knit family, bound together by a shared sense of duty and privilege. In a few vivid scenes at the beginning of the novel, Auchincloss establishes their solidarity, and nowhere more divertingly than in chapter four when fifteen-year-old Ivy Trask is sent to Europe as chaperone to her grandmother.

Grandmother Trask, a widow from Brooklyn who relishes her annual summer trip to Europe with Mr. and Mrs. Robbins, is forced to cancel in 1903, "for the first time since the Franco-Prussian War," because of the death of Mrs. Robbins. In 1904, Mrs. Trask and Mr. Robbins, septuagenarians both, decide to resume their European travel. Ida's mother, Lily Trask, is dubious about the propriety of their trip. Her concern and subsequent deeds in her mother-in-law's behalf exemplify Denison family values in action.

"It's really only the boat, I suppose that makes any matter. There's something about two at table that looks so—so connubial."

"And think of those deck chairs, side by side," Father continued with a small smile. "And down in the hold, Vuitton trunk by Vuitton trunk."

"Ida," Mother said suddenly, "how should you like to go over with your grandmother this year?"

Despite the chaperonage, Grandmother Trask's Brooklyn neighbor, Miss Florence Polhemus, who happens also to be aboard the *Mauretania*, objects to her friend's traveling arrangements. For the sake of appearances she strongly suggests that Mrs. Trask and Mr. Robbins stay in separate hotels, travel on different trains, and return on different ships. Such were the times, the summer was reorganized to conform to Miss Polhemus. Later, in Paris, Mr. Robbins proposes marriage, which Mrs. Trask declines. Ida asks why.

"In the first place, it would not be loyal to your grandfather. He was a very fine and good man."

"But how can you be loyal to someone who's dead?"

"He seems dead to you, Ida, because you never knew him."

"But he's still dead, isn't he?" I protested. "Hasn't he been dead for years and years?"

"Years and years seem longer to some people than to others."

"If you died first, do you think he'd never have remarried?"

Ida realizes by the look on her grandmother's face, "she had really startled her now."

Having been apprised of recent developments, Ida's mother arrives, unannounced, in Paris to take matters in hand. "Poor grandma," Ida soon learned, "was suffering from an apprehension common to her generation; she was afraid of confronting grandpa with Mr. Robbins in the next life." Lily Trask succeeds in sweeping away her mother-in-law's religious scruples and, soon after, her practical objections.

> Everybody in the family always thought that mother did a wonderful job that summer. Father used laughingly to describe it as the time when she made an 'honest woman' of her mother-in-law. But I have often wondered if she didn't overdo it. . . . Far from home and faced with a strange bewildering problem, Grandma allowed herself to be taken in hand by her big, kindly, reassuring, fast-talking daughter-in-law. But I doubt very much if, left to herself in Brooklyn, she would ever have married again. Marriage to her meant grandpa and love, and that had been over three decades before. All that she wanted from Mr. Robbins was the continuation of the schedule of bygone summers, lightly flavored with the atmosphere of an indefinitely protracted courtship. . . . But, no, they could not be allowed so little. . . . Grandma and Mr. Robbins had to do the sound, sensible, up-to-date "Denison thing." Miss Polhemus was much less demanding than Mother; she insisted only that they be proper. Mother insisted that they be happy. When grandma had at last been induced to yield to the respectful importunity of Mr. Robbins, she was frightened by the burst of congratulation in the messages from relatives and friends. Aunt Dagmar cabled from Long Island, and Uncle Victor and Aunt Sophie came up from Dinard and Uncle Philip from the château country. The Denisons seemed to be claiming poor

Grandma as one of their own. She became Mrs. Robbins in the private episcopal chapel of one of mother's expatriate friends in the presence of her son and daughter-in-law, two of her daughter-in-law's brothers, a granddaughter and Miss Polhemus, who wept copiously throughout the ceremony.

In establishing Denison allegiance and affection, Auchincloss recreates the sense of life his mother had conveyed about her own family in her introduction to a Dixon genealogy, but nostalgia for the simpler New York of the brownstone era is not the point. Above all else, *Portrait in Brownstone* is a delineation of the decline of clan loyalty and traditions and its eventual outcome, the collapse of a settled society. In telling Ida's part of the story in the first person and of other characters' parts in the third person, Auchincloss shows how Ida emerges as the strongest force for unity in a family disintegrating from external and internal pressures. Although she marries the cold, calculating, and brilliant Derrick Hartley, who disdains her idealization of family and who has an affair with her beautiful cousin, Geraldine, she bows always to duty and discipline, never letting anyone down—not even Geraldine, who, after trying to steal her husband, becomes a dreary alcoholic. Ida turns out to be the most pragmatic character in the novel, for "she learns," Auchincloss has written, "from all that Geraldine has cast aside, that there must have been something worthwhile in what their family stood for, and that even if that something should turn out to be her illusion, it is a surer standard for the good life in a changing city than anything in Derrick's coarser creed." Geraldine and Derrick rebel against a rigid social code, not understanding it is the only discipline to be had in changing times and therefore not to be lightly discarded. In *Portrait in Brownstone*, Auchincloss embodies one of the central problems of the modern world; namely, the lack of a moral community, the absence of shared values that give a society a commonalty that confers an identity on a collection of competing individuals.

Like its predecessor, the novel became a best-seller (Houghton Mifflin alone sold almost thirty thousand hardback copies);

Literary Guild chose it for a main selection, and *The New York Times Book Review* gave it front-page coverage on July 15, 1962. "This book does seem to be getting off to a good start," Auchincloss wrote Houghton Mifflin, "and I still blink when I think of being on the front page of the Sunday Times Book Review. It's been a long time coming, but I finally made it." These successes were to be eclipsed by the triumph of his next novel.

The Rector of Justin is the fictional biography of the clerical headmaster and founder of Justin Martyr, a New England Episcopal church school, the crucible in which the kind of men who people *The House of Five Talents* and *Portrait in Brownstone* were fired, tested, and formed. "I always reserved the subject of a headmaster for the time when I should feel ready to handle it," Auchincloss wrote years after the 1964 publication of the novel. Even as he wrote during 1963, he "had an inkling that it was going to be [his] major theme."

The Reverend Francis Prescott's story is told by six people: the finicky, fastidious old Horace Havistock, Prescott's boyhood friend; malicious, destructive Jules Griscam, Justin student, 1922, who hates the Rector; David Griscam, Jules's father, alumnus 1893, longtime trustee, and millionaire; Cordelia, the Rector's neurotic, rebellious daughter; Charley Strong, football captain and senior prefect of the class of 1911, shrapnel victim of the war, and Cordelia's lover; and, finally and principally, Brian Aspinwall, fifty years younger than the Rector and unlike him except in his strong faith. Aspinwall decides shortly after arriving at Justin as a master to be the Rector's biographer, and his journal provides most of the chapters in the novel. Each narrator speaks in his own distinctive voice, from the histrionic, narcissistic, almost hallucinatory style of Charley Strong, a style the antithesis of Auchincloss's own, to the precious, mincing speech of Horace Havistock.

While the feat of writing *The House of Five Talents* in the voice and from the perceptions of a woman, a voice far less intelligent than Auchincloss's, is impressive, the use of six distinct voices in *The Rector of Justin* is a tour de force. In his memoir, *A Writer's Capital*, Auchincloss claims to have acquired this skill in 1943 in

Panama when he represented all-too-obviously guilty sailors in trials by court-martial. Their only chance for acquittal or a lessened sentence was to make a credible statement of mitigation, which they had to deliver themselves. If it appeared that their lawyer had prepared the statement, it did them no good. So Auchincloss's job, as he saw it, was to write and rewrite a statement in each sailor's voice until he got it right, and then to have the sailor memorize and practice delivering it. He became so adept in this technique that the presiding officer in his last court-martial congratulated the defendant for his frank plea and censured Auchincloss "as a lazy, good-for-nothing counsel who had done nothing but plead guilty and leave the job of defense to his poor client." He must also have learned something about voices from Ruth Draper, the great monologist, who lived in the same apartment building as his parents on East Seventy-ninth Street. He had seen all her monologues on stage and went often to the parties she gave for her nieces and nephews, for whom she performed. Writing in another's voice is exactly like doing a monologue: Writer and performer put on different hats and strut about their stages.

The purpose of the shifting points of view in *The Rector of Justin*, besides the realization of a multiple portrait that matches the complexity of Francis Prescott, is to examine the Rector's influence on the people in his power so that, Auchincloss has said, the reader will ask whether the education he provides is more of an asset than a liability. Never does the reader nor did the author question the headmaster's faith.

A man of faith like the Rector assumes that the family of Justin Martyr believes in and practices the faith he holds so strongly. Very near the end of his life, he learns otherwise. At a gathering of the school's principal trustees, a proposal to liberalize admission policies is discussed. "Do we want to jettison altogether the principle of a Protestant school for boys of Anglo-Saxon descent?" one trustee asks. "But there never was any such principle," Dr. Prescott objects.

"Not in your eyes, sir," another trustee interrupts. "But in the eyes of most of the country Justin, along with other New

England prep schools, has that reputation. And why should we be ashamed of it? Haven't our boys come of the families that made America great? Isn't there something in traditions and responsibility handed down from generation to generation? Look at the aristocratic tradition in England."

The Rector *has* looked, and he sees that the English aristocracy gave something in return: service in the army or church or government. But Justin has no such tradition. "It has always been my chief regret," he says, "that Justin has sent so few men into public service." Another trustee disagrees, insisting that producing the leaders of corporate America has been good for Justin. "Would families like the Griscams occupy the position they occupy today if they'd gone into the army or navy or wasted their time in politics? . . . Business is our aristocracy. . . . Finance is our aristocracy. . . . You should be proud, Dr. Prescott, that you have sent your boys to take their places in the front ranks of American progress."

Finally, a defeated and despairing headmaster concludes "that Justin Martyr is like the other schools. Only I, of course, ever thought it was different. Only I failed to see that snobbishness and materialism were intrinsic in its makeup."

This theme, coupled with certain Groton customs and characteristics, convinced nearly everyone in the "Groton family" that Louis Auchincloss had traitorously criticized Dr. Peabody and his school. No matter that certain historical facts of Prescott's career differ from those of Peabody's (far too slightly, most believed), and no matter that the famous Dr. Peabody of Groton, identified as a contemporary of Prescott's, appears in the novel as a separate character, harsh was the censure of present and former Grotties. Endicott Peabody's biographer maintained that no book about Groton had caused such a stir as this one. He conceded the preponderance of dissimilarities between the fictional and actual headmaster, but "to old Groton hands," he insisted, "much of the setting, many of the details, some of the minor characters, and at least one major episode were familiar. The result was confusion and unhappiness. Many felt it a pity that such an important work of fiction should be popularly considered as an authoritative picture of a man, his school, and his family." Even Peabody's children acted as if they believed Prescott was Peabody.

Exasperated by this reaction, Auchincloss was mollified when Marietta Peabody, the Rector's granddaughter, told him that it showed how few people had really known her grandfather. The character of Endicott Peabody was too simple and direct to dramatize "the troubled story of the Protestant church school," Auchincloss had realized, so he used traits of the more complicated Judge Learned Hand for his fictional Rector, and even made Justin Martyr larger (more like the size of St. Paul's) than Groton, for he wanted his fictional school to be "characteristic" rather than "special." These distinctions went unnoticed by angry Groton alumni. Years later, Auchincloss said he probably would not have attempted a book like it without the self-confidence analysis had given him. He had worried some about his parents' reactions, but his mother thought the book was good, "and she actually began to defend it."

So, too, did a majority of the critics: "the finest novel Mr. Auchincloss has written"; "not only the best novel Louis Auchincloss has written . . . [it] will assuredly have a place among the best American novels written in the 1960s"; "passionately interesting . . . spiritually important"; "the richest of his books . . . witty, perceptive, and beautifully written"; "I was swept along by it, for the revelation of Prescott's character is fascinating"; "I don't think an American novelist of his generation has matched it either in technique or content"; "with it Auchincloss must be reckoned in the front rank of mid-American novelists." Not surprisingly, *The Rector of Justin* rose quickly to the top of the best-seller lists and for thirty-five weeks it vied with Saul Bellow's *Herzog* for first place. Houghton Mifflin sold eighty thousand hardcover copies and twenty thousand paperbacks; New American Library had sold 2 million copies by 1966. It was Auchincloss's first Book-of-the-Month Club selection, a Franklin Library leather-bound "classic," and a nominee for the National Book Award and the Pulitzer Prize. So confident was his publisher that he would win one or the other, it had prepared two dummies of releases for the daily papers to announce each prize. "As you see," editor-in-chief Paul Brooks wrote Jim Brown, "we are prepared for anything or everything."

The day of the Pulitzer announcement, Auchincloss worked off the suspense of waiting by writing Gore Vidal. "I write with an eye on the clock for it will soon be 3 p.m. at which time the Pulitzer awards are announced. . . . Do I care? Of course, I care. I have reached the age [forty-six] when I want prizes, *any* prizes. . . . Even the glory of the Literary Guild, the spectacular heights of Book-of-the-Month have not sated my middle-aged lust." He realized, he told Vidal, that his eagerness to win was foolish. "It is true [the Pulitzer] went to *The Age of Innocence* and *The Late George Apley*, but so did it go to the worst of Willa Cather (*One of Ours*) and the worst of Faulkner (*A Fable*). And to a lot of writers one has never heard of." He got neither the Pulitzer nor the National Book Award. "The absurd thing about prizes," the disappointed author reflected, "is that they are *supposed* to *encourage* the arts and they have precisely the opposite effect. The winners either know how little the prizes mean or else decidedly should *not* be encouraged. The losers are disproportionately discouraged by seeing what words are preferred to their own. What a silly racket and how silly of me to mind. But I do."

Although many serious critics believed *The Rector of Justin* was the best book of 1964, and said so, no one should have been surprised it did not win. In a period of ethnic, racial, and feminist upheaval, this was a book upholding tranquillity, order, and practical Protestant restraint. Civil rights and race relations had been the burning issues of 1964, and it was Shirley Ann Grau's *The Keepers of the House*, a fast-paced narrative of miscegenation that exposes the absurdities and cruelties to which prejudice leads, that won the Pulitzer Prize. Saul Bellow's *Herzog*, a subjective, well-wrought, rambling study of a contemporary Jew trying to shore up his disintegrating life, won the National Book Award. Auchincloss even conceded his irrelevance, telling a Houghton Mifflin editor he had deliberately set out "to display the strange phenomenon of the New England school as a burning white light, oddly irrelevant to the contemporaneous world, but nonetheless admirable in its isolation and all the brighter for being surrounded by the grayness of materialism.''

Virgilia Peterson, in a front-page *New York Times Book Review* assessment of *The Rector of Justin* correctly predicted protest about Auchincloss's subject matter, which the book did elicit—a different kind of protest from the cries of offended Groton alumni. "Voices will no doubt be raised—as they always are when a novel is centered upon what we now call upper-upper and upper-middle classes—to protest that these classes no longer represent our country, that white Anglo-Saxon Protestantism has ceased to be our distinguishing mark, and that to attempt to define American culture in such narrow terms is like trying to define an elephant in terms of its ears.'' As if on cue, the critic for *The New York Review of Books* depreciated "life in our better prep schools'' as trivial material and, in this case, badly executed. "Perhaps someone better qualified can report if living, breathing people ever spoke the way Brian Aspinwall and Frank Prescott—with their repeated solicitation of the Deity's help to solve small, severely practical problems—are made to speak in this novel.'' (Anyone who has attended a church boarding school can attest to Auchincloss's bull's-eye accuracy in just this respect.) Granville Hicks, the regular book reviewer for *The Saturday Review*, consistently dismissed Auchincloss's fiction because it was about " 'good' society, the well-to-do and the well bred,'' and of course *The Rector of Justin* was no exception. Although Auchincloss conceded that "since 1776 the very existence of a fashionable world has seemed to many the perpetuation of an arch heresy in the shrine of democracy,'' he was nonetheless irritated by Hicks, who often came close to "denying that a rich man can be a valid subject for fiction.'' *The New York Review of Books* and *The Saturday Review* were by no means alone in deprecating Auchincloss's subject matter. Even so sympathetic a critic as James Tuttleton called Auchincloss's world "small'' and "narrow'' and criticized him for writing of no other. Reviewers obviously considered "Baldwin's slums, Malamud's ghettos, O'Hara suburbia, Nabokov's motel routes, O'Connor's parishes, and Faulkner's Yoknapatawpha County" the real America, yet as Virgilia Peterson pointed out in his review of *The Rector of Justin*, "like it or not, and justly or not, the preponderance of our leadership in government, the professions and business comes, still today, out of that social minority which preempts Mr. Auchincloss's field of vision." Leadership in government, the professions, and business was exactly where Auchincloss cast his eye next.

Wall Street in the 1930s was the battleground between the epic forces of big finance and big government, a struggle that began when the Securities and Exchange acts of 1933 and 1934 established the SEC and brought the securities industry under its control and ended when Richard Whitney, five times elected president of the New York Stock Exchange, was sentenced to prison for embezzlement. The clash of finance and government was an ideal story for a novelist like Auchincloss, and he started to work on *The Embezzler* even before *The Rector of Justin* was published. Richard Whitney, a caste-proud patrician, was chronically in debt from various investment schemes. Twice he had "borrowed" bonds from his deceased father-in-law's trust to use as security for personal loans, but when he raided the New York Yacht Club's treasury and the Stock Exchange Gratuity Fund, a quasi-pension endowment for families of deceased members, he began to worry about detection. About to be exposed in 1937, he turned to his brother George, a partner of J. P. Morgan & Company, for help. Although George was appalled, having spent years in Washington hotly defending the House of Morgan against insinuations of impropriety (in 1933 federal legislation forced it to divide into what became Morgan Guaranty Trust, for commercial banking, and Morgan Stanley, for investment banking), he lent his brother a million dollars, thereby implicating himself and the bank in the crime. Less than a year later, when the mess was exposed, the Richard Whitney story set off a colossal scandal. Even Franklin Roosevelt was shocked. "Not Richard Whitney!" was all he could mutter.

Howland Auchincloss was a friend of George Whitney. His firm, Davis Polk & Wardwell, did all of Morgan's legal work. Priscilla Auchincloss and Martha Whitney, George's wife, had known each other for years as members of the Junior Fortnightly and the Colony Club, and they spoke to each other often by telephone. When rumors that Louis was writing about the thirty-year-old family humiliation reached Mrs. Whitney, she hurriedly dashed off a plea to her friend's son to stop.

> What Dick Whitney did is impossible to understand [she wrote], and of course he deserved his punishment. He has taken his guilt like a true man and never ran away from it and has spent the rest of his life trying to atone. He is not well and has only a few more years of life expectancy and it does not seem quite fair to have the knife continually turned in the wound. His children love him and his grandchildren, and they have all been loyal. When my husband died, [Richard's daughter] burst into tears and said, "The papers will all harp on Daddy again." I said, "Oh, no. They wouldn't be so unkind," but they did. Now I cannot bear to have it all rehashed and publicized once again and of course it will be. My information that you were writing the book came from my grandson in Wall Street, so it is already known and talked about there, and your book is labeled "Dick Whitney" no matter how hard you try to camouflage it. Of course you have the right to write on any subject, but the wounds are still sore and Dick is still alive and he has paid heavily. If you could only wait for a few years until he died. . . . It's all so sad, and in spite of not condoning his actions, I can't help feeling sorry for him now. I forgive him for all that he did to my husband, but the world will never forgive or forget.

Louis was not inclined to postpone the book, but he politely went to see Mrs. Whitney. He pointed out to her that what interested him about her brother-in-law was not the man but the deed. He told her, quite accurately, that the protagonist of his novel was an entirely different person from Richard Whitney, with different motivations and family. Understandably, Mrs. Whitney remained unmollified. She appealed to her friend Priscilla.

Ever since *The Indifferent Children*, Louis had been submitting every manuscript to his mother's inspection, though he dreaded the arguments each elicited. That he wrote about the New York business and social worlds to which his mother felt so connected and that his characters might be (and often were) identified with persons she knew seemed to Priscilla Auchincloss a betrayal of "an allegiance from within the citadel." Although she often begged him to change this or that character so as to camouflage a resemblance to someone or other she felt too identifiable, he always refused, yet he kept showing her subsequent work, so highly did he value her opinion. He knew, then, that this character and this subject would cause her real pain.

> If any one person could have represented everything that Mother valued in the 'establishment,' it was Martha Whitney. Not only her husband, but her father before him, had been Morgan partners, and she herself was a kind of Roman matron, with great presence and personality. Even before *The Embezzler*, Mother had admitted that when she apprehensively turned to one of my manuscripts and tried to imagine what the world would say of it, "Martha's are the eyes that I feel reading over my shoulder." And now! Martha was not only reading it, she was vociferously protesting. The nightmare had come true. First the Groton family and now the House of Morgan were reacting exactly as she had feared they might.

Although Auchincloss insisted that Martha Whitney had nothing to lose from the appearance of a novel "based on a crime of which all the world was only too aware," it would have been odd if she had not been upset, and odder still if his parents had not objected. In addition to the close friendship with the Whitneys, Louis's grandfather Stanton had been an officer of the Standard Trust Company, an adjunct of the Morgan empire, and his grandmother Stanton's best friend had been Mrs. Charles Steele, the wife of one of the great Morgan partners. After they sold their Locust Valley house in the mid-1940s, Howland and Priscilla Auchincloss had lived gratis in a cottage on Mrs. George Nichols's place in Cold Spring Harbor. Mrs. Nichols was none other than Jane Morgan, daughter of J. P. Morgan, Jr. Robert Whitney, Richard Whitney's nephew, had been in Louis's Groton form. The Morgan-Whitney-Auchincloss connections were close and long-lived. For Louis to say he changed Richard Whitney (and Groton) for his fiction and that therefore no one should be upset is disingenuous, but, like all writers, he has to make himself something of an outsider. How else could he observe life around him so dispassionately? He claims not to be a satirist, yet he possesses the perspective to judge what he sees ironically. From the time he perceived his mother's need to dress up her family, her husband's partners, and the Morgan bankers as paragons of virtue, he learned to look at his environment realistically. In his writing, he never shows noble traits without their accompanying flaws, and his authorial voice always sees more humor in any given situation than do the characters that create the situation. It is precisely his dissection and criticism of a world he is both part of and drawn to that makes these 1960s novels so convincing and trustworthy.

The Embezzler was another big success: his fourth time on the front page of *The New York Times Book Review*, his second Book-of-the-Month-Club main selection, his second National Book Award nomination (Bernard Malamud's *The Fixer* won), and his fifth appearance on the best-seller lists. The novel is the story of Guy Prime, scion of an old Knickerbocker family, who misappropriates bonds to keep afloat during the Depression. He is caught and brought to trial. The New Deal pillories him as a flagrant example of the kind of men who run Wall Street like a private club. He goes to prison and after release exiles himself to Panama. The crime and the punishment are Richard Whitney's; the perpetrator is not.

The reader is never certain why Guy Prime acted as he did, for his story has no central narrative voice but is told from three different points of view. His memoir, his friend Rex Geer's memoir, and his wife Angelica's memoir present overlapping and contradictory versions of the man that tantalizingly illustrate the psychological and moral mystery of human motivation. Blanche Knopf rightly called it a rare book, "completely civilized," and reminiscent "of the Galsworthy era and elegance," but it just misses the greatness of the three preceding novels. Guy Prime is not Francis Prescott, so the unraveling of the mysteries of his character does not lead to the larger ethical and moral issues raised by Prescott's life. Moreover, the memoirists seem too literary to be altogether believable and they sound too much alike, for as John Mason Brown wrote in the *Book-of-the-Month-Club News*, "the one premise of his novel, necessary though not always easy to accept, is that Prime, Rex Geer and Angelica are all able to write with Mr. Auchincloss's felicity." Finally, he fails to give readers the richness of detail of the preceding three novels. Still, *The Embezzler* is an exciting book, an accurate picture of the great world of finance before World War II, especially of the widespread speculation and wholesale borrowing of the 1920s and 1930s before the New Deal tamed Wall Street, and a picture of the disintegration of old New York.

Auchincloss used the device of multiple narrators only once again after *The Embezzler*—in *The House of the Prophet*, a novelistic interpretation of the underlying motivation of Walter Lippmann's aloofness—and that was fourteen years later. He explains that differentiating and sustaining various voices requires an inordinate expenditure of time, energy, and effort, yet even his third-person narration has been criticized. He creates characters who sound alike, critics complain, frequently literary, like himself. He was aware of the problem, as an observation he made about Henry James, the novelist he admires above all others, shows.

What James never learned was how to make his characters reveal themselves in dialogue. They all talk alike, and artificially. This makes no difference in the novels. There the characters are so vividly presented in the prose that we are delighted to have them speak beautifully—as if they were declaiming poetry or singing. Stylization of dialogue occurs in many of our greatest works of fiction. But when the curtain rises on a drawing room of our own day, the actors have only the vernacular in which to introduce and describe themselves. James never addressed himself to this problem. I doubt he recognized it.

Auchincloss began publishing literary criticism such as this at the same time he started historically and culturally exploring New York's ruling class. *Reflections of a Jacobite*, his first collection of critical essays (one of which had appeared in *Partisan Review* and two in *The Nation*), came out in 1961. Between then and now he has produced fifteen books of nonfiction, including one memoir, two books of edited diaries, five collections of literary essays, and seven books of biographical essays.

If "criticism is the highest form of autobiography," as Oscar Wilde wrote, a reader should learn something about the man as well as the writer from the nonfiction. What the essays reveal is Auchincloss's deep love of literature, his pragmatism, his strongly held views, his humor, clearheadedness, and good judgment. To make the "unfashionable and unrepentant" point that the Albertine passages in *Remembrance of Things Past* harm the artistic unity of Proust's masterpiece, he read through its seven novels in reverse order. Not surprisingly, he has written several essays on Proust, as well as pieces on Daudet, Bourget, Corneille, Racine, Saint-Simon, Richelieu, and Versailles. He has neglected neither the English, publishing essays on Shakespeare and the nineteenth-century novelists, nor the Americans, writing frequently about Henry James and Edith Wharton, but also about Emily Dickinson, Henry Adams, Theodore Dreiser, nine women novelists (including Willa Cather, Katherine Anne Porter, and Carson McCullers), John P. Marquand, and John O'Hara.

When Auchincloss pointed out in 1960 that O'Hara's "strange, angry world" was really the old-fashioned novel of manners in disguise, O'Hara wrote, "I can best reply by pointing out the fact that you obviously have read all my novels, and I have not read one of yours. I don't know anything about your importance as a lawyer, but in my league you are still a bat boy, and forty-three is pretty old for a bat boy." As it turned out, Auchincloss was more and more compared to O'Hara by critics. Clipping each article or essay that paired the two, Auchincloss mailed it to O'Hara with the signature, "The Bat-boy." Eventually, O'Hara's wife, an Auchincloss cousin, drew her relative aside at a clan gathering and asked him to stop. O'Hara had not been amused.

Clear thinking and sound judgment permeate Auchincloss's nonfiction. The first principle of good writing, one he takes seriously, is to entertain. "Her tragedy as a writer," he says of George Eliot, "is that she never learned the simple lesson that an entertainer must entertain." In defense of Proust and implicitly of himself, he takes the reasonable position that since "snobbishness reigns on all levels [of society], why does it matter which level one selects to study?" Eminently pragmatic, he writes, "*King Lear* strikes so directly into family life that I suspect that many parents since 1605 have had the old man's dread example in mind while considering settlements on their offspring. As a lawyer I can think of more than a few." Never afraid of strong opinion, he ranks George Meredith's *The Egoist* "among the ten finest novels in the English tongue." Not shackled by abstract principles of criticism, he writes with no "other object but to induce [his] reader" to read the book under consideration. He believes writers today are too conscious of literary fashion, and that the idea that a particular literary technique is out-of-date is silly. "I would not hesitate to write a novel in letters like *Clarissa Harlowe*, if I felt the urge." Nor does he like the nonobjective in art. "I loved Albee's *Virginia Woolf*, but I could make no sense of *Tiny Alice*. I like everything that is meaningful and sensible. . . . I am not the least interested in guessing games." Techniques that Auchincloss praised in the critical essays are exemplified in his fiction; sometimes, his literary analyses are even incorporated into his characters' dialogue. Much of his literary criticism can be read as a gloss on his own work.

In the eighteen months immediately following *The Embezzler*,

however, Auchincloss wrote short stories (some for magazines) not
nonfiction. They were published in 1967 in a collection called *Tales
of Manhattan*. He still had not started a new novel, an unusual
hiatus for this extraordinarily prolific writer. "You will be
amused(?) to hear," he wrote Gore Vidal in March, "that for once
my well is dry. Nothing in progress. What can it mean?" And again
in May, he wrote, "Still no new book, but a faint theme may be
stirring."

The "faint theme" had first been heard in "The Money Jug-
gler," one of the stories in *Tales of Manhattan*. Auchincloss ex-
panded this into the novel *A World of Profit*. In the story, four
college classmates discuss a fifth, who, after a tremendously lucrative business career, had gotten into trouble with the law. To the
foursome, he represents the parvenu's refusal to abide by a moral
code, and they conveniently overlook their own willingness to
profit from his entrepreneurial schemes. The career of Jay Livingston, the protagonist of the novel, recalls that of Edward M. Gilbert, a businessman who, after a series of misappropriations, fled
to Brazil in the mid-1960s. Like his fictional counterpart, Gilbert
had been caught between his desire to get a divorce and his attempts to take over a company, for which he eventually resorted
to crime. Having made his fortune in real estate, Jay tries to marry
into an old New York family by the name of Shallcross, a greedy,
unattractive, ridiculous group who are even more corrupt than he
is and only too happy to feed on him, according to Sophie Shallcross. Yet shady as his dealings are, he is the only character halfway
interesting due to his energy and a certain odd naïveté in the sense
that "the world to him never loses its aspect of a shop window."
Despite the novel's grand theme—confusion in the contemporary
world, "where there is no accepted code of what is right and
wrong, [where] marital infidelity, financial fraud, even violence
have become acceptable, [where] about the only thing which is
morally wrong is racial discrimination," according to Auchincloss—
the book is a letdown after its predecessors. Auchincloss, too, was
disappointed and said so in a letter to his agent.

I have a big batch of reviews in, and they are pretty bad. Certainly the worst in my career. But I am beginning to pull myself together. I have been much helped by Vol. 4 of Edel's life of James (*The Treacherous Years*) and how he came back (at about my age) from being booed in the theatre and went on to the climax of his career which he hit at sixty. May I do the same! May I come through this slough of despond. But these things have to be faced alone. Nobody at home (including Adèle) or at Houghton sees what has happened. They see the big sales and the big ads and think I am a grumbler. But I know it has been a long time of judgment and that I have been found wanting. It is not all spite or jealousy or modernism. There is some truth in it. And to go forward I must improve. I know I am at the crossroads and no one (not even you) can help me.

A World of Profit does have shortcomings. It introduces too many characters, some one-dimensional, and repeats ideas encountered in previous books. The character of Jay Livingston is new, however, a kind of Jay Gatsby, different from any of Auchincloss's other characters. Yet it seems odd that someone as intelligent as Jay Livingston is unable to acquire more polish as he climbs the social ladder. If he knows enough to shed his birth name of Levermore for Livingston, why does he not discard his ruby cuff links and diamond ring and curb his habit of combing his hair in public with a small gold comb? Finally, the novel is less complex and vigorous than its predecessors, most likely owing to its having been written in third-person omniscient-narrator style. Even so, the novel was the Literary Guild's Main Selection for January 1969, featured on the cover of its magazine, condensed in *Ladies' Home Journal*, and appeared on the best-seller list for thirteen weeks. But looking back, Auchincloss recognized *A World of Profit* as the beginning of "a capital slump." "It got worse and worse and finally I ceased to sell paperback rights. I did that for a long time and then I slowly turned around critically and started to come back." Still, he never again achieved the literary heights of his three greatest novels, *The House of Five Talents, Portrait in Brownstone,* and *The Rector of Justin.* In his earliest novels, he had adhered strictly to people, events, and places he had observed with his own eyes, but in the 1960s novels, he made a sustained and eminently entertaining examination of the fate of the WASP elite from the late nineteenth century to the 1950s. In taking a long, hard look at inherited money, at an old New York family, at exclusive schooling, and at Wall Street, he showed in these social chronicles how it came to pass that his own class lost its exclusive control over America. "To have witnessed the disintegration of an economic ruling class in the 1930s from a front row seat," he has said, "was all a novelist could ask." It was indeed, and he made the most of it.

The 1960s was an incredible decade for Louis Auchincloss, writer: five novels, three books of essays, two books of short stories, four book-club selections, five best-sellers, four front-page reviews in *The New York Times Book Review,* stories published in *The Saturday Evening Post, Town & Country, Cue, Coronet, State Department Magazine, The New York Times, New York Herald Tribune, The Saturday Review, American Heritage, Virginia Law Review, The New York Times Book Review, The Nation, Partisan Review, The New Yorker, Good Housekeeping, Cosmopolitan, McCall's,* and *Redbook.* By 1964, he was able to tell Gore Vidal that he made "as much money from writing as from the law." For tax reasons, in the early part of the decade, he had asked Houghton Mifflin to pay him $25,000 the first of every year (it was later increased to $40,000) and to keep the rest in his account. By the end of the decade, he had over $200,000 in the account. Auchincloss had become an easily recognized New York celebrity—a frequent guest of Mayor John Lindsay's at Gracie Mansion, one of *Town & Country*'s one hundred most "in" people of the decade, a guest at Truman Capote's famous 1966 Black and White Ball at the Plaza Hotel for New York's best-known personages, even appearing as an occasional clue in *The New York Times* crossword puzzles—and a considerable literary figure. A wide variety of academic, literary, and journalistic critics wrote in praise of him. Requests to serve on juries for literary awards, for blurbs, from publishers, and for speeches before the likes of the American Booksellers Association and Harper & Row's 150th anniversary reception attest to his renown. In 1965, along with John Berryman, Alfred Kazin, Richmond Lattimore, Howard Nemerov, and Isaac Bashevis Singer, he was elected to the Department of Literature of the National Institute of Arts and Letters, an august assembly founded in 1898 and limited to 250 creative artists and intellectuals. In 1968, the National Arts Club awarded him its First Gold Medal for distinction in literature. He had certainly proved himself a major American writer, and against a powerful popular tide. His fiction consistently stood for preserving what is valuable in the culture of the past—stoicism, duty, order, all values directed toward maintaining a stable society—during a decade that discarded the past and spurned its values as repressive. Moreover, he upheld these values in an even, decorous, reserved, lucid style. Auchincloss's writing was decidedly unlike the often inward-oriented fiction that celebrated the subjective self alienated from the social order—a style that was much revered during the 1960s.

CHAPTER 9

Louis S. Auchincloss, Lawyer

The world Auchincloss writes about, the domain of Wall Street bankers and lawyers and stockbrokers, is thought to be irrelevant, a faded and fading genteel-gentile enclave when, in actual fact, this little world comprises the altogether too vigorous and self-renewing ruling class of the United States—an oligarchy that is in firm control of the Chase Manhattan Bank, American foreign policy and the decision-making processes of both divisions of the Property Party.

GORE VIDAL, 1974

Four decades of the practice of law on Wall Street brought me close to the pulse of our legal and financial systems, both notoriously neglected by American novelists often sheltered in universities.

LOUIS AUCHINCLOSS, 1990

Every weekday morning, Louis Auchincloss rode the Lexington Avenue subway from Eighty-sixth Street to Wall Street, reading all the way. Never without a leather-bound first edition of one of his favorite novelists, he was an oddity among the early-morning commuters, many of whom (though never having met him) recognized the familiar tall, slim figure hanging on to a subway strap with one hand and a volume of *A la recherche du temps perdu* with another. (Convinced that no one reads *Remembrance of Things Past* because of its formidable length, Auchincloss tried in vain to convince English and American publishers to publish his edited and much shorter version.) If he was an oddity on the subway, he was a downright curiosity on Wall Street. What other downtown lawyer lined the walls of his office (a large boxlike corner space on the eleventh floor of Hawkins, Delafield & Wood's quarters at 67 Wall Street) with a collection of marriage contracts from the court of Versailles and a framed montage of Richelieu? "There is nothing he doesn't know about French history," a friend and client has observed. "He knows every picture at Versailles as if he lived there." A handsome glass cabinet displayed not law books but first editions—the complete Edith Wharton, the first poems of Emily Dickinson, an early novel of Evelyn Waugh, a mint copy of *Swann's Way*—and all his own books bound in leather.

Auchincloss became head of Hawkins, Delafield & Wood's trust and estates department in 1966. When he had come to the firm in 1954, Dexter Hawkins was the department's partner in charge, but Hawkins died in 1964. His successor, Lawrence Morris (a cousin of Adèle Auchincloss), died two years later. Louis, as the third partner in the department, assumed responsibility for the firm's trust and estate business for the next twenty years, until his retirement. Although he had been doing most of the work in the department before his two predecessors died, business fell off when he took over, so much so that the department eventually consisted of Auchincloss and one associate only. "I never recovered from the general belief that Dexter Hawkins and Lawrence Morris did everything, and I don't think people like their lawyers writing novels. Many people think you can't do two things at one time." He knew of at least one client who admitted she went elsewhere for her will because, she complained, anyone who wrote as prolifically as Louis Auchincloss must be neglecting his legal work. "I think it's hurt me, has impeded my career. That doesn't mean it wiped me out. I produced clients, but not substantially. We lived on Larry's clients."

Since one big estate can carry a firm for years with little work (there is not much difference between administering a $100 million estate and a $1 million estate), Morris's clients were indeed worth holding on to. Two of these included a cousin of Morris's who left an estate in the high eight figures ($35 million of which became the Macy Foundation, on which Auchincloss as administrator of trust and estates served—and still does as trustee) and the art collectors Mr. and Mrs. Robert Bliss, who turned over Dumbarton Oaks, their historic house and grounds in Washington, D.C., to Harvard University for a research center in Byzantine and medieval studies. Other partners provided some estate work. Charles Kades, for example, brought in General and Mrs. Douglas MacArthur (as an army colonel, Kades had chaired the steering committee for the revision of the Japanese Constitution of 1889, residing in Tokyo for three and a half years after the war), and Auchincloss attracted clients on his own, such as a cousin of Edith Wharton, writers Stephen Birmingham and Gore Vidal, Yale classmates Jack Pierrepont (as well as his mother) and Robin Brewster, and Walter Lippmann. But large estates were not what they had been in Morris's prime, because of changes in tax laws and because increasing numbers of New Yorkers retired to other states, such as Florida. In the 1970s, New York lawyers started following their clients south, opening one- and two-man offices to handle trusts and estates. "They have to," Auchincloss quipped, "as nobody dies in New York anymore."

The key to profitability for a law firm is the partner-associate ratio. The more associates a firm has in relation to its partners, the more money it will make, because the firm bills clients for associates' work at rates that more than compensate for their salaries and overhead. Since Auchincloss did not bring in substantial new business, his department, with a ratio of one partner to one associate, did not generate profit. When he started practicing law, the business of the great firms was institutionally generated. Davis Polk was general counsel to J. P. Morgan & Company, for example, and Milbank, Tweed to the Rockefellers and their bank. Today, a firm's business is apt to be transactional in nature: The firm might handle a merger or acquisition for a company but not its other legal affairs. When Auchincloss returned to the law, Hawkins, Delafield & Wood had a dozen partners. Its growth to almost 40 partners occurred in the 1970s, and this growth was primarily transactional. Not surprisingly, the partners who brought in this business—"rain-makers," as they are called—became the best-paid and most influential men in the firm. At Sullivan & Cromwell, presumably, the institutional business was so great, Auchincloss could have comfortably serviced clients, letting others worry about attracting them. "Resigning Sullivan & Cromwell was the worst mistake I ever made," he has said recently.

The chief rainmaker at Auchincloss's firm was Donald Robinson, who had been an associate and John Mitchell's protégé at Mudge, Rose, Guthrie and Alexander (Richard Nixon's old firm) until 1969, when he moved to Hawkins, Delafield & Wood as a partner. At the same time, two of Hawkins, Delafield's partners went to Mudge, Rose, taking the Washington subway-bond business with them. "No one would suggest that Mudge, Rose is going to get all the 2.25 billion Washington Metro business because President Nixon is in the White House and another former partner, John Mitchell, is Attorney General," *New York Post* columnist Jack Anderson wrote on February 26, 1970, but it was a fact that "while the subway was in its dreaming stages, from 1966 to 1969, Hawkins, Delafield & Wood did a highly acceptable job of working up plans for the bond issues," and it is also a fact that after the Hawkins partner assigned to the subway-bond deal had been snatched away by John Mitchell for Mudge, Rose, "the Nixon administration and the Washington, D.C. government, both subject to the president, swiftly began to break the logjams that had blocked the much-needed subway."

Meanwhile, at Hawkins, Delafield, thirty-five-year-old Robinson was given responsibility for four major clients Mudge, Rose also coveted—the Port Authority of New York and New Jersey, the Power Authority of the State of New York, the New Jersey Turnpike Authority, and the Delaware River Port Authority. Although Attorney General Mitchell offered him the post of White House counsel to President Nixon, Robinson declined. (Had he accepted, Auchincloss has said, there would have been no Watergate cover-up. "He would have stood up and said, 'You

can't do that—it's illegal!' and that would have been the end
of it.")

Auchincloss had been dismayed by the firm's loss of two partners, appalled that they had "moved over and became partners of
Mudge, Rose—bam, just like that; it made us look namby-
pamby." The conclusion to his short story "The Kingly Crown"
illustrates just this aspect of the episode. "When a man's in a jam
and is looking for a tough lawyer is he going to the smart cookie
who walked off with half the firm's business or to the firm that let
him do it?" Yet for all Hawkins, Delafield lost in 1970, it made up
tenfold in subsequent years owing in large measure to Robinson's
business-getting prowess. By the mid-1970s, he was one of the
best-known bond lawyers in the country, and it was New York's
fiscal crisis that provided his renown.

New York City was on the verge of bankruptcy in 1975. When
the federal government refused to bail the city out, financier Felix
Rohatyn came up with the idea of MAC, the Municipal Assistance
Corporation, inevitably dubbed "Big MAC" by the tabloids, and
turned to Donald Robinson, by the mid-1970s the presiding partner at Hawkins, Delafield, who with two other partners, Charles
Kades and Henry "Ike" Russell, worked out the fiscal provisions
of Big MAC. The negotiating, which involved the unions, the
financial community, and the city and state governments, was resolved minutes before the default deadline. From that time forward, money poured into Hawkins, Delafield. It may not have had
the prestige of a Sullivan & Cromwell or of a Davis Polk, but its
partners made more money than their counterparts in the larger
firms. "I rode a bonanza," Louis Auchincloss has said. "Three of
our partners regularly made over a million dollars a year." Of
course, the non-bond partners shared in this largess. That he
reaped the benefits of other departments' success made Auchincloss reflect, with typical irony, on the widely held belief that
earned money was morally better than inherited money. "Any distinction is silly. I was running a department that actually ran a loss.
I might just as well have inherited money. I was living off other
people."

After Auchincloss retired in 1986, the end of the calendar year in which he reached sixty-nine (following the firm's mandatory policy), his successor in trusts and estates began an aggressive pursuit of new clients, indicating some disappointment on the part of the firm that Louis's department had not grown. Yet most (if not all) members of the firm believed he was worth every penny he got. Everyone on Wall Street knew that Hawkins, Delafield & Wood was Louis Auchincloss's firm, so at the very least his presence distinguished it from its downtown Manhattan counterparts. John Sullivan, partner in charge of the firm's banking practice, testified to the value of this name recognition, expressing "great satisfaction when people say, 'Oh, Hawkins, Delafield & Wood— you mean Louis Auchincloss's firm!' " In 1986, *The New Yorker* ran a cartoon that pictured the door of a law firm listing the not-quite-readable names of partners, below which was the caption, "A Louis Auchincloss–type firm."

Of course, much of Auchincloss's celebrity resulted from his dual career, which he claimed was "the most boring subject of my life" and one that people found the most interesting. He was forever being asked how he managed to combine two such demanding professions and what effect one had on the other. "I think my practice in law has enhanced my writing in providing all kinds of thoughts, ideas, and inspirations; and of course I've written a good deal about the law. I would not think my writing has in any way enhanced or helped my practice of law." But of course it had.

Several times lawyers and clients had come to him because they felt "that the imaginative qualities required by a writer of fiction might be of some help to them," demonstrating the symbiotic kinship of his two spheres. A nice illustration of this is the 1956 case of the Edith Fabbri trust, which shows he was more than an excellent draftsman. As his former partner Charles Kades has said, "His Fabbri brief reads like a short story. Louis could not only make fact into fiction, as in many of his books, but he was also adept at making fiction into fact. I would have bet my last dollar he'd have lost that case," yet he won in a case that was appealed twice, ultimately triumphing for Edith Fabbri's heirs.

The Fabbri estate matter was first heard in the surrogate court, which decided in Auchincloss's favor, then the intermediate appellate court overturned the decision of the surrogate court, and finally, the court of last resort, the court of appeals, reversed the intermediate court and reinstated the decree of the surrogate court.

Alessandro Fabbri, a bachelor, and his brother Ernesto Fabbri were Florentines who had settled in Bar Harbor, Maine. Alessandro and Ernesto left a brother and four sisters in Florence. Alessandro drew a will in 1920 that created two trusts, with the income of one to go to Ernesto and the income of the other to Ernesto's wife, Edith. (Edith Fabbri was a first cousin of Adèle Auchincloss's grandmother and an aunt of Lawrence Morris.) Upon the death of Ernesto, the principal of the first trust passed to his three married sisters. Upon Edith's death, the principal of the second trust was to be distributed to the children of Theresa Clark, Ernesto and Edith Fabbri's only child, "as I may designate in writing," as the will stated. Alessandro died in 1922. At that time, only one of Theresa Clark's two children had been born, and Alessandro had made no further designation. The difficulty arose when Edith died in 1954. If Alessandro's will could be shown to be invalid, then Edith's principal had to pass by the rules of intestate succession. Alessandro's other heirs at law decided to try to prove an invalid will on the grounds that it was incomplete. Auchincloss represented the Clark children. If the will was valid, the principal of the Edith Fabbri trust would pass to the two Clark children. If the will was invalid, the estate would be divided among all of Alessandro's living descendants. In order for the court to decide who was entitled to receive the principal, Alessandro's intention as expressed in the will had to be determined.

Auchincloss argued that Alessandro's intent had to be gleaned not from a single word or phrase but from a sympathetic reading of the will as an entirety. Not surprisingly, he invoked Judge Learned Hand ("the greatest human being that it has ever been my privilege to know"), who observed that courts should be wary of making "a fortress out of the dictionary" since there "is no more likely way to misapprehend the meaning of language . . . than to read the words literally, forgetting the object which the document as a whole" seeks to achieve. Since all of Alessandro's siblings, except two, were left money in his will, there could be no doubt of intent as far as they were concerned. But the words that referred to Edith's grandchildren—"such as I may designate"—indicated only the reservation of a right to prefer certain of Theresa Clark's children, Auchincloss reasoned. At the time the will was written, Mrs. Clark only had one child, who was under two years of age, Auchincloss continued, and so Alessandro probably expected there would be more children. At this point in his argument, the fiction writer took charge. Here he read Alessandro's mind, just as he might read the mind of a character in one of his books. "It was entirely possible," Auchincloss contended, "that over the years some of the grandnieces and grandnephews might assume different places in the affection of [Alessandro]. Aware of this possibility, [he] desired to allow their personal relationships to develop while at the same time preserving the inheritance for the grandnephews and grandnieces as a class." After presenting his own interpretation of the will, he turned to refuting the interpretation of the opposing lawyers.

[Their] argument that the language is clear and free from any ambiguity, as they interpret it, would compel a conclusion on our part that the testator deliberately did not dispose of a substantial portion of his estate and intended that, in the event of his death, without making a further writing, the property should pass by the laws of intestacy. It would be tantamount to saying that he intended by the language employed to indicate a temporary disinheritance of the grandchildren of Ernesto and Edith, the brother and sister-in-law between whom he had divided the income of his residuary estate and who were apparently his favorite relatives, in favor of relatives for whom he had already provided, or relatives he had not mentioned in his will. Such a result contradicts not only the testamentary scheme and dominant purpose discernible in the will but runs counter, also, to experience. A testator, by the act of making a

will, casts grave doubt on any assumption that he expressly
intends to chance dying intestate as to any portion of his property.

Conceding in his summation that the search for intention was difficult, Auchincloss urged the court look at the whole document and
the circumstances surrounding its formulation.

The Fabbri case deals with an interesting legal issue—the
scope of intent—and is still cited often. One of the judges made
the point that to guess what the testator should have done with his
property or what he would have done had he done anything was as
likely to be wrong as right. Nevertheless Auchincloss's case was
persuasive, for the court of appeals decided four to three in his
favor. No wonder Mario Cuomo, at the time clerk to the presiding
judge on the court of appeals, said the author of that brief should
be a novelist. He is, he was told.

According to Charles Kades, "It takes a very good lawyer to
win a case like this," and it also requires the lively, creative imagination of the fiction writer to make what would ordinarily be a dull
case lively and literary as well as cogent. Surprisingly, Auchincloss
never used the story in fiction, although almost two decades later
he wrote "Agreement to Disagree," the story of a divorce case,
which carried the stretching of intent to an implausible degree. In
it, a lawyer argues that a marital partition agreement is invalid,
since the wife intended to use it as a weapon to inflict physical
harm on her estranged husband, for which assertion there is not a
shred of evidence. "Sometimes we lawyers have to be novelists,
too," a fictional character says in another short story, and "Agreement to Disagree" is a case of the novelist overriding the lawyer.

The Fabbri matter was the only case Auchincloss argued in
court; his day-to-day practice was strictly office-bound. As soon as
he arrived in the morning, he took care of mail, memos, and phone
calls. "On the phone, he got right to the point, which is not always
a successful approach, and then hung up, often without saying
good-bye," an assistant has noted. He read so quickly and perceptively and wrote so clearly and effortlessly, he had finished routine

chores before many of his colleagues had begun. Then he met with Paul Golinski, the trust and estates associate who did much of the department's work, for their daily conference. In that meeting, they came up with a relevant legal principle for whatever matter was under consideration. "Louis was fascinated by how law fit into things," Golinski has said. "As a theoretician, he's a great lawyer. Some lawyers can't see the forest for the trees. But Louis hated the nitty-gritty of the law, like dealing with the billing department. When he wanted to be lawyering, you couldn't find a better lawyer, but there were few occasions when he'd get absorbed." Finally, Auchincloss made his daily phone call to his agent, Jim Brown, and then, if there was no further business to attend to, turned to writing. Lawyers walking by his always-open office door sometimes observed him carrying on a whispered dialogue with an imaginary character.

He was a popular partner, always in demand for lunch, which he usually ate at one of a handful of downtown spots—Michael II, Harry's of Hanover Square, the Down Town Association—frequently with partners Charles Kades, John Sullivan, and Donald Robinson. The Down Town Association, which occasionally shows up in his fiction, is a century-old private luncheon club on Pine Street. Paneled walls lined with portraits of club officers and nineteenth-century engravings of ships provide an understated setting for uninspired food and the dozens of partners' luncheons. The Hawkins, Delafield table was always lively. The liberal Kades and the conservative Robinson could be counted on to provide political arguments, and Auchincloss, whose ramrod-straight posture and forbidding gaze belied a wicked wit, repartee. "Rarely would Louis be neutral on any issue," Kades says. "That's what made lunch with him such fun. You'd come back with some new and humorous slant on the news of the day. And he'd surprise you with things he knows." Twice a month, Auchincloss ate lunch with an informal club of twenty-five to thirty lawyers from the largest firms. They called themselves Coram Nobis, a reference to an old writ: "Bring the thing before us." They met to discuss the problems of managing large firms. "You find out that when you have a problem," Auchincloss explains, "everyone has it. What to do about retired partners is a good example." For years, Coram Nobis met at the Down Town Association, but when so many firms moved uptown, the group alternated between it and the Century Association on Forty-third Street.

Auchincloss also represented the firm as an active member of the Association of the Bar of the City of New York, the country's most prestigious local bar association and, because all the top Wall Street firms had members on its key committees, more influential and powerful in New York City than either the New York State Bar Association or the national American Bar Association. Auchincloss joined in 1946 and over the years served on three committees —the ethics committee, the trust and estates committee, and the executive committee. During the years before the Supreme Court allowed lawyers to advertise, the ethics committee responded to telephone and letter questions primarily about what constituted advertising. Auchincloss has shown himself to have always been sensitive about this issue. In *The Rector of Justin*, when Justin Martyr trustee David Griscam announces his intention to take a year's sabbatical from his firm to solicit funds for the school, he is surprised by the delight of the founding partner. "It's precisely the push that your career needs . . . you should see every big man in New York, Philadelphia and Boston. . . . We lawyers have to take advantage of these things. . . . After all, we can't advertise." Griscam is dismayed by this reaction, and so, too, was Auchincloss, who neither permitted Houghton Mifflin to mention his own firm's name on book jackets nor even to suggest any resemblance between his fiction and an actual law firm. A letter to his editor about the marketing of *Powers of Attorney* illustrates his sensitivity and vigilance.

> I have already talked with David Harris about the small print on the bottom of the advertisement on the front page of the May 20 issue of *Publishers Weekly*, ("Its resemblance to a law firm in Wall Street is uncanny"). It seems to me that the inference of this sentence is that I have drawn an actual law firm,

roughly disguised. Whether or not this was intentional, it certainly could be and has already been so interpreted.

As I am a member of the Committee on Professional Ethics of the Association of the Bar of the City of New York and as Mr. Herbert Brownell, our President, has consulted me on the whole problem of advertising by lawyers, I am in a peculiarly vulnerable situation with relation to advertisements of my own book and particularly so where the book deals with the practice of law. . . .

Under all the circumstances, I would appreciate it if you would give me proofs of advertisements before they appear. I hate to bother you with this for your advertising in the past has always been most tactful, but the little sentence in *Publishers Weekly* has given me a jolt.

The trust and estates committee lobbied at the state legislature in Albany, a useful role certainly, but not as interesting for Auchincloss as the four years he spent on the executive committee. Once a month, "the most brilliant group of lawyers I'd ever been in session with" met at the bar association's building on West Forty-fourth Street to determine the makeup of the association's other committees, to discuss issues of importance to the membership, to advise the president, to manage the nitty-gritty of building maintenance, dues collection, and the like—in short, to run the association.

Auchincloss had had abundant management experience as a member of his own firm's management committee throughout most of the 1970s. The committee, made up of five and sometimes seven members who met every two weeks before the regularly scheduled firm luncheon, ran the firm. Technically, the partnership could outvote the committee, but it never did. Its most crucial and delicate task, and that which gave it power, was the distribution of the firm's yearly profits. "I never had any voice that was important," Auchincloss claims, "because my department didn't contribute money to the firm." Yet in his colleagues' eyes he did have an important role. He brought to the management committee, Donald Robinson says, "judgment, kindliness, gentlemanliness. In my mind, his type of character is important to a firm, and he didn't have a personal agenda. He pushed for what was good for Hawkins, Delafield & Wood." Partner Ralph Brown concurs.

> He was a peacemaker. On one occasion, after a power play within the firm, a person positioned himself to get on the committee, to the chagrin of some members. Louis averted trouble by quoting LBJ on J. Edgar Hoover: "Is it better to have the camel inside the tent pissing out or outside pissing in?" Louis was always the modulating influence, even-tempered and never angry. "Let's get back to the point," he'd say after ad hominem remarks had entered an argument. He could get annoyed and impatient, though.

Several partners commented on his dislike of unimportant detail, and everyone knew when he considered something unimportant. He would rise, give his vote, and leave. Other times, "he'd cut off long-winded discussion," Kades remembers, for he had the gift of getting to the core of an issue.

Paul Golinski, who worked with Auchincloss every day for twenty years, knew him best, and his remarks corroborate the partners' assessments. "He wasn't as money-conscious as many of his colleagues, having a higher view of the social utility of the law, and he had *very* high ethical standards." More than once, Golinski had suggested that Auchincloss deduct his European travels as a business expense on his income tax. After all, he frequently wrote about England and France in both fiction and nonfiction. "Louis, you're an author. You have justification," he said. "But Louis never took a penny of deduction." Like the partners, Golinski had seen Auchincloss annoyed on occasion but never angry. "Of course," he added, "Louis never showed any feelings. Nor was he involved in the politics of the firm, for he believed everything should be settled in a gentlemanly way. He hated confrontation." This might partly account, Golinski thinks, for his having never become a member of the firm. (He is now a partner in an old and distinguished Brooklyn firm.) "Louis wouldn't beat on the table," Robinson says, "but Golinski's not being made partner is one of his great disappointments." A nonlawyer friend of Auchincloss agrees, adding that "Louis probably views it as one of his real failures in life." Partnership at Hawkins, Delafield & Wood is won only by the unanimous vote of existing partners. In Golinski's case, the two dissenting partners argued that the trust and estates department could not reasonably support two partners. Despite the disappointment for both Auchincloss and Golinski, the two men worked well together, and during many summers in the 1970s, Golinski and his wife and children lived in the Auchincloss house in Bedford, New York. Thinking the family would enjoy country living, Louis and Adèle gave them use of their house when they were away.

In their twenty years as colleagues, the two men never had an argument about legal issues, but Auchincloss had much to say about Golinski's writing style and grammar. The writer-lawyer admitted that "his belief in the importance of English to the lawyer amounted almost to a religion." His own plain, unfussy, precise style of writing dovetailed nicely with the needs of the legal world, wherein words and phrases are constantly defined and redefined in relation to specific human conflicts. Moreover, the language of the law provided a source of ready reference for the fiction, frequently showing up in his stories throughout his writing career. Linn Tremain's question to a young associate about the courtship of his niece in *Portrait in Brownstone*, for example, means that "Derrick, as the lawyers put it, was 'on notice.' " In the same novel, a childless marriage is said to be "in default of issue." Legal terms such as these, as well as legal situations such as probate and divorce matters, appear from time to time, but only peripherally. Auchincloss has, quite naturally, written several novels and short stories that deal primarily with the world of law.

The legal fiction is about lawyers being lawyers, "the rich untapped areas of the inner working of the big law firm and its clients," and not about lawyers winning dramatic courtroom battles. "What goes on within the lawyer's office is . . . packed with drama," Auchincloss has said. "I have always found that this field makes for the quickest writing as the stories seem to write themselves. When I published a group of connected stories about a fictional law firm entitled *Powers of Attorney*, I got dozens of letters from people in firms all over the country asking how in God's name I had known about their Mrs. X or Mr. Y. What they did not realize was that human types abound in certain territories." Every large law firm has had the senior partner who, having served in Washington and having "been bitten by the federal bug" thereafter, disdains prosaic everyday practice; the corporate men who "looked down on everything outside their department"; the litigator who treats his department as a firm within the firm; the elderly partner, terrified that he has not kept up; and the secretary of the deceased founding partner who feels it beneath her dignity to serve anyone else. In Auchincloss's short stories, plots turn on the mundane and sometimes trivial interactions among these types.

At the same time as these sketches of Manhattan legal life show lawyers at work, they give an accurate sociological portrait, not in depth but in sharp focus, of the twentieth-century New York bar. Sweeping changes have made the practice of law today different from practice in 1939 when Auchincloss went to Sullivan & Cromwell as a summer boarder. When he tried to write a one-act play based on an early story, "The Mavericks," for PBS, a simple update from the 1950s to the 1980s proved impossible. "I had to do the whole thing from scratch," he marveled. "I might as well have been writing in the Renaissance. It was incredible how things had changed—how law offices are run, the coming of women into the firms, the change in moral standards." The most obvious difference is the change in the size and structure of firms, which resulted in a change in the character of practicing law.

In the early part of the century, the precursors of the present Wall Street firms were small. When Howland Auchincloss started practicing in 1911, his firm had seven partners; when he retired in the mid-1950s, Davis Polk had grown to forty partners, and today it has well over three times that number. In the small firms, practice was general, but as they grew, they necessarily became specialized and compartmentalized, with an increasing percentage of business from corporate work. The growing process often generated tensions between the old-fashioned general practitioners who, in professing adherence to firm traditions, romanticized the past and the younger attorneys who accepted the modern reality of law firms with specialized departments and powerful corporate clients.

Sheffield, the aged head of Sheffield, Stevens, Knox & Dale, the fictional firm in *The Great World and Timothy Colt,* is a survivor from the nineteenth century, an era of legendary legal individualists who looked down on the dictates of the marketplace and who regarded a law firm as "a group of gentlemen loosely associated by a common enthusiasm for the practice of law." Henry Knox, the senior partner in Sheffield's firm, teaches young associates the idealistic notion that lawyers "were the men who greased the wheels of finance and business. That [their] contribution to the general welfare was direct and creative. That it was [their] glory to have worked out the relationship between the government and industry." Loosely based on Lansing Reed, a warm and engaging man who had been the leading partner to guide the growth of Davis Polk during Howland Auchincloss's days and a friend of the family, Henry Knox expresses an outlook that was prevalent in the great firms, at least until the middle of this century. According to Louis's oldest son, the lawyers of his grandfather's era believed that they had brought order to the business world before the government stepped in. They were actually, they believed, the keepers of the moral order. "I grew up," John Auchincloss says, "with the received notion that my grandfather was not only someone who contributed to the national welfare but who kept American corporations honest."

A young associate in another of Auchincloss's fictional firms, Tower, Tilney & Webb (the firm-protagonist of the twelve episodes that make up *Powers of Attorney*), claims to see through such high-mindedness; if senior partners did not make their associates feel like missionaries, how else could they work them so hard for so little pay? High-mindedness, however, is necessary to the partner who shepherds a firm from sleepy obsolescence to sleek modernity without sacrificing its distinctive traits. Clitus Tilney, as administrative head of his firm, is simultaneously "capable of re-calling the difference in price between roller towels and evaporat-ing units for the washrooms" and of scolding another partner who planned to represent a controversial client: "It depends on what your philosophy of being a lawyer is. Do you want to be the kind of person who helps society to make a better thing of itself, or do you want to make your money out of simple blackmail?" An elderly partner of Arnold & Degener, the fictional firm in the short story "Foster Evans on Lewis Bovee," thinks Lloyd Degener was not high-minded enough. "Lloyd, in his near half century of Wall Street, has developed the firm from what we used rather super-ciliously to describe as a 'gentleman's chaos of prima donnas in high white collars at roll top desks' to the huge, bright, humming legal machine that occupies two glass stories at Number One Chase Manhattan Plaza. It is not even a detail to him that we may have lost our soul in the process." Albert Ellsworth of Carter & Ells-worth makes it "his policy to keep the spirit of Elihu Cowden Carter alive." He "made his memory and his image the trademark" of the firm, and, if anything, he overdoes it. Each associate gets an Ellsworth-penned biography of Carter, slain by a Latin American assassin; Carter's French furniture lines the reception area; a Sar-gent portrait of him hangs in a spot no one entering the firm can miss; bronze tablets with his sayings adorn the watercoolers; a glass topped case with his decorations from foreign governments stands in the library; and his bloodstained vest gilds the main conference room. "You coolly manufactured a religion and a creed to hold your office together," Ellsworth's grandson charges. "The Double Gap" is a wonderful, Chekhovian story that clearly pre-sents two opposing attitudes toward Wall Street's mythologizing. Ellsworth believes that a "law firm is something much more than its clients' problems," that lawyers "must be dedicated to some-thing higher than monetary reward," yet he admits to looking the other way when the Great American Fruit Company, a major client, bribed courts in Dutch Honduras, accepting that practice as the only way to do business in Central America, and he has allowed the firm to try a case before a judge whom he knew had been fixed. His grandson fails to see why he should join his grandfather's firm, in which lawyers preach high ethical canons that have "the function, at least in the minds of your generation, of raising the lawyer to a higher moral plane than that of his client" and yet practice law as tools of clients.

Robert Service, the fictional Yuppie of the 1986 novel *Diary of a Yuppie*, thinks senior partners "invoking the ideals of the past while garnering the profits of the present" are hypocritical. "The basic greed and selfishness of human beings" should be permitted to be pursued, he believes, except when they lead to actual crime. His law firm is different from the type of firm Henry Knox strove to build, for Robert Service believes the law is "a game, but a game with very strict rules. You have to stay meticulously within the law; the least misstep, if caught, involves an instant penalty. But there is no particular moral opprobrium in incurring a penalty, any more than there is in being offside in football." Service's attitude illustrates what Auchincloss thinks is Wall Street's biggest change; and that is, Wall Street's reflection of society's attitude toward morality. Take the Richard Whitney case, he says.

> Richard Whitney was considered a traitor to his class! His crime just *rocked* society. Many of his friends wouldn't speak to him until his dying day. They felt he had let them down. Nowadays, you commit a crime and you write a book about it.

Robert Service commits no crimes, unless throwing out cant can be considered criminal. He is hated, Auchincloss says, because he points out that lawyers who espouse the higher road "are largely hypocrites and fools." Auchincloss agrees with his character to a point. Old-fashioned notions of what constitute proper lawyerly behavior that many of his characters espouse are "partly illusionary," he says. "You look back at their record and wonder if there isn't a nostalgic illusion, and yet there's also a certain underlying truth to the stories."

Far from becoming extinct, Auchincloss told an interviewer,

mythmaking may become more pervasive as firms grow even larger. In the past twenty years, the large firms have gotten even larger owing primarily to friendly mergers and acquisitions. At first, the most powerful corporate firms refused to handle hostile takeovers, so companies interested in acquiring unfriendly target companies and the target companies themselves turned to firms that did not look on this activity as unseemly. Since takeover practice is extremely lucrative—for the company that is the target of a takeover effort, the struggle is a life-or-death effort in which no expense is spared, and even a friendly merger needs a lawyer experienced in hostile takeovers to look out for and fend off any potential raiding companies—it was soon embraced even by firms at the pinnacle of the legal world. "Could lawyers in the past have done that?" an Auchincloss character asks. Auchincloss answers that "it's perfectly true that when the takeovers started, a lot of the big firms looked very much down their noses at that kind of practice, where you sort of crept up on somebody and then pounced. ["I guess it's the huggermugger of the thing that sticks in my craw," one of his lawyers says.] It didn't seem consistent to them with the dignity of an older practice. But they all do it. If they were going to be corporate lawyers, that was the name of the game." They may all do it, but not all, including Auchincloss, like it. "On each side of a hostile takeover, lawyers bring lawsuits that are not motivated, merely harassing; I was brought up to believe lawyers who did that were shysters." A fictional partner in a "flourishing" midtown firm who disdains corporate takeovers reflects the novelist's thinking when he says, "Even the vocabulary gets me down. Terms like 'bear hug' and 'blitzkrieg,' and 'shark repellent!' " Even so, Auchincloss claims that "when people adapt to a market like that, it is not to criticize them to point out that they *have* changed."

For over a decade, the largest law firms have acquired the characteristics of the corporations they represented, so now they find themselves suffering corporate afflictions. A century-old tradition of partner job security is gone, for example; partners are being fired. The profession of law has become the business of law.

Fictionally, Auchincloss takes no side on these matters; he simply reports them. If pressed, however, he says he would side with the older-style lawyers because, "those people are much more attractive, amiable, lovable. . . . They're slightly less rapacious and cutthroat." Beeky Ehninger, a fifty-six-year-old attorney in *The Partners* dedicated to the old-fashioned, "gentlemanly" practice, is one of these. He decides quixotically to set up a new firm with all the rejects (he calls them duplicates) who were to be let go after his firm merges with another. Auchincloss sees his act as generous rather than practical. "I suspect the firm probably isn't going to do very well." Practical or not, his sympathy tends to come down with the idealists, but it is a tempered sympathy. "After all, look at the game they're in. If they were really totally idealistic people would they really be in the practice of law at all? Wouldn't they be missionaries of some sort? Or working for legal aid?"

Auchincloss's legal stories confirm what outsiders have always believed about Wall Street lawyers, namely that money is all-important. Lawyers, after all, serve a society that is bent on making money. Elihu Root's hardboiled adage "The client never wants to be told he can't do what he wants to do; he wants to be told how to do it, and it is the lawyer's business to tell him how" is their credo. A fictional lawyer is a useful foil for exploring moral restraints of such an ethic because a lawyer is paid to be an energetic servant of and not moral auditor of his clients' interests. "If ever you have the good fortune to secure a big company for your client," a partner in Tower, Tilney & Webb informs a subordinate, "you will learn the word 'unbiased' has no further meaning for you. . . . A good lawyer eats, lives and breathes for his clients." Clitus Tilney wistfully acknowledges the truth of this remark: "I wish we could return to the old days of great integrity. . . . Before we were captured by the corporations. Before we became simple mouthpieces." Both men are suggesting that the successful practitioner keeps his sense of ethical outrage within the boundaries of his clients' interests. To do otherwise is not to live in the real world. Several stories indicate that many partners are not cynical opportunists but frustrated idealists who have learned to temper their idealism. The rhetorical question "Well, did you and I make the world?" brings to pragmatic conclusion two stories that raise complex moral questions.

The public, Auchincloss knows, has a highly negative image of the lawyer. "He's shifty. He's another man's mouthpiece. So how can he have superior ethics?" Criticizing lawyers today, he has said, "is nothing but another way of criticizing the nature our civilization has taken. . . . Everything is essentially a market today, and whatever is demanded is going to be found." The law, he thinks, is as good as the rest of the professions and a great deal better than most. Moreover, he believes the Wall Street lawyer can keep his integrity and clients, though he admits the tax lawyer presents a special case. "The tax system has probably done more to destroy morality in this country than anything else. . . . Even the highest-minded lawyers find it difficult to thread their way through the subtleties of tax avoidance versus tax evasion." Beeky Ehninger, who counsels an associate to specialize in tax law, speaks for Auchincloss. "What better seat on the grandstand of life can I offer you than that of tax counsel? . . . Public and private morality, where are they? Submerged in a sea of exemptions and deprecations, of write-offs and loopholes, of fabricated balance sheets and corporate hocos-pocus. What is hospitality but deductibility? What is travel but business expense? What is charity, charity that was greater than faith and hope, but the taxpayer's last stand?"

All of Auchincloss's legal stories give insight into the internal character of Wall Street firms—even to the end-of-the-day accounting of billing hours—and its effect on the individuals who practice there. Most of their plots turn on the management and office politics of firms, the real world of most attorneys. While the courtroom trial may be theatrical, the essential spirit of the law is not dramatic. After all, the law's purpose is to mediate, often to diffuse, not to incite conflict, which is why the majority of disputes are settled out of court (and which is also why Auchincloss deplores the harassment suits that deliberately foment conflict as part of the hostile-takeover strategy). So, with an economy of style and alertness of eye but without moralizing, Auchincloss depicts the ethical complexities inherent in a profession whose ethos is so client-centered. Lawyers read the stories avidly: They are regularly reviewed in bar association journals and legal magazines, and the wear and tear of the Auchincloss holdings in the library of the Bar Association of the City of New York indicates heavy use.

In general, Auchincloss's fellow lawyers like his legal fiction, though some see in it a simplification of complicated issues. He is excused on the grounds that he is reaching out for an audience composed primarily of nonlawyers and thus focuses on personal rivalries, foibles of character, comic predicaments, sexual adventures, and other aspects of conduct and character that lawyers share with other people, rather than on things that set them apart. Even when a story does genuinely deal with legal issues, a writer's first allegiance is to his art: He is free to compress, blend, exaggerate, omit. In other words, he sometimes bends the law for the sake of the plot. For example, a lawyer cannot talk to a person who is represented by other legal counsel about a matter that is within the scope of that representation, yet in the first story of *Powers of Attorney*, Clitus Tilney not only discusses with a friend, Mrs. Granger, the litigation that Tilney's partner, Francis Hyde, is prosecuting against her, but he conspires with her against his partner. Tilney is guilty of breaching several rules: First, he advises another attorney's client; second, he breaches the rule that says a lawyer owes his first loyalty to his own client; and third, he breaches a rule that prohibits the disclosure by a lawyer of information entrusted to him by a client when he reveals to Mrs. Granger information about her case that his partner has obtained from the firm's client, Mrs. Crimmins. Auchincloss excuses this disregard for ethical canons of the profession when he says, "The trouble in writing fiction is that the oddballs are always more amusing than the average person."

Lawyers who forgive such fictional license often complain, along with his cousin Judge Louis Stanton, that there is "no whisper of lawyers liking law" in his books. Other readers question the large number of highly educated, formidably cultured lawyers, sounding suspiciously like their inventor, that people Auchincloss's fiction. These readers forget that Auchincloss is writing about the elite bar, the 3,000 or so lawyers out of 500,000 nationwide who practice in the handful of top firms with blue-chip corporations and financial giants as their clients. As for the charge that his fictional counterparts do not like practicing law, three major characters, Henry Knox, Clitus Tilney, and Beeky Ehninger, provide easy refutation. Even self-destructive Timothy Colt "loved the abstractness of the practice of law":

> he found it actually exciting that on the signing of the final paper, the passing of the final check, after the hurly-burly of the conference table and all the talk, there would have been no change in anything physical, no alteration in the appearance of a mill smoking by a sleepy river, no shift in the vast, ordered weight of bales in a soot-stained warehouse. If this was sterility to a vulgar mind, it was beauty to him, the approach to the essence of things without disarrangement.

Most of Louis Auchincloss's legal stories are gems of irony, ambivalence, ambiguity, metaphor: all techniques by means of which two or more views of experience may be expressed simultaneously. How else could he so vividly embody the inherent difficulties of occupying, as lawyers do, a unique position within society, for they are located on the boundary between clients and the law, between private and public interests.

Louis Auchincloss owes a literary debt to the law. "I think it is a profession ideally married to writing because both deal with the written word and an emphatic need for probing and analyzing." Though he has never concealed the fact that writing has given him more fulfillment than the practice of law, the law has provided limitless capital and has helped shape his writing. Legal thought encourages precision through the imagining and denial of alternative actions available to the client. In an address before the American College of Probate Counsel, he commented on how much time lawyers spend "dressing up the world to look better than it is. The legislator and the judge, perhaps, have to deal with raw reality. But the lawyer deals with the imagined world of what would be best for his client. To the extent that he is able to superimpose this imaginary world on the actual one, he is a success." This is true not only for the lawyer but also for the writer. A much-quoted remark of Samuel Johnson sums up the profitable union of law and literature for Louis Auchincloss: "Lawyers know life practically. A bookish man should have them to converse with. They have what he wants."

CHAPTER 10

The Public Man

New York has absolutely everything today except a past . . . and the only way to create a past that's already been destroyed is in a museum.

LOUIS AUCHINCLOSS

What I've been trying to do is see the New York I know in depth. . . . That's the heart of my work.

LOUIS AUCHINCLOSS

After meeting Louis Auchincloss at Brooke Astor's, First Lady Lady Bird Johnson described him as "very good company, and easy to talk to—polished, very Eastern. I couldn't imagine him living or writing about life west of the Mississippi River." She could have said Hudson River and been just as accurate. When an Auchincloss character leaves Manhattan, his destination is most often Newport, Bar Harbor, Southampton, or the North Shore of Long Island, all upper-middle-class appendages of that great city on the Hudson. Like his fictional lawyer who "decided he wanted to paint a picture of life in New York for a subsequent generation," Louis Auchincloss has, in three dozen books, conveyed his own vision of New York, the bygone city as well as the contemporary. "I have always been fascinated by the history of New York," he has said. "I think I would rather see the old reservoir on Forty-second Street or the original Madison Square Garden than I would any of the lost wonders of the ancient world."

He has been called a "New York institution," "Mr. New York," and a "New York file" because he can walk down almost any city street and tell a companion what family lived where and what home had been torn down there, showing himself worthy of the oft-repeated epithets. Promoted to the American Academy of Arts and Letters in 1991, that most honorific assembly of fifty creative artists and intellectuals chosen from the 250 members of the National Institute of Arts and Letters, Auchincloss had the choice of three chairs that had become available. He opted to replace Isaac Bashevis Singer because he, too, had made New York his ken. When President James Hester of New York University conferred an honorary degree on Auchincloss for his "evident love of the city and its past" and the National Arts Club gave him its first Distinction in Literature Award for being "a quiet but persuasive cheerleader for the best in urban values," they merely stated the obvious: the man and his books are unimaginable separated from New York City.

Yet Auchincloss insists that "these geographical things are enormously exaggerated. I could move into different cities without an essential difference. I couldn't move my settings to Harlem, for what I write has to do with upper-middle-class America." If he lived in and wrote about any other American city but New York, however, he could not write about the "great world," his milieu of wealth and power, of those persons and institutions that shaped, for better or worse, the rest of the country. "I have always dealt with the great world," says one of his characters, who could be speaking for the novelist, "the top of the heap. How people climbed up and what they found when they got there." And only New York as "the center ring of the American circus," as the critic Lewis Lapham puts it, had the requisite raw material. The "great world" after World War II, Auchincloss understood, was not the reasonably homogeneous aristocracy of his parents' New York but a more open meritocracy, to his mind, more stimulating for its emphasis on talent rather than on birth. His mother is responsible for this attitude. For all her stories about family connections, she was far more impressed by achievement than ancestry, and her son enthusiastically adopted her viewpoint. Although he feels that his novel *A World of Profit* fails literarily, Auchincloss likes the book for its portrayal of the protagonist, who embodies "the spirit of New York itself" in his worship of success.

Auchincloss's own appreciation of making one's mark on the world explains why he so readily resigned from the venerable Knickerbocker Club in 1953 (even though he had been a governor) when he was invited to join the intellectual and celebrity-garnering Century Association. "I much preferred the Century and I didn't think that I could afford two uptown clubs," he says today. "To his achievement-oriented mind," his agent James Brown has said, "the Century was a more exciting place." It was also a club to which his father and grandfather had belonged. The Knicker-bocker, the most glamorous and fashionable of the men's social clubs, had been formed in 1871 by men such as John Jacob Astor and William Cutting who were impatient with the delay of getting into the Union Club, the oldest of the men's social clubs in New York. Modeled on men's clubs in London, the Union from the start attracted the wellborn and well-off. "Louis likes to go to the Union," Brown says, "but, though he's never said it, he thinks it is stuffy." Nevertheless, Brown believes that his friend properly belonged at the Union; not only had the brother of one of his ancestors been a founder but one of his Stanton relatives had been president. The Century, founded in 1847, eleven years after the Union, for "gentlemen engaged or interested in letters and the fine arts," was a meeting place for extraordinary talent, and thereby more desirable to the novelist. In its first century, its membership included distinguished American painters of the Hudson River School whose works hang throughout the clubhouse on West Forty-third Street; all three partners of the towering architectural firm of McKim, Mead & White that did so much to make the classical style popular in America and that built in 1891 the present clubhouse; writers Henry Adams and William Dean Howells, financier J. P. Morgan, and politicians Theodore Roosevelt, William Howard Taft, Woodrow Wilson, Franklin Roosevelt, Herbert Hoover, and Wendell Willkie. The Century appears as the Arts and

Letters Club in a short story in *Tales of Manhattan* and by name in
a short story in *Powers of Attorney*. The latter, entitled "The Single
Reader," is a fascinating story about a would-be fictional Saint-
Simon, a diarist obsessed with getting down on paper a picture of
New York for subsequent generations, who allows a woman into
his life for the sole purpose of confirming the quality of his writing
and observations. At the end of the story, she nervously returns his
work while saying she cannot marry him. He reacts by apathetically
noting:

> It was only seven-thirty; he still had time to dine at the Cen-
> tury Club. When he got there he hurried to the third floor and
> glanced, as he always did, through the oval window to see who
> was sitting at the members' table. There was an empty seat
> between Raymond Massey and Ed Murrow. Opposite he noted
> the great square noble face and shaggy head of Learned Hand.

For most New Yorkers, making money is the achievement
that counts most, and Auchincloss, like his fictional character
"Duke" Ehninger in *The Partners*, is "a mine of information about
the source of every fortune in New York." "His mother's family
were never social climbers," James Brown explains, "but they
were conscious of money. They had to be in this city. Money is *the*
criterion." Auchincloss realizes that "everything is based on money
today. It's money that determines your rise or fall. If you have
money, you can get almost everywhere, unless you are really repulsive." His favorite subject, the storming of the social and business citadel of New York's exclusive alliance of founding families
by pushy newcomers, turns on money, and money turns the great
world. "To get to the roots of that world," which is "the heart of
my work," he has said, is to deal with the moral issues that grow
out of the lives of the very rich. After all, "money is power," as
George Will has written, "and power involves moral responsibility,
so the pursuit of money is a subject for serious literature, and
Auchincloss has made it his specialty." No city could provide Auchincloss with a larger field of vision, for as he himself has said,

"New York is mesmerized by money. Half the people want to make it for themselves and the other half for their charities." As the president of the Museum of the City of New York for the last quarter of a century, Auchincloss knows New York's charity world well. "I'm very much in the New York cultural scene," he told an interviewer, "so a large part of my social life is with people who work in and out of museums and other cultural institutions."

The Museum of the City of New York was the first museum in the country to be founded solely as the keeper of a city's past. In 1923, Henry Collins Brown, the president of the Society of Old New Yorkers and the author of nine books and numerous articles on the city's history, gathered together a group of equally devoted New Yorkers to establish a museum. Their inspiration was the Carnavalet, the French museum devoted to the history of Paris, but, with no large donation of money or of an existing private collection, they started from scratch in Gracie Mansion, a 1790s landmark house at Eighty-eighth Street and East End Avenue that the city had owned since 1891. (It has since become the residence for the mayor.) Too small for a sizable collection, Gracie Mansion was home to the museum for a scant nine years—time enough, though, for Priscilla Auchincloss to have taken her small children through its rooms several times. Louis Auchincloss is today probably one in only a handful of living New Yorkers to have visited the original site of the museum. Offered land on Fifth Avenue between 103rd and 104th streets, the museum's trustees raised $2 million for a building large enough in which to grow. Shortly before the 1929 crash, New York's dapper and soon-to-be disgraced Mayor Jimmy Walker laid the cornerstone for the new museum, designed by Joseph Freedlander, which would occupy an entire city block. The good-looking five-story redbrick Georgian-style structure with its graceful marble portico was completed in 1932. Three decades later, Louis Auchincloss joined the museum's board. When Mrs. Winthrop Aldrich (a friend of Louis's mother) had asked John Pierrepont to become a trustee of the museum, he suggested that Louis Auchincloss also be invited to become a board member.

As trustee, Auchincloss was expected to attend all benefits for the museum. His first, a performance of the musical comedy *Ben Franklin in Paris,* simultaneously bored and inspired him. Disgusted that a museum devoted to preserving the cultural and historical past of a city should sponsor a play that he called "a travesty of history to the point of insult," he complained to the trustees' chairman of the ways and means committee. "Shouldn't our benefits have *some* relation to the aims of the museum? Shouldn't they have some bearing on the history of New York?" "Fine," she answered. "Why don't you arrange one that does?" And so it happened that Auchincloss conceived the idea of a benefit exhibition of paintings of old New York families. He reasoned

> that a record in painting, covering the history of a great city, of how its rich and fashionable families wished to see themselves, against the interiors in which they liked to immerse themselves, had to have some kind of sociological message for us today. After all, if *that* was what they had wanted to look like, it must have been how thousands upon thousands of their less privileged contemporaries had also wanted to look. It is startling to consider, as we look back into history, how much our conception of any period is dominated by the costumes of its upper class. When we say Elizabethan, don't we think of a ruffled collar and jewels?

To collect the paintings, he wrote every museum and historical society in New York. He managed to borrow from these institutions twenty-five of the fifty-eight pictures that made up the show. The rest came from families he knew. No Auchincloss hung in the exhibition, but Reginald Auchincloss had loaned his 1902 Benjamin Porter portrait of his mother, Ruth, and grandmother, Mrs. R. Fulton Cutting, and Hugh Auchincloss and his wife loaned Tatia Francetti's 1955 slightly surrealistic study of her two daughters, Jacqueline Kennedy and her sister, Lee, playing checkers. The show did include several portraits of his wife Adèle's family, however.

Adèle Auchincloss's maternal grandmother, the daughter of one of Commodore Vanderbilt's grandchildren, had married a Burden. Two Burden family pictures by the well-known nineteenth-century portraitist Eastman Johnson were among the best exhibited. One, a drawing on which an oil painting was based, hangs today in Louis Auchincloss's dining room; the other was the painting of the four members of the family, including Adèle's grandfather. The earliest of the Vanderbilt pictures shows Mr. and Mrs. William H. Vanderbilt in their cluttered Victorian parlor on Fifth Avenue with their eight children, three in-laws, and two servants. The Commodore was still alive when Seymour Guy painted them in 1873, so they had not yet inherited the vast fortune whose spending defined the phrase *conspicuous consumption*, providing fifty years later the raw material for *The House of Five Talents*. One of the children, Emily Sloane, recently married to the dashing rug merchant who is buttoning her glove in the portrait, is Adèle Auchincloss's great-grandmother. The belle epoque, or the Mauve Decade, as Auchincloss referred to the opulent 1890s in a publication he edited and annotated of a diary of Emily Sloane's daughter, was represented in Giovanni Boldini's 1905 painting of the Duchess of Marlborough and her son, Lord Ivor Churchill. The duchess, as everyone at the exhibition knew, was born Consuelo Vanderbilt.

Auchincloss wrote the text for the show's catalog. "Three Hundred Years of New York City Families" proved to be an absorbing pictorial history of upper-middle-class New York and a popular and successful benefit. Three months later, Auchincloss became president of the board of the Museum of the City of New York, and, once again, Mrs. Aldrich was responsible. Harriet Aldrich "made" him take the chairmanship, he says. "She sat me down one day and said, 'Do you want just to sit on a fat-cat museum board for social reasons, or are you going to pitch in and do something worthwhile?' Mrs. Aldrich was a woman who always got what she was after; she delivered the goods."

If ever there was a perfect match of man and job, this was it. With his own roots deep in New York—a portrait by Rembrandt

Peale of his great-great-great-grandfather John Hone, the elder brother of a former New York mayor, hangs in the museum—he is and always has been absorbed in the city's past. "History is not only when things happened but where," he wrote in an introduction to a history of New York based on the collections at the museum. From the time he was a young student at the Bovee School, Auchincloss had been alert to the pulling down of old buildings and wrote about this fifty years later in *A Writer's Capital*. "The noisy destruction of the great Renaissance palace which Richard Morris Hunt had reared for the Astors on the north corner of 65th Street helped to develop my early sense of the transiency of the city landmarks." Elsewhere he noted that in a city "whose buildings replace themselves like cells of the human body," structures that have escaped the wrecking crew less than a quarter century are regarded as landmarks.

And it has ever been so. When Prince Bernhard of the Netherlands visited the museum's Dutch gallery with Auchincloss and viewed the fanciful diorama of New Amsterdam as it might have appeared to Peter Stuyvesant, he asked his host, "How many of these buildings are still standing?" "None," Auchincloss replied. "None!" the prince exclaimed. "You do things thoroughly in New York." Auchincloss had to admit that only four seventeenth-century structures existed in the five boroughs that make up the city, and not many more eighteenth- and nineteenth-century buildings. The situation was not much better in the twentieth century, at least until the mid-1960s, when the great marble Pennsylvania Station was leveled, and the station itself was reduced from a recreation of the Baths of Caracalla to a subterranean concourse. This so outraged people that the city set up a Landmarks Preservation Commission with real power.

In 1963, an index of the city's designated landmarks was published, and Auchincloss became "a kind of fanatic on that book," he wrote Jean Stafford, visiting each building listed, early every Sunday morning. These Sunday-morning meanderings turned up in "The Landmarker," a tale about an aged bachelor who "took long walks to recapture the old New York that was dying with him" and was happy "to pass a morning traveling . . . to the center of Brooklyn for a glimpse of the Gothic gates of Greenwood Cemetery," Auchincloss's favorite landmark, according to his letter to Stafford. In his fiction, Auchincloss has meticulously delineated the texture of life during various times in New York's history: in the mid-eighteenth century ("The Martyr" in *The Winthrop Covenant*), in the Civil War (*Watchfires*), in the robber baron era (*The House of Five Talents*), in the brownstone period (*Portrait in Brownstone* and *The Book Class*), in the 1930s (*The Embezzler* and *The Country Cousin*), in the 1940s (*The Indifferent Children* and *The Injustice Collectors*), in the 1950s (*The Great World and Timothy Colt*), in the 1960s (*Honorable Men*) to the present (*Diary of a Yuppie*).

Ardent resident and city chronicler, such a man was an inspired choice for the presidency of a museum devoted to preserving New York's history. As a journalist wrote, "Any casting director worth his salt would assign the role of president of the Museum of the City of New York to Louis Auchincloss." The very embodiment of the museum's purpose, the president fervently believed that "if the past is to be saved at all in our cannibal city, which eats itself every generation, it can only be in a museum." The museum, quite naturally, profits from New Yorkers' compulsion to tear down and rebuild, becoming as a result the repository of their heirlooms. Like the Museum of North America in one of Auchincloss's novels, the real-life Museum of the City of New York "had been the beneficiary of the migration of wealthy New Yorkers from mansions to brownstones, and from brownstones to apartments, and from there to the suburbs, each step necessitating the shedding of quantities of furniture, porcelain, silver, gold, clothes, and even jewelry." Curators estimate an aggregate of more than 2 million objects have been donated since 1923, items that range in size from a ticket for a concert by P. T. Barnum's Swedish singer, Jenny Lind, to a giant two-ton zinc statue of Robert Fulton, and in value from two Childe Hassam oil paintings to a postcard depicting New York scenes.

Frequently subjected to critical disapproval for celebrating the very rich, Auchincloss delivers a decisive attack on these rich in

"The Prison Window," an extraordinary short story redolent with Rod Serling–style eerie atmosphere about the distinction between the artifacts people collect and people themselves. An "ancient rusted piece of iron grillwork" that had been used in the Revolution as "the sole outlet to a large, dark storage room in which Yankee prisoners were miserably and sometimes fatally confined" is brought into the Museum of Colonial American Art. The window becomes the vehicle by which a spinster curator is forced to "take a new look at [her] eighteenth century," all beautiful objects like Bogardus tankards, Copley portraits, and Beekman breakfronts.

The artifacts rich New Yorkers have given to their museum are organized by departments, some very distinguished. Over a half a million photographs of the city make this a definitive archive. Equally important are the Currier and Ives Collection, the largest assemblage of prints of this famous New York firm; the Theatre Collection, including an important Eugene O'Neill archive; the collected work of New York cabinetmaker Duncan Phyfe; and the departments of Decorative Arts and Costumes. The museum's most visited collection is toys, with its thousands of dolls, intricate dollhouses, and ingenious mechanical playthings from every decade.

In 1970, four years after becoming president, Auchincloss had to replace the director, who had retired, and the new director, Joseph Veach Noble, almost immediately conceived an innovative audiovisual multimedia show that caused quite a stir in the museum world. Entitled "Drug Scene," the exhibit marked the first time a museum had put together a show on addictive drugs. At the entrance of the museum, a fifteen-foot-high photomural of a boy probing his forearm for a good vein towered over three coffins, representing the three New Yorkers who would die that day from drug abuse. "I thought I'd try drugs just once," a recorded voice boomed, "and then, before I knew it, I was hooked." In one place, strikingly lifelike three-dimensional photomurals of all manner of drug addicts lined the walls; in another, the hardware of narcotics use as well as real drugs were displayed; in yet another, a screen projected dozens of images, including a picture of Judy Garland singing; and patrolling all areas were several ex-addicts who wore red and white buttons that read, ASK ME. Children as young as third graders wanted to know how long the addicts had been on drugs and what they took. At the end of the exhibit, a red hot-line telephone was provided on which anyone could call an addiction control center for help. The show was praised in newspapers and magazines, imitated by other museums, most notably the Smithsonian, attended by four times as many youngsters as usually visited the museum, and enthusiastically supported by a president who, had he been less willing to take risks, might have insisted on safer projects. Later, he insisted that "all of us on the board agreed [the show] was appropriate because New York then had the nation's worst drug problem."

Right from the start, Auchincloss believed in and supported Noble, whose style, he said, enlivened exhibits, boosted attendance, and attracted money. On his part, Noble credits the excellent working relationship he had with the president as the reason for the museum's resuscitation from its former self—a sleepy and dangerously underfunded institution. "Louis took the trustees in hand. 'They are my responsibility,' he said; 'the museum is yours.' He never interfered, because he said the job of a board is to hire a director and if necessary fire the director but never, never to interfere with the director's day-to-day management of the museum." Auchincloss governed by this conviction, even when Noble did a show on venereal disease of which he disapproved. "Drug addiction . . . could properly be attributed to [a] particular culture and studied as [a] social symptom by a history museum," he supposed, "but V.D. was more like tuberculosis or infantile paralysis and belonged to the field of medicine rather than of history. In any event, it was certainly approaching the line where the board could legitimately assert itself." Auchincloss decided, however, to go ahead and raise money for the project. "One of the board asked me where, if ever, I would be willing to draw the line. I replied very firmly: 'At a show on hemorrhoids.' " Like Noble, who retired in 1985, the museum's current director, Robert Macdonald, appreciates Auchincloss's sure grasp of the function of a board. As a member of several boards over the years—trustee of the New York Society Library, the French Institute, St. Bernard's School, and the Macy Foundation, as well as a member of the administrative committee of Dumbarton Oaks Research Library—Auchincloss had logged hundreds of trustee hours, and, being "a quick read of people and situations," learned governance, which Macdonald says is most museums' major problem. "I've directed four museums, and Louis is the best president I've worked with. He understands various roles not widely understood."

When the museum opened in the depth of the Depression, it had no endowment and no opportunity to build one. Even today, although the city maintains the physical plant, money is in short supply. Still, the museum had never done serious fund-raising until Auchincloss took over. Twenty-five years ago, he called in professional fund-raisers and executed their recommendations. He created a President's Council, an in-group of almost a hundred, to provide a proving ground for board membership and to help financially by giving and attending the museum's fund-raising balls, and set up several board committees to lobby the mayor and the New York State Council on the Arts for funds and to solicit corporations and foundations. Today, the museum needs far more major funding for expansion and has embarked on a $30 million fund-raising drive. Auchincloss, now chairman emeritus, is not directing the drive, but he made radio promotions for it. It is hoped that the new president, an investment banker, will provide the forceful money-getting initiative that Auchincloss lacks. Raising such a sum will be difficult, for, as a part-time development officer says, "The Museum of the City of New York is not in the big leagues, but without Louis for the past twenty-four years, it would have been nothing." Donald Robinson, a trustee since 1978, concurs. "Louis came into the museum at a time it really needed some life. He brought a presence it did not have. Under his presidency, the museum became much better known, and it played a major role in the education of the children of the neighborhood."

The best way to comprehend the demands put upon a contemporary president of a New York cultural institution is to read Auchincloss's fiction set in this world, a world as rife with ethical perplexities, giant egos, and petty scheming as the world of big-time law. Tom Wolfe claims Auchincloss "struck a theme . . . never . . . struck before in fiction. It's contemporary, absolutely of the moment, namely, the whole business of art motivations in the city and jealousy within the world of art." In a recent story in *False Gods,* an heiress married to a self-made man sets up and runs her own foundation, failing to see that officers of charitable institutions often believe "that the ends justify almost any means, certainly flagrant misrepresentation." As a result, she is "badly taken in by a couple of her biggest 'investments.' " In another story in the same collection, the chairman of a major fund-raising drive for a zoo of which he is trustee momentarily succumbs to the temptation to cajole a wealthy widow into technically complying with while essentially violating a promise made to her late husband about the disbursement of a marital deduction trust, thereby enriching his zoo's endowment. Later, he comes to his ethical senses when his wife convinces the widow to do exactly what her deceased husband had expected. In still another story about the ethics of respecting the intent of the donor, Beeky Ehninger, chairman of the board of the Colonial Museum, uncovers a curator's forged memo that results in a $300,000 grant to the museum. He fires the curator, who shortly after commits suicide. "Of course, he wouldn't have killed himself if I hadn't discovered him, but it was he who lit the powder fuse, not I," Beeky tells his concerned wife. "It's sheer sentimentality to avoid doing the right thing because somebody might get hurt."

Not many people do the right thing in Auchincloss's only full-length portrait of a New York museum, which, in *The Golden Calves,* is dominated by duplicity, greed, and self-aggrandizement. Set in and around the fictional Museum of North America, the novel depicts wealthy collectors as people "who want art for social recognition and conspicuous consumption." The title is an allusion to art as a new religion—"worship of artifacts in a world where religion is dead except for phony television evangelists"—says Auchincloss. Very like the Museum of the City of New York in its lack of endowment, the Museum of North America first opened its doors in 1930, but the banker who built it subsequently lost his fortune, with which he had planned to subsidize it, and it had been dogged by financial problems ever since. In a plot-heavy story, the novel raises questions about the nature of collecting, the role of museums, and what it means when curators and collectors glorify art instead of God. It is a tale of corruption and betrayal in which the bequest of a rich but high-minded old lady is vandalized by her scheming estate lawyer, who also heads the museum's board of trustees. (The scenario suggests the real-life case of Adelaide Milton de Groot, who left the Metropolitan Museum a sizable bequest of art, which the museum, against her written wishes, deaccessioned and sold.)

Auchincloss's knowledge and love of art permeate his fiction. From the time of his first novel, whose protagonist works for an art gallery, his favorite pictures, sculptures, even pet theories about art, show up in book after book. "You can't educate people to appreciate beauty by showing them beautiful things," a character in *Honorable Men* tells another. "That's the fallacy of the museums. What good does it do to show people masterpieces if they've never seen anything *but* masterpieces? . . . [They] think they can take in art by osmosis. They'd be better off at the movies." Even his own art appears in the fiction. "Tell me about Walter Gay," a character asks a curator in a *Skinny Island* story. "He did his friends' châteaux," the curator answers. "He was one of those exquisite expatriates of Edith Wharton's world," who painted rooms with no people in them. "You don't even feel that anyone just left the room," the curator continues. "They are totally empty voids," for "Gay believed that rooms have souls even if their owners don't." This description of Gay's style of painting exactly fits an oil of a room at Versailles that hangs in the author's apartment. Other artworks in his collection include a William Sidney Mount portrait of his great-grandfather Charles Handy Russell; an Eastman Johnson drawing of Adèle's grandfather James Burden as a child; portraits of novelists Edith Wharton and Samuel Richardson; a bronze figure of a girl by Gertrude Vanderbilt Whitney; a bust of Priscilla Auchincloss by Dorothy Draper; a Kensett marinescape; and, favorite of all, a Lucien Pissarro landscape in oil over the living room mantel, replaced today by a French view of a Louis XIII house that reminded Adèle of one of her grandmother's houses.

James Brown has always insisted his most prolific client would never have written so much had he not married a woman so eager to get out of the city on weekends. Left to his own devices, Auchincloss is perfectly content in town, visiting the museums, the New York Society Library, or the Century Association, or just walking around his Carnegie Hill neighborhood. As spiritual kin to his maternal grandmother's good friend "Aunt Marie," who admonished him whenever he left the city for the country, "If you see a tree, give it a kick for me," he is happy to remain on the "skinny island" of Manhattan. In New York, he has written, "One could do anything if one cared enough. Perhaps that is why I have always regarded it as so particularly ignominious for a New Yorker of my generation and upbringing to have failed to enjoy life."

CHAPTER 11

The Private Man

One's life seems to divide into chapters of much varying length. In the beginning
we need a new one for each school that we attend, sometimes each vacation,
certainly each love affair. But there come periods when whole years, maybe even
decades can be lumped into a single division, when our existence resembles
nothing so much as a long western train trip over prairies that stretch uniformly
to a constantly receding horizon. Such periods, however, need not be unhappy
or even boring. Indeed, they can be the best of one's lifetime.

LOUIS AUCHINCLOSS

L
ouis badly needs what he won't accept: a brutally candid
editing," one editor at Houghton Mifflin wrote another in
a confidential memorandum in 1971. Both had been bemoaning the uneven quality of his newest novel, *I Come as a Thief*,
and wondering what had happened to the author of *The Rector of
Justin*. Auchincloss, too, was concerned about his work, fearing his
Groton novel might have represented his "peak and a dangerously
large expenditure of the precious capital of childhood impressions." He need not have worried. In 1974, when he wrote a direct
and moving account of the process that led to his becoming a writer
(which included sympathetic and warmhearted portraits of his recently deceased parents), he produced some of his finest writing—
modest, precise, beautifully controlled yet emotionally revealing,
polished, humorous, deliberately understated. *A Writer's Capital*
is easily the nonfictional equal to *The Rector of Justin*. Its dedi-

cation—"For Adèle and my sons, John, Blake, and Andrew, who came into my life after this memoir ends but who have been responsible for the good things that have happened ever since"— suggests some measure of the happiness and peace of mind that Auchincloss found in family life.

Family life for the Auchinclosses, like family life for most people, settled into an unvarying routine, which nicely accommodated the writer-lawyer-museum man. "My life doesn't vary," he wrote Gore Vidal in the early 1960s, "but then I don't want it to," and twenty years later, he was obviously of the same mind. "Routine . . . brought . . . liberation," the Lippmannesque Felix Leitner says in *The House of the Prophet.* Daily life in Louis's own family, for all its regularity, differed considerably from that in his parents' home. As casual as Priscilla Auchincloss was correct, Adèle managed her family of five with a live-in housekeeper for weekdays; weekends the family went to the country alone. Everyone shared chores. "The boys did the vacuuming, Louis the mopping, and I the cooking," she told an interviewer. Adèle was an enthusiastic cook, making everything from scratch. "I've a little collection of cookbooks I depend on, even when we have guests. In town, we like sit-down dinners for six, eight, or ten. Then I always have extra help come in at 5:00 P.M., so that once we sit down to dinner, my activity is over." A sea change separated upper-middle-class lifestyles in the sixties and seventies from those in the twenties and thirties, when Priscilla and Howland Auchincloss had employed ten in help. The first time Priscilla Auchincloss beheld her son changing a diaper exemplifies this transformation. "Do you like changing diapers?" she asked in a voice that registered her astonishment at seeing her son so occupied. "No, I don't like it. I'd be perverted if I liked it," Louis answered emphatically. Despite her having reared four children, his mother had never changed a diaper, a circumstance not the least unusual for one of her era and background.

When Priscilla Auchincloss was still alive, the younger Auchinclosses generally ate Sunday lunch at her apartment—"not one you romped in," Blake remembers—and once a week Adèle

was expected to have her for tea or a visit of some kind. Because
everything had to be done just so, Adèle said, nothing was much
fun at her mother-in-law's, either in the city or in Bar Harbor (and
later in Newport, where the senior Auchinclosses summered after
Howland's stroke). Adèle's own parents were more relaxed and
easygoing, so of course the family preferred visits with them, and
in fact spent July in Charlotte in a cottage on the Lawrences'
property. Charlotte, with its sailboats and canoes, its islands for
overnight camping, its cows and pigs, was an idyllic spot for the
boys, and they always looked forward to their Vermont holidays.

Although Adèle complained that her mother-in-law "treated
[her] like a child," she admired her, as a letter she wrote Louis
after Priscilla's death in 1972 indicates.

I'm sitting on the porch as the boys must go to bed—it's
sprinkling with a warm slightly fishy Florida breeze. Shells are
stacked on the sides of the porch and we are salty and warm
from the sun. There is little to do—which I find peaceful, but
I do know that's not your thing.

We first wrote each other fifteen years ago—basically from
here—with—at least on my part—excitement, attraction, a
great deal of uncertainty. I write tonight with certainty, attraction and with true love. . . .

I don't know how to tell you about your mother—because
as you well know, I don't understand my own feelings about
her. I realize how very much I will miss her and I realize what
she has given to us and our children—in spite of my resent-
ments. I also know she gave me (if not threw at me) you!

I sat with [friends] last night—arguing that conventionality and niceness produces the best in humans—I, thinking of
history and in a way of your mother (who sure as hell was
conventional) felt that independence of deed and thought and
morals produced a greater spirit than either [friends and Adèle]
who are so scared to be different. What I guess I'm trying to
say is your mother, in spite of conventionality, did dare to be

herself—one of the reasons she was such a marvelous friend. I will miss her, your mother, more, perhaps than you will.

Despite what Adèle Auchincloss wrote, she was not conventional herself. She cared not a whit about fashion, for example, although the social life she and Louis were accustomed to—receptions at Gracie Mansion, Jacqueline Onassis's Christmas parties, Malcolm Forbes's excursions around Manhattan on his yacht—put her in steady touch with the most stylish New Yorkers. She did not seem to notice or care that she wore the same outfits over and over; to acquaintances, she appeared oblivious to fashion. Reasonably content with art classes and volunteer work in town, she was far more comfortable and at home in blue jeans in the country. At Bedford, she delighted in long walks and, despite its ceaseless demands, in gardening. The Auchincloss's white clapboard house sat on a spacious lawn that rolled down to a rock-lined stream; across the road, the boys could fish on Aspetong Pond. Despite the rustic appearance of the property, at least in the 1960s when they purchased their four and a half acres, Adèle had plenty of outdoor work to do, and "she loved it all," a friend has said, "the planning, digging, pruning, weeding, raking. She would return from weekends exhausted but triumphant." Adèle once wrote about her Bedford garden.

Two small orange poppies bought from an Haitian gardener have spread and fill every sun-filled rocky wall. Campanula and columbine, jack-in-the-pulpit, violets, and oenothera, black eyed Susan and feverfew are almost weeds. Lettuce grows in the unsprayed rose plots; parsley and verbena are a pretty combination; squash like the cosmos patch and marigolds and nasturtium planted next to tomatoes are a must. Not even gypsy moths eat mint or garlic and both add form and texture to a small garden. I like my mess. My husband is nice enough to say it looks a bit like one of the gardens that Vuillard painted. No one would photograph it for a seed catalogue or a garden magazine, but it remains a constantly changing kaleidoscope of images on my mind.

People who knew Adèle comment that she was as ardent about nature as Louis is about literature. Her husband wholeheartedly concurs. "Adèle was passionately interested in the environment, flowers, and the park system." An accident in Central Park touched off what turned into a hardworking dedication to New York City's parks. As a three-year-old, John was hit by a steel swing, requiring eight stitches. When the pediatrician treating the wound blamed it on Robert Moses's ill-conceived playgrounds, Adèle complained about them to city officials. "They have cutting edges and they weigh about twenty-five pounds," she noted. No one listened, so she joined an organization called the Park Association of New York City, a group that had been founded by Iphigene (Mrs. Arthur Hays) Sulzberger. The Park Association set about rebuilding the city's playgrounds. Not only were the parks made safer, children learned something about nature along the way. "We saw kids were playing baseball in the bird sanctuary," Adèle explained, citing one example, "so we had to teach them what a bird sanctuary was, so they would play elsewhere." To accomplish this and to cultivate in these city children sensitivity to the out-of-doors, they put together an annual summer program. In 1967, Adèle became president of the association. "Don't ever think that volunteer work is ineffective," she said at the time. "Once you're inside an organization in that capacity, you can offer unbiased and unbuyable opinions, and the people who set the policies will listen to you." In 1968, the association became the Parks Council when the Council for Parks and Playgrounds, another private group, joined the association. Adèle was elected president of the newly formed Parks Council. Mayor Abraham Beame rewarded her volunteer efforts with a paying parks job in 1974. "Adèle is now Deputy Administrator for Parks, Recreation, and Cultural Affairs with a secretary, a driver and car!" Louis wrote to a friend. "She finds it exhausting work (everyone is always *angry*) but she finds the challenge exhilarating. I am happy I made her take it when the offer came in and she was dubious." During one month, she was left in charge of the entire department of three thousand men. The post, which fell victim to the city's fiscal crisis after a year, was an 8:00 A.M. to 9:00 P.M. job and an unparalleled opportunity to get to know every environmental group in the city. "I learned how the city runs or doesn't run" was her summation of her stint in government.

Adèle Auchincloss's conservation efforts first came to the public's attention in 1971 when she, well ahead of the times, set out to prove how much environmental waste can be eliminated by conscientious grocery shopping. She enlisted the aid of a friend to act as the thoughtless consumer. The friend simply bought the usual groceries for her family of five for a week. Adèle, as the thoughtful consumer, shopped with a string bag for vegetables and fruit, discarded outer wrappings of other foods at the checkout counter, and bought soft drinks and milk in reusable glass bottles. The result—that the Auchincloss family accumulated one half the amount of garbage as the friend's family—was published in *New York* magazine. As a trustee for the New York Botanical Garden, she was in charge of community relations for the country's largest botanical garden. As one of her many public relations tasks, she undertook the research for a book on the history of the Botanical Garden that was published for its centennial in 1991. Her finest environmental achievement, however, was helping to found the National Resources Defense Council, a group dedicated to the wise management of natural resources. Today, the NRDC has a staff of 125, a budget of $12 million and a membership numbering 95,000. As one of the five founding trustees, Adèle was involved in a number of projects on the council, once directing its capital campaign, which entailed a full-time, everyday, year-long commitment, working on endangered plant issues, and a dozen times introducing a group of twenty Easterners to the wonders and problems of Alaska aboard the *Observer*, the NRDC's luxurious touring vessel. Alaska was Adèle's nirvana; she never tired of what had become an annual tour. Louis accompanied her three times, then announced "three times to Alaska is enough." She even induced her sons to take summer jobs at the NRDC. Small wonder its executive director, John Adams, called her "our most devoted trustee" and "New York's first lady of conservation."

Even Adèle's artistic gifts served conservation. Her book, *Tongass Tides*, for example, captures the fragility of the Alaskan environment in etchings, as many of her drawings wryly suggest Alaska's urban antithesis—fish coming out of faucets, octopuses in sewer pipes. In some ways, the making of prints, drawings, and designs gave Adèle as much pleasure as the natural world. In the early years of her marriage, she did the jackets for several of her husband's books, among them a severe New England steeple for *The Rector of Justin*, a facsimile of the stock-market page of the daily newspaper for *The Embezzler*, and a circle of several skyscrapers encased in a floral motif that suggests Tiffany glass for *Tales of Manhattan*. Seeing that her middle son had inherited her artistic and environmental bent, she encouraged Blake to make a three-dimensional model of Jamaica Bay Park, which was used for a long while in the visitors' center. Another summer, she got him to do a scientific study of Aspetong Pond. She helped all three boys with any science or math problems, while they turned to Louis for anything to do with culture.

Math, science, even sports did not particularly interest Louis. "Athletically, he was zip," Blake says, yet he found ways other than throwing balls or attending sporting events to amuse his children. He loved reading to them when they were small, and all three particularly remember Kipling's *Jungle Book*, a book Louis's mother had frequently read to him. In the country, he organized long walks, when he talked "about anything and everything, even about nature, but not as my mother could," Blake recalls. In the city, he took them to museums—"he accused us of leaving paintings flapping on the walls, we'd go by so fast," Blake says with a laugh—to the opera and theater, and regular "boys night out," which usually meant dinner with James Brown at the Century Association. During the fourteen years one or other of the boys was at St. Bernard's, the private boys' school in New York that each

attended for eight years, their father was on the board of trustees
of the school, which involved "a certain amount of work," he has
said, as "St. Bernard's has a very concerned board." "Dad spent
time at St. Bernard's finding out what I did," Blake remembers.
"Unlike my brothers and my father, I'm not good at English and
history, and I felt a stigma about that. I just don't have the mind
to remember." What Louis had decided, according to John, was
that Blake would probably do better not following his older brother
to Groton, and so he "devoted himself to finding a school where
Blake could make his own mark. He brings real imagination to the
job of parenting, coaxing us to go in directions he thinks are right.
He gets you to do what he wants and has you think it was your
own idea." "I looked at Groton," Blake says, "and even liked it,
but I didn't want to go away to school. My father told me Peabody
had founded a sister school, and so we sent for the Brooks catalogue. I fell in love with the school." Blake did well at Brooks: he
was senior prefect, and he was accepted on the early-admission
plan by Williams College.

During the 1970s, Louis and Adèle started taking the boys
abroad, to France one summer, to England and Scotland another,
to Italy, Switzerland, and Germany for a third. Louis's favorite of
the European trips was a cruise on a luxurious passenger barge
with a crew of five down the Canal du Midi in southern France.
Besides the five Auchinclosses, the Lawrence grandparents and
two of Adèle's sister's children boarded the barge at Toulouse for
the tour that ended a week later at Aigues-Mortes, a medieval
seaport on the Mediterranean. The trip was a delight. Auchincloss
described it in *The House of the Prophet*.

> We reclined in deck chairs as the big, slow craft nosed its way
> down the placid narrow waterway, past hot, still fields and
> misty hills, which succeeded each other like Cézanne land-
> scapes in an exhibition, and through small, sleepy white-
> washed villages. A motorcar followed and met us at the docks
> to take us on excursions to castles and churches, to Roman

ruins and caverns. I enjoyed strolling ahead on an old towpath
while our barge waited its turn in the little locks; sometimes I
would lend a hand at the crank or with the lines.

Adèle also enjoyed the barge; European landscapes captivated her
as much as or more than historical and literary sites enthralled
Louis. "I got a garden for every château," she jokingly told an
interviewer. She was also amused by the deal she made with her
more frugal husband to get two or three nights in the most luxurious available hotel or castle in exchange for two or three nights in
a "fleabag." Some summers, they traveled with all three boys, and
on others with just one. (The two left behind went to camp.)
Twice the whole family went to a ranch, to the Bliss Ranch in
Montana and to a ranch in Arizona, where the boys got mumps.
Every spring vacation, they headed south—to Mexico, the Caribbean, and once by car to the Everglades—but only once, Adèle
emphasized, because the boys quarreled all the way to Florida.

Louis Auchincloss has written that the strongest influence on
children today is not parents but peers. The judgment may be
applicable to less close families than his own, but not, certainly, to
his children. They speak of his influence. "My father is a strong
personality and a stronger influence on Andrew and myself than on
Blake," John believes. Like their father, John and Andrew graduated from Groton—a far more permissive place than the Groton of
the 1930s—Yale, and the University of Virginia's law school. All
three sons see their father as forever rational, exceedingly annoying
to them as teenagers; rebelling against someone so evenhanded as
Louis was impossible. "They resent the fact that I never raise my
voice, that I am always reasonable, always willing to hear both
sides" could be Auchincloss describing his sons' teenage feeling
about him, but it is actually the fictional David Griscam, Justin
Martyr trustee, speaking. Griscam, Auchincloss writes, was "admirably adapted" to the law, by "nature reserved, patient, of even
temper and a good listener," all qualities the boys saw in their
father. Excerpts from a few of John's letters written to him during
law school provide an illustration of just how good a listener.

I realize that I have been whining with self-pity about all the pressures I have, enough even to tax *your* capacity to be understanding. . . . Considering the worries that you and Ma have had in recent months [Blake had been seriously ill], it was unfair of me to burden you with my anxieties.

I write you all this because I know that you worry about my emotional state. [John had been upset by a broken engagement.]

This must seem silly to you, who have been so patient through my emotional bellyflops this past year or two.

Perhaps you will understand my distraction better, though maybe I haven't revealed anything unknown to you. I would appreciate your keeping the essential details of this letter away from Ma, who always takes it upon herself to give me lousy practical advice about emotions. I love her, but she doesn't always understand.

Adèle Auchincloss, in contrast to her husband, habitually responded to everyday life emotionally. "My mother," John says, "tended to express her concerns in emotional terms. With my mother, you jumped around in a startling fashion. She had no patience with a discussion that resembled a rational argument, making it so easy to rebel against her." Blake, who looks like his mother, maintains that "from early on I aligned myself with my mother. Perhaps I was more Lawrence and my brothers more Auchincloss. Certainly aspects of this are true." Like the Lawrences, he revels in the out-of-doors and, like his mother, he majored in art history in college, which led to a career in architecture following graduate training at Columbia. After his parents bought four hundred acres on the Neversink River near Liberty, New York, having sold their Bedford house after a quarter of a century on Aspetong Road, they asked Blake, by 1987 an architect, to design a house. Blake declined, as he had just taken a job with an architectural firm in Boston, but he recommended a Columbia classmate, Peter Pennoyer, John Auchincloss's brother-in-law. The Auchinclosses started with a budget of $350,000, which turned out to be grossly inadequate. The site preparation alone cost $100,000. The house was positioned 140 feet up on the side of Wildcat Mountain, which required the construction of a wall to keep the hill from burying the house. The drawings took a year to complete and ended up very different from what Adèle had originally conceived, and the construction consumed another year. As the costs continued to soar, Louis sold off eighty of the acres, as well as his Pissarro and Kensett oils, several volumes of Shakespeare from the first, second, third, and fourth folios, and a collection of the dramatist's poems.

Louis loved the place every bit as much as Adèle, although everyone referred to it as her house. Since she had been the owner of the Bedford property, which was sold to help pay for this house, technically it was hers, so she undertook the project, and the result is substantially Adèle. The house was a fabulous success, and as Blake describes it, "a blend of a villa for my father with vernacular Catskills for my mother." Outside it was rustic, a long, gabled shed constructed of beaded board with exposed rafters, and inside slightly more formal, with French doors and copper swags and a spectacular library for Louis—"a bribe to compensate so devoted an asphalt hound," he said—set in the center of the house and rising two stories, with a circular opening to a book balcony under a dormer window on the roof that floods the area with light. Because Adèle wanted to minimize upkeep, she used local materials that never require painting; and to conserve energy, she divided the structure into three parts so different sections could be closed down. She and the architect succeeded in bringing about a close relationship between house and environment.

Sadly, 1989 was her first and last summer in this house. She had not been feeling well during the spring of 1990, even though she and Louis spent two weeks driving around Sicily in April and two weeks in Moscow at a writer's conference (along with William Gass, Arthur Schlesinger, Jr., Elizabeth Hardwick, and David Halberstam) in May. By June she was in and out of hospitals with every kind of mysterious symptom. Not until August was she diagnosed with multiple myeloma, a cancer in the bone marrow. Told it was a cancer that could be held at bay indefinitely, she underwent radiotherapy treatment, but during the short times she was allowed to go home, she had to use a walker to get around. Her mother died in November; she succumbed on February 6, 1991, at fifty-nine. Her beloved Catskill retreat now belongs to her sons.

Her funeral, conducted in the large Gothic Episcopal Church of the Heavenly Rest, the parish where John, Blake, and Andrew had attended kindergarten, was packed with a well-dressed crowd who came out on a cold, gray February 11 to honor her. The choice of music—Bach and "Amazing Grace"—and of speakers—her close friend Martha Sutphen and NRDC director John Adams, whose eulogies accurately described her life—her warmth and humor and her deeply felt values, the importance of family, art, and ecology—conveyed the sense of a person who "worked hard for her family, her friends, and her planet." In summing up her last six months of life, eulogist Sutphen paid tribute to Louis as well as to Adèle. "I had known that she and Louis were partners in an extremely happy marriage. Seeing them as they faced Adèle's increasing illness was a privilege. They were quietly courageous, never bemoaning what seemed to be a great unfairness. Each sang the praises of the other's cheerfulness and bravery. Each was sustained by the other's love."

*   *   *

The seventy-five-year-old widower continues to occupy the same apartment he and Adèle shared for thirty-one years. The museum president and the lawyer have retired; the writer maintains his course.

Auchincloss is a phenomenon: a writer who likes to write. "Writing is terribly necessary to me," he insists. "I had been determined to give it up, but I had to put my little stamp on the world any way I could." An inscription in a collection of short stories reveals his fear, however, that he has perhaps written too much. "This book has not had a good press, but I feel that [I] would have done better had I published less." Twenty years ago, *New York* magazine asked a number of writers, including Auchincloss, about how they handled writer's cramp. He replied, "As my twenty-second book since 1947 appeared in December, I do not think I should write on this subject. The critics . . . think I need a cramp." The count is now forty-nine. This most prolific writer has averaged a book a year for almost a half century, and now that he has retired from the downtown world, he will undoubtedly produce at an even faster clip. "Because I'm a person with a nervous personality," he once admitted, "I operate in all things with a certain speed," which results in an "impatience with what I have on my desk. I always have the desire to go on to the next thing." "He's always been in a hurry," says lifetime friend Robin Brewster. Auchincloss never appears hurried or harried, but haste does affect the quality of his fiction.

A perfunctoriness of treatment has marked much of the recent work. His interest in the conception and plan of these books is evident; in fact, the plots of some are quite complex. But an impatience to fill them out results in a thinness, a two-dimensionality. This speed affects dialogue, too. Too many characters speak like Louis Auchincloss, full of literary allusions, witty anecdotes, and old-fashioned expressions, just as some historical characters sound too contemporary. Occasionally, he requires dialogue to perform too much work, to carry too great a load of information. Characters, too, get compressed treatment, so that they sometimes lack flesh and blood. For all his sophisticated reading of his characters' psyches and understanding of the ironies of their relationships, he seems to be looking at them from the wrong end of the opera glasses, generating, thereby, acute observations from afar. To borrow his own frequently used image, a scrim between the characters and the reader lessens the reader's emotional response. Many of the books do not make a lasting impression, so that after reading several, it is difficult to set one apart from another.

For all that, however, Louis Auchincloss is an accomplished

artist who has not gotten his due. Critics do not hold all of Shake-speare's plays to the standards of *King Lear,* yet they seem to expect every Auchincloss book to be as brilliant as *The House of Five Talents, Portrait in Brownstone,* or *The Rector of Justin.* A writer must be judged not by his average but by his best, and Auchin-closs's best is in the first rank of American literature. Moreover, his twelve collections of short stories and twenty-two novels docu-ment his accomplishment as a storyteller. Everything he writes is entertaining and at the same time wise. He has a hard, penetrating view of the world, a world in which no force is exerted without a consequence.

As a person who harbored creative impulses in a professional family, he had been full of self-doubt as a young man as to whether he belonged anywhere but on Wall Street, the "real" world accord-ing to just about everyone he knew, but "from the beginning," Gore Vidal has written, "Louis was a writer: word-minded, gossip-prone, book-devouring." Although Auchincloss's story is one of the reconciliation of the "real" and artistic worlds in his makeup, the resultant dual career bemused legal colleagues and led writers to slight his oeuvre. Still, lawyer Auchincloss made himself an authentic man of letters, one who writes critical essays, plays, and biographies, as well as fiction. He has transformed the material of his life into narratives that have their own dynamics and causation and counterpoint in a lucid, simple, and elegant style that is, in its plainness and unfussiness, characteristically American.

The self is revealed in the style. Louis Auchincloss's writing manifests a way of thought; his control of words implies a corre-sponding control of emotions. As Benjamin DeMott has said, Au-chincloss never writhes in print. In his conduct, his detachment is the source of his forbearance; in his art, it yields lawyerly logic, common sense, and precision. "A fine literary style always means sincerity," an early fictional character says; and for Auchincloss, "it was the candor of good manners and not self-revelation." Good manners, Auchincloss said on Lewis Lapham's "Bookmark," are not so different from morals. "The very moral person usually has quite good manners because good manners are usually some sort of basic consideration." When he puts the good manners of twelve women (very like his mother and her friends) under the microscope in *The Book Class*, he concludes that although they have been ministered to by servants and rich fathers and/or husbands, who have relieved them of pressing obligations, they have not wasted their lives, as so many people do. "They knew they were . . . privileged, and they thought that placed them under [the] duty . . . to be good." So, too, has Louis Auchincloss.

As a writer, he offers his readers unimpeachable observations of the rich and powerful in twentieth-century Manhattan, reminiscent of Edith Wharton's portrayal of an older New York. His appraisal of Wharton's career points to the way his own may be evaluated in the future.

> The intensification of interest in American history and letters . . . has assured a permanent place for the fiction of Edith Wharton. She has become required reading for students who want a picture of Eastern-seaboard upper-class living at the turn of the century. The very aspect of her writing that has put off so many readers—her concern with rich and cultivated Americans, usually New Yorkers, who did not have to earn their living—ironically enough, has contributed to her enduring fame. . . . If anyone says that what she did was not worth doing, I can only answer that the society of which she wrote was an integral part of the American dream.

Yet Edith Wharton's New York had a recognizable power structure —civic, business, and social leaders came from the same families; Auchincloss, in recording the breakup of this monolithic control, brings her story up to date and in so doing illuminates the upper reaches of the business and legal worlds he inhabits with understanding of its complexities and conflicts. His work gives a more complete accounting of America, a story, after all, of money and its resultant power, or as Gore Vidal has written, "the real protagonist of America."

"I do not presume to compare myself with our great novelist,

Edith Wharton," Auchincloss said recently, "but I feel as she did when she wrote to an old friend, toward the end of her life, to speculate on the final assessment of her work. In speaking of the 'densities of incomprehension' of some of her critics she wrote":

> You will wonder that the priestess of the life of reason should take such things to heart, and I wonder too. I have never minded before, but as my work reaches its close, I feel so sure that it is either nothing or far more than they know. And I wonder a little desolately which.

At the very least, Auchincloss has done for his world what the Duc de Saint-Simon, about whom he has written so much, did for Versailles. The Versailles people know today is Saint-Simon's creation, not Louis XIV's. The writer who acutely observes and cogently and elegantly relates what he has seen is more enduring than any critic or king.

Bibliographic Note

    The reader will find citations in the notes for the books, articles, and letters that I have consulted and the interviews that I have conducted. I have, therefore, omitted a formal bibliography. Below are the Auchincloss books I refer to in the text. The page references to *False Gods* are to the manuscript pages, since the published book was not yet available at the time I finished this biography. All the books have been published by Houghton Mifflin except when otherwise noted.

NOVELS

1947	*The Indifferent Children*
1951	*Sybil*
1953	*A Law for the Lion*
1956	*The Great World and Timothy Cold*
1958	*Venus in Sparta*
1959	*Pursuit of the Prodigal*
1960	*The House of Five Talents*
1962	*Portrait in Brownstone*
1964	*The Rector of Justin*
1966	*The Embezzler*
1968	*A World of Profit*
1972	*I Come as a Thief*
1977	*The Dark Lady*
1978	*The Country Cousin*
1980	*The House of Prophet*

1981	*The Cat and the King*
1982	*Watchfires*
1983	*Exit Lady Masham*
1985	*Honorable Men*
1986	*Diary of a Yuppie*
1988	*The Golden Calves*
1990	*The Lady of Situations*

SHORT STORY COLLECTIONS

1950	*The Injustice Collectors*
1954	*The Romantic Egoists*
1963	*Powers of Attorney*
1967	*Tales of Manhattan*
1970	*Second Chance*

1974 *The Partners*
1976 *The Winthrop Covenant*
1983 *Narcissa and Other Fables*
1984 *The Book Class*
1987 *Skinny Island*
1989 *Fellow Passengers*
1992 *False Gods*
1993 *Three Lives*

NONFICTION

1961 *Reflections of a Jacobite*
1962 *Edith Wharton* (University of Minnesota pamphlets on American Writers, No. 12, University of Minnesota Press)
1964 *Ellen Glasgow* (University of Minnesota pamphlets on American Writers, No. 33, University of Minnesota Press)
1965 *Pioneers and Caretakers: A Study of Nine Women Novelists* (University of Minnesota Press)
1969 *Motiveless Malignity*
1971 *Henry Adams* (University of Minnesota pamphlets on American Writers, No. 93, University of Minnesota Press)
Edith Wharton, A Woman in Her Time (The Viking Press)

1972 *Richelieu* (The Viking Press)
1974 *A Writer's Capital* (University of Minnesota Press)
1975 *Reading Henry James* (University of Minnesota Press)
1979 *Persons of Consequence, Queen Victoria and Her Circle* (Random House) *Life, Law and Letters*
1983 *Maverick in Mauve*, ed. (Doubleday & Co.)
1984 *False Dawn* (Doubleday & Co.)
1988 *The Vanderbilt Era* (Charles Scribner's Sons)
1989 *The Hone & Strong Diaries of Old Manhattan*, ed. (Abbeville Press)
1990 *J. P. Morgan, The Financier as Collector* (Harry N. Abrams, Inc.)
1991 *Love Without Wings*

Notes

ABBREVIATIONS

For brevity, I have used certain abbreviations in these notes, as follows:

LA   Louis Auchincloss
PSA   Priscilla Stanton Auchincloss
NYRB   *New York Review of Books*
NYT   *New York Times*
NYTBR   *New York Times Book Review*
LA to PSA   All letters from Louis Auchincloss to his mother, cited thus,
              are in the Louis Auchincloss Collection, Accession 9121 g,
              Alterman Library, University of Virginia.

PREFACE

ix   "associated with the tinkle . . .": written by Louis Auchincloss for
     Niagra, a forthcoming Russian publication about American writing,
     in 1990.

ix   *WASP*: This acronym was first used in print by E. B. Palmore in *The
     American Journal of Sociology* in 1962. E. Digby Baltzell claims credit
     for popularizing it in his 1964 book, *The Protestant Establishment.*

ix   "I especially want . . .": quoted in Roy Newquist, "Louis Auchin-
     closs," *Counterpoint* (Chicago: Rand McNally, 1964), 35.

ix   "In my youth . . .": "The Fabbri Tape," *Narcissa and Other Fables,*
     153.

x   "a wider than ordinary perspective . . .": written for *Niagra.*

x   "As a child . . .": ibid.

xi   "is the only serious writer . . .": John Leonard, "What Have Amer-
     ican Writers Got Against Businessmen?," *Forbes Magazine,* May 15,
     1977, 121.

xi   "The assumption that the people . . .": EW to William Crary Brownell, 6/25/1904, quoted in R. W. B. Lewis, *Edith Wharton* (New York: Harper & Row, 1975), 131.

xi   "constantly downgraded . . .": written for *Niagra*.

xi   "I can believe . . .": Thomas Edwards, "News from Elsewhere," *NYRB*, October 5, 1972, 22.

xi   "thin slice of privileged rich . . .": Virgilia Peterson, "In a World Without Passion," *New York Herald Tribune Book Review*, October 1, 1950, 12.

xi   "that little world": Sarah Henderson May, "Poor Sinner in a Labyrinth," *Saturday Review*, October 3, 1953, 28.

xi   "exists like Shangri-La . . .": Webster Schott, "The Partners," *NYTBR*, February 24, 1974, 2.

xi   "claustrophobic and rigid": James Glassman, *Washington Post Book World*.

xi   "characters called WASPs . . .": Patricia Kane in *Dictionary of Literary Biography: Yearbook, 1980* (Detroit: Gale Research Co., 1981), 6.

xi   "an arrogant neo-aristocrat": Angus Wilson, "The Short Story Changes," *The Spectator*, October 1, 1954, 402.

xi   "little world . . . detached . . .": Granville Hicks, "I Come As a Thief," *NYTBR*, September 3, 1972, 6.

xi   "What bothers me . . .": Granville Hicks, *Literary Horizons: A Quarter Century of American Fiction* (New York: New York University Press, 1970), 205.

xii   "Such is the vastness . . .": Gore Vidal, "Real Class," *NYRB*, July 18, 1974, 10–11. (Reprinted as "The Great World and Louis Auchincloss" in Vidal, *Matters of Fact and of Fiction* [New York: Random House, 1977].)

CHAPTER 1: ANCESTRY

1   "When I am told . . .": *A Writer's Capital*, 15.

1   "See that? . . ." to "Knock it off . . .": author's interview with LA, July 1989, NYC.

1 "I checked . . .": ibid.

2 "I felt . . .": ibid.

2 "Genealogy amuses me": author's interview with LA, March 1991, NYC.

2 Collection of cards: author's interview with J. Howland Auchincloss, Jr., July 1989, Cazenovia, NY.

2 Two plays: The handwritten manuscripts of *Henry VIII* and *The Temple* were given by LA to his Yale classmate and lifetime friend Robin Brewster, NYC.

2 "a chest of information . . .": *A Writer's Capital*, 27.

2 "My mother told me . . . LA,": "Eastside Brownstone: A Cinderella Story," *Architectural Digest*, November 1991, 35.

2 "I was fascinated . . .": *A Writer's Capital*, 71.

3 "Years before . . .": ibid., 27.

3 "It became a rather sour . . .": ibid., 26.

3 "Louis is very proud . . .": author's interview with Gordon Auchincloss, July 1989, Lenox, MA.

3 "Looking for my answer . . .": introduction to *John and Elizabeth (Buck) Auchincloss, Their Descendants and Their Ancestry* (Freeport, Maine: Dingley Press, 1957) 3, compiled by Joanna Russell Auchincloss and Caroline Auchincloss Fowler.

3 "a certain proportion . . .": *A Writer's Capital*, 12.

4 "you have the beginnings . . .": ibid.

4 "but that was a tremendous feat . . .": LA to Stephen Birmingham, 9/27/1966, box 46. Stephen Birmingham Collection, Boston University Library.

4 "but he had to lop . . .": ibid.

4   Electronic high jinks: author's interview with Gordon Auchincloss.

4   "realistic about the family's pretensions . . .": Gore Vidal, "Real Class," *NYRB*, July 18, 1974, 12.

4   "were really 'Johnny-come-latelys' ": Mary Tannenbaum, "The Tastemakers," *Cue*, April 6, 1968, 14.

4   "There never was . . .": *A Writer's Capital*, 13.

5   *Fanny Taylor* order: Customs Declaration, Butler Library, 2/12/1806, Special Collections, Montgomery Collection, Columbia University.

5   "Forty miles from Tidewater . . .": *John and Elizabeth (Buck) Auchincloss, Their Descendants and Their Ancestry*, 60.

5   "provided the family . . .": author's interview with LA, July 1989, NYC.

6   "It's not exactly . . .": Gore Vidal, *People Weekly*, May 11, 1981, 36.

6   "Sooner or later . . .": Vidal, "Real Class," 12.

6   Gore Vidal's connection: The marriage of Nina Gore Vidal to Hugh Dudley Auchincloss II lasted from 1935 to 1941.

6   "For idle hypergamy . . .": Gore Vidal, "Reflections on Capital Glories," *The Washington Post*, July 7, 1991, 131, reprinted from an earlier article in *The Threepenny Review*.

6   "No Handy ever . . .": *Watchfires*, 71.

7   Lincoln's letter: In *The Golden Calves* (p. 102), the Lincoln letter gets fictional treatment. "When they go to Newport in the spring the one not driving holds in his lap the framed Abe Lincoln letter congratulating Arleus Speddon for his work on the sanitary commission. It's the same when they come back in the fall. The holy document is never trusted to a servant or left in an empty house."

7   "A square brownstone mansion . . .": *Watchfires*, 41.

7   "Were of English origin . . .": *A Writer's Capital*, 13, 14.

7 "soft-shell crabs . . .": Maud Howe Elliott, *This Was My Newport*, n.d.

7 "with the tin roof . . .": Edith Wharton, *The Age of Innocence* (New York: Grosset & Dunlap), 205.

7–8 Chronicling post–World War II New York: letter from LA to Allan Nevins, 1/27/n.d., Special Collections, Allan Nevins Collection, Butler Library, Columbia University.

8 Facts about Charles Russell: Charles Howland Russell, *Memoir of Charles H. Russell* (New York: DeVinne Press, 1903).

8 "filled with decades . . .": LA, "Oaklawn," *History-Bulletin of the Newport Historical Society*, XLIV (Winter 1971): 1924.

9 "Only Uncle Russell's . . .": author's interview with LA, March 1991, NYC.

9 "living in Paris . . .": "Aunt Mabel," *Fellow Passengers*, 5.

10 "a polite, agreeable . . .": LA, "My Mother, Priscilla Stanton Auchincloss," in *Family Portraits, Remembrances of Twenty Distinguished Writers*, ed. Carolyn Anthony (New York: Doubleday, 1989), 19.

10 "sent his shirts . . .": *The Vanderbilt Era*, 145.

11 "I cannot sing . . .": Walter Damrosch, quoted in Francis Robinson, *Celebration* (New York: Doubleday, 1979), 46.

11 "Don't get Dixonized": *Family Portraits*, 25.

12 "Homesickness . . .": Priscilla Auchincloss, "Foreword to Members of the Dixon Association," in Evalena Dixon Stevens and Louise Dixon DuBois, *The Ancestors of Courtlandt Palmer Dixon and His Wife Hannah Elizabeth Williams*, privately printed, 1927, courtesy LA.

13 Dixons going to church: author's interview with Priscilla Auchincloss Pedersen, July 1989, New Canaan, CT.

13 "All 'foolishness . . .' ": Pauline Dixon, "My Daughter's Friends," unpublished, courtesy LA.

13 Denison: Denison is the name of Louis's great-great-grandmother on his mother's side.

13 "even a small desire . . .": *A Portrait in Brownstone,* 27.

13 "Increasingly idealized . . .": *Family Portraits,* 25.

13 "she played the role . . .": *A Writer's Capital,* 23.

14 "hearing one end." "Foreword to Members of the Dixon Association," vii–viii.

15 "the symbol of that world . . .": C. D. B. Bryan, "Under the Auchincloss Shell," *NYT Magazine,* February 11, 1979, 66.

CHAPTER 2: FAMILY

16 "It has been said . . .": *A Writer's Capital,* epigraph.

16 Louis's weight: cable from Howland Auchincloss to Gordon Auchincloss, 9/28/1917, group N. 580, series II, box 4, folder 040044, Gordon A. Auchincloss papers, Sterling Library, Yale University.

16 Brownstone: house at 37 West Forty-ninth Street.

16 Ninety-third Street: 27 East Ninety-third Street was rented.

16 Ninety-first Street: The Auchinclosses bought the five-story house at 67 East Ninety-first Street.

17 "It was his . . .": *A Writer's Capital,* 20.

18 Howland as an expert: J. Howland Auchincloss's obituary, *NYT,* September 1, 1968.

18 "He was always . . .": author's interview with Helen Stanton (Mrs. L. Lee Stanton), July 1989, NYC.

18 "When you asked . . .": author's interview with Judge Louis L. Stanton, July 1989, Federal Court House, Foley Square, NYC.

18 Meticulous records: author's interview with J. Howland Auchincloss, Jr., July 1989, Cazenovia, NY.

18–19 Howland's attitudes about parenting: ibid.

19 "My older brother . . .": author's interview with LA, March 1991, NYC.

19 "Howlie adored Louis . . .": author's interview with Priscilla Auchincloss Pedersen, July 1989, New Canaan, CT.

19 "quite a jock": author's interview with LA, March 1991, NYC.

19 "not . . . interested in any sport": Groton Archives.

19 "Mother would protest . . .": *A Writer's Capital*, 20.

19 Howland's temper: author's interviews with Priscilla Auchincloss Pedersen.

21 "He never wavered . . .": LA, "My Mother, Priscilla Stanton Auchincloss," in *Family Portraits, Remembrances of Twenty Distinguished Writers*, ed. Carolyn Anthony (New York: Doubleday, 1989), 24.

22 "Father claimed . . .": Vincent Piket's interview with LA. Piket interviewed LA in NYC on Oct. 8, 1985; in Bedford, NY, on July 2, 1987; and in NYC on July 8, 1987, and furnished me with undated transcripts of those interviews. I have cited them jointly as "Vincent Piket's interview with LA."

22 "even after Father's stroke . . .": *A Writer's Capital*, 22.

22 Trip to Belgium: author's interview with Helen Stanton.

22 "By 1927 . . .": *A Writer's Capital*, 16.

23 "one of the great matriarchs . . .": author's interview with Howland Auchincloss, Jr.

23 "Mother was inclined . . .": "Aunt Mabel," *Fellow Passengers*, 19.

23 "loved her sense . . .": *A Writer's Capital*, 26.

23 Priscilla's daily regimen: author's interview with Howland Auchincloss, Jr.

24 "Speculative conversations": author's interview with Eleanor Elliott, July 1989, NYC.

24 Members as exceptionally strong individuals: author's interviews with John Pierrepont, Robin Brewster, Eleanor Elliott, and Louis

Stanton. All made the point that these matriarchs were strong-willed and strong-minded individuals.

24 "Quick and omnivorous . . .": *A Writer's Capital*, 22.

24 "But don't you know . . .": *Family Portraits*, 29.

24 "She put her finger . . .": Piket's interview with LA.

25 "came out with . . .": author's interview with Eleanor Elliott.

25 "the illumination of her . . .": Eleanor Belmont to LA, 10/3/1972, courtesy of LA.

25 Louis's reading: Piket's interview with LA.

25 "My relation with her . . .": LA to Waller Barnett, 5/22/1972, acc. 9121 h., Alterman Library, University of Virginia.

25 Capital versus living: author's interview with LA, July 1990, NYC.

25 "She wouldn't open . . .": author's interview with Adèle Auchincloss, July 1990, NYC.

26 "Priscilla and Louis had . . .": author's interview with Judge Stanton.

26 "He was the apple . . .": author's interview with Pat MacManus, July 1989, NYC.

26 Favorite child: author's interview with Eleanor Elliott.

26 "The other three children . . .": author's interview with Sam Shaw, July 1989, NYC.

26 "It goes all the way back . . .": *Contemporary Authors*, New Revision Series, vol. 29, 1990 (Detroit: Gale Research, Inc.), 29.

26 "She was always . . .": author's interview with Helen Stanton.

26 "If I wanted . . .": Piket's interview with LA.

27 "The unknown . . .": *A Writer's Capital*, 25.

27 "Behind the impressive barricade . . .": ibid., 23.

27 "grandma questions": author's interview with John W. Auchincloss II, July 1990, NYC.

27 "She would listen . . .": author's interview with Judge Stanton.

28 "That did more . . .": author's interview with LA, February 1991, NYC.

28 "very firm opinions . . .": author's interview with Helen Stanton.

28 "She had an uncanny sense . . .": *A Writer's Capital*, 22.

28 "She didn't care . . .": author's interview with Judge Stanton.

29 "a school of social standing": *A Handbook of the Best Schools* (Boston: Porter E. Sargent, 1915 and 1925).

30 "developed a tiny . . .": *A Writer's Capital*, 32.

30 Bovee sold to a developer: *NYT*, April 18, 1929.

31 "She had a lofty . . .": *A Writer's Capital*, 30.

31 "Miss Eleanor's faith . . .": ibid.

31 "protesting that the school . . .": ibid., 33.

32 "Mother tried to see . . .": ibid., 25.

32 "The difficulty was . . .": ibid.

32 "silly side": ibid., 26.

32 "silly social types"; "utterly ridiculous"; "the worthy . . ."; "innate decency"; and "high moral standards": ibid.

33 "Oh, how wonderful! . . .": Piket's interview with LA.

33 Gymnasium in Oyster Bay: Mrs. James Blackstone Taylor was the woman who owned the gymnasium. Years later, Louis became her lawyer, handling her estate. When he told her how upset he had been by her offer, she was horrified to think she had caused hardship when she had meant to give pleasure.

33 "I observed . . .": *A Writer's Capital*, 26.

34 "Our living . . .": author's interview with Howland Auchincloss, Jr.

34 "He knew all their makes . . .": author's interview with Priscilla Auchincloss Pedersen.

34   "All the drama . . .": *A Writer's Capital*, 27.

34   "she could see . . .": ibid., 27.

34   "Was coming back . . .": ibid., 21.

34   "He meant it . . .": ibid., 24.

35   "Dull, soul-breaking things": ibid., 21.

35   "I shuddered . . .": ibid., 21.

35   "to learn the dusty task . . .": ibid.

CHAPTER 3: BOARDING SCHOOL

36   "I spent six years . . .": statement made by LA for Russian writer's trip, to be published in *Niagra*, a Russian journal devoted to American literature.

36   Kissing mother good-bye: Groton Oral Reminiscence, Anne Auchincloss interviewing LA, 10/18/1983, 3.

36   "become necessary . . .": PSA to Endicott Peabody, 12/3/n.d., Groton Archives.

37   "this stuffy little group . . .": LA to PSA, at sea, n.d./1945, acc. 9121 g, Louis Auchincloss Collection, Alterman Library, University of Virginia.

37   "I did it . . .": *A Writer's Capital*, 43.

37   "It no more . . .": quoted in C. D. B. Bryan, "Under the Auchincloss Shell," *NYT Magazine*, February 11, 1979, 61.

37   "You have one eye out . . .": Vincent Piket's interview with LA.

38   "I don't think . . .": Groton Oral Reminiscence, 4.

39   "My father and brother . . .": "Groton School Centennial Address," *Groton School Quarterly* (September 1985): 19.

39   "Rickey, do you believe . . .": ibid.

39   "He never spent . . .": ibid., 18.

40 "The overt teaching . . .": David Halberstam, *The Best and the Brightest* (New York: Random House, 1969), 51.

41 "the central problem . . .": "Writing *The Rector of Justin*," *Afterwords: Novelists on Their Novels*, ed. Thomas McCormack (New York: St. Martin's Press, 1988), 4; originally published by Harper & Row, 1969.

41 Ten out of one thousand graduates: "Twelve of America's Best Schools," *Fortune*, January 1936, 106.

41 "A man who considers . . .": *The Rector of Justin*, 43.

42 "Something has troubled": quoted in George Biddle, "As I Remember Groton School," *Harper's*, August 1939, 300.

42 "The 1932 presidential campaign . . .": 1935 Groton yearbook, 40, Groton School Archives.

43 "our view . . .": Endicott Peabody to PSA, 5/29/1931, Groton Archives.

44 "a cancer in America . . .": *The Rector of Justin*, 44.

45 "One could get . . .": Oliver LaFarge, *Raw Material* (Boston: Houghton Mifflin Company, 1945), 43–44.

45 "I am convinced . . .": quoted in Frank Asburn, *Peabody of Groton* (Cambridge: Riverside Press, 1967), 195.

46 "I found a nice . . .": Groton Oral Reminiscence, 14.

46 "Fun was defined . . .": *The Rector of Justin*, 246–247.

46 "Then, bit by bit . . .": LaFarge, *Raw Material*, 45.

47 Time for recovery: J. Howland Auchincloss to Endicott Peabody, 4/8/1930, Groton Archives.

47 "scandalized and actually . . .": *A Writer's Capital*, 45.

47 "fellow prisoner . . .": Vincent Piket's interview with LA.

47 "I never turned over . . .": LA to PSA, at sea, n.d./1945.

48 "which made [his] line . . .": *A Writer's Capital*, 47.

48–49 LA in fifth place: Records in Groton Archives.

48   "a key at last . . .": *A Writer's Capital*, 48.

48   "Louis demanded respect . . .": Vincent Piket's interview with Sam Shaw.

49   Debating prize: LA to Franklin Delano Roosevelt, 6/16/1933, Groton Archives.

49   "At Groton . . .": quoted in Roy Newquist, "Louis Auchincloss," *Counterpoint* (Chicago: Rand McNally, 1964), 32.

49   "with students and teachers bowing . . .": Piket's interview with LA.

50   "titanic transition": *The Grotonian*, October 1934, 3.

50   "It seems impossible . . .": LA, "Marie Antoinette," *The Grotonian*, November 1933, 18.

51   "My 'accent' is . . .": LA to PSA, 7/20/1945. (This is one of his letters written to his mother during WWII. The letters have been typed, photocopied, and deposited at the Alterman Library at the University of Virginia. The collection is comprised of 411 pages.)

51   LA's clothes and gait: author's interview with Samuel Shaw, July 1989, NYC.

51   "Louis had style . . .": author's interview with Richard Irons, July 1989, Groton, MA.

51   "I feel I must write . . .": LA to Oliver LaFarge, 9/9/1945, Harry Ransom Humanities Research Center, University of Texas, Austin.

52   Peabody and Theodore Roosevelt: Ashburn, *Peabody of Groton*, 63.

52   "I believe . . .": Frank Ashburn, *Fifty Years Out: Groton School 1884–1934*, privately printed, 33.

52   TR influencing FDR: Edmund Morris, *The Rise of Theodore Roosevelt* (New York: Ballantine Books, 1979), 579.

53   "He was the first . . .": unpublished prize-day address, 1982, year that LA's son Andrew graduated from Groton. Although LA had vowed no son of his would go to Groton, the school had so changed,

he, too, changed his mind, sending two of his three sons to his alma mater.

53   "I don't know when . . .": LA to PSA, at sea, n.d./1945.

54   "helpful and a real source . . .": LA to Endicott Peabody, from Yale, n.d., Groton Archives.

54–55   Tilney, Roosevelt, and Gardner: author's interview with Gordon Auchincloss, August 1989, Lenox, MA.

55   "sensitive young men . . .": ibid.

55   "infinite variety . . .": Piket's interview with LA.

55   "His character . . .": LA, "Writing *The Rector of Justin*," in *Afterwords: Novelists on Their Novels*, 3–4.

55   "had complete faith . . .": Piket's interview with LA.

55   "this huge, magnificent . . .": *A Writer's Capital*, 38.

56   "when I was reaching . . .": Groton Oral Reminiscence, 11.

56   "presented a model . . .": *A Writer's Capital*, 59.

56   "Malcolm cared nothing . . .": ibid., 55.

57   "I thought at first . . .": author's interview with Howland Auchincloss, Jr., July 1989, Cazenovia, NY.

57   "Do you know . . .": *The Rector of Justin*, 115–117.

58   "an act of religious devotion": author's interview with LA, March 1991, NYC.

59   "Oh, I remember . . .": ibid.

59   Peabody as a saint to Strachan: Strachan and Louis discussed the Rector's character often.

59   "was so intense . . .": "Groton School Centennial Address," 22.

59   "He was the dearest . . .": author's interview with LA, March 1991, NYC.

59   "whether my own education . . .": LA, "Writing *The Rector of Justin*," in *Afterwords: Novelists on Their Novels*, 6.

59 "was utterly engrossed . . .": ibid., 4.

59 "Mother was an intellectual . . .": author's interview with LA, July 1990, NYC.

60 "Massachusetts church school . . .": *The Indifferent Children*, 20.

60 "I suspect . . .": *The House of the Prophet*, 243.

61 "I don't have . . .": author's interview with LA, March 1991, NYC.

61 "a case can be made . . .": unpublished prize-day address, 1982, 4.

CHAPTER 4: UNIVERSITY

62 "You couldn't go . . .": Vincent Piket's interview with LA.

62 "It wasn't till Virginia . . .": LA to PSA, 9/n.d./1945, Alterman Library, University of Virginia.

62 Auchinclosses' apartments and rent: author's interview with LA, July 1989, NYC.

63 Auchinclosses' trips: ibid.

63 Groton graduates' college choices: from 1935 Groton yearbook, Groton Archives.

63 "My father went to Yale . . .": Piket's interview with LA. LA's younger brother, Howland, also went to Yale.

63 Movies: Yale's yearbook of 1939, Sterling Library, Yale University. LA went to *The Thirty-Nine Steps* with his brother John the first night he arrived in New Haven.

64 "paradise of . . .": LA quoted in "New Haven for a Film Fan," *My Harvard, My Yale*, ed. Diana Dubois (New York: Random House, 1982), 190.

64 "the last of the serious debs": LA, "The Last Serious Debs," *NYT Magazine*, part 2, November 9, 1986, 58.

64 "I was perfectly clear . . .": *A Writer's Capital*, 71–72.

64 "When Louis went . . .": author's telephone interview with Marshall Green, October 1991.

65   "Well, if that . . .": "Leonard Armster," *Fellow Passengers*, 56–57.

66   "I was fascinated . . .": "Early Reading and Alphonse Daudet," *Reflections of a Jacobite*, 2–3.

67   "I was drunk . . .": quoted in *My Harvard, My Yale*, 191.

67   "arty and individualistic": LA to PSA, 9/n.d./1945, Alterman Library, University of Virginia.

68   Dramat information: Dramat Archives, box 23, folder 28, Sterling Library, Yale University.

68   "the only convincing": *New Haven Register*, October 17, 1936.

68   "a zenith": *Yale Daily News*, October 16, 1936.

68   "Father came backstage . . .": author's interview with LA, March 1991, NYC.

69   "I didn't foresee . . .": Piket's interview with LA.

69   "exercises": *A Writer's Capital*, 78.

69   Jack Woods's prizes and honors: *New York Herald Tribune* obituary, June 13, 1941.

69   "It was as if . . .": *Fellow Passengers*, 50.

70   "I was terribly . . .": Piket's interview with LA.

70   "But the great thing . . .": *A Writer's Capital*, 77.

70   "was a thing . . .": *Portrait in Brownstone*, 40.

71   "the vulgarity of . . .": *A Writer's Capital*, 80.

71   "I learned . . .": ibid., 78.

71   "Buckley, Chelton, Yale . . .": "A World of Profit," 144.

72   "hands fluttered": ibid., prologue.

72   "clung around buildings . . .": ibid., 8.

72   "Isn't it a . . .": ibid., 9.

72   "Rows of brownstone . . .": ibid., 67.

72 "I was not indignant . . .": *A Writer's Capital*, 80.

73 "I know why . . .": Piket's interview with LA.

73 "I was afraid . . .": *A Writer's Capital*, 82.

73 "He would put his finger . . .": author's interview with LA, March 1991, NYC.

73 "romantic university . . .": *Honorable Men*, 118.

74 *Wood* v. *Duff-Gordon*: In this case, he decided for plaintiff Wood, who, when he did not make enough money for Lady Duff-Gordon and she bestowed her endorsement on another, sued.

74 "The defendant . . .": *A Writer's Capital*, 85.

74 "Like every author . . .": *A Writer's Capital*, 86.

74 "the most imaginative . . .": LA, "Amelie Rives," from page 15 of an unpublished portion of a biographical essay, Ms. Collection, Curtis Brown, Rare Book and Manuscript Library, Columbia University.

75 "Legislatures . . . drowned in . . .": Foreword to Mordecai Rosenfeld, *The Lament of the Single Practitioner* (Athens, Georgia: University of Georgia Press, 1988), xi.

75 "I saw my dear . . .": Amelie Rives to LA, 12/15/1938, Letters of Amélie Rives Troubetzkoy, acc. 6020 j, Alterman Library, University of Virginia; also quoted in part in *A Writer's Capital*, 141–142.

77 "I've gone left . . .": author's interview with LA, March 1991, NYC.

77 "The book speaks . . .": LA, "Book Note," *Virginia Law Review*, vol. 27, 5.

78 "I loved being . . .": author's interview with LA, March 1991, NYC.

78 "It was a joke . . .": Piket's interview with LA.

78 "I wasn't in the circle . . .": ibid.

78 "very happy . . .": LA to William S. Wilson III, 3/8/1952, William S. Wilson Collection, acc. 6524-b, Alterman Library, University of Virginia.

78 "to bring together . . .": Constitution and By-laws of the Raven Society of the University of Virginia, April 6, 1939, in Rare Virginia Pamphlets, vol. 789 (F221), Alterman Library, University of Virginia.

79 "Serene dome," "noble lawn," "graceful pavilions," and "multitudinous columns": *False Gods*, ms. 4.

79 "It was at once . . .": *A Writer's Capital*, 89.

80 Jack Woods's military draft: In 1940, the Selective Service System was created to administer the draft. Men classified 1-A were available for induction.

81 Woods's obituary: *New York Herald Tribune*, June 13, 1941.

81 "He had the exquisite . . .": *A Writer's Capital*, 82.

81 "how deeply . . .": LA to PSA, 5/29/1942.

CHAPTER 5: WAR

83 "There had always . . .": *A Writer's Capital*, 90.

84 "Virginia encouraged . . .": LA to PSA, 8/29/1942.

84 "evaded the sordid . . .": *The Indifferent Children*, 23.

85 "if you're going to be . . .": author's interview with Judge Louis L. Stanton, July 1989, NYC.

85 "Although an ardent . . .": *A Writer's Capital*, 91.

86 Building that stank of formaldehyde: author's interview with John Pierrepont, July 1989, NYC.

86 "New York in the autumn . . .": *The Indifferent Children*, 41.

86 "and after that . . .": ibid., 54.

86 "All life centers . . .": LA to PSA, 2/27/1942.

86 "It's impossible . . .": LA to PSA, 3/19/1942.

87 " 'When through scudding . . .": LA to PSA, 8/21/1942.

87 "flat-footed American Zonites . . .": LA to PSA, 6/3/1942.

87 "Inevitable disillusionment . . .": LA to PSA, 10/n.d./1942.
   More than three decades later, Louis felt the same way. When the renegotiation of the treaty for the Panama Canal was being discussed, Auchincloss expressed his views in a letter to the editor published in *The New York Times*, April 23, 1976.

When the United States acquired the canal rights of the French Canal Company in 1903, it found Colombia, which then owned all of Panama, unwilling to come to terms about the building of a canal. Rather than negotiate the matter, we induced the Panamanians to revolt and sent a warship, which effectively prevented the Colombians from suppressing the rebellion. The price of Panama's independence was the Panama Canal Treaty.
   It is perfectly true that later, in 1921, Colombia by treaty released its rights to the Canal Zone. But if Panama will not abide by a treaty, why should Colombia? It seems to me that if we stand on treaties, the canal should remain in American hands under the present agreement. If we discard them, the Canal Zone should be returned to Colombia.

88 "They keep wanting . . .": LA to PSA, 7/23/1942.

88 "to be thankful . . .": *A Writer's Capital*, 93.

89 LA letters home: These war letters to his mother, 411 pages of them, are in the Alterman Library (acc. 9121, box G), University of Virginia.

89 "The district intelligence officer . . .": *A Writer's Capital*, 93.

89 "It is a little . . .": LA to PSA, 8/4/1942.

89 "Don't, please, use . . .": LA to PSA, 8/10/1942.

89 "For an active . . .": LA to PSA, 12/26/1942.

89 "I don't enjoy . . .": LA to PSA, 4/22/1942.

90   "The most trivial . . .": LA to PSA, 3/12/1942.

90   "Panama's spiffiest organization": LA to PSA, 5/25/1942.

90   "Some of the new arrivals . . .": LA to PSA, 8/10/1942.

90   "The Tropics can . . .": LA to PSA, 3/19/1942.

90   "I disagree . . .": LA to PSA, 5/20/1942.

90   "I have suddenly decided . . .": LA to PSA, 11/9/1942.

90   "Henry Adams . . .": LA to PSA, 12/19/1942.

90   "Oh, how wrong . . .": LA to PSA, 12/7/1942.

91   "It was dull duty . . .": *Honorable Men*, 142.

91   "I enclose a street photo . . .": LA to PSA, 2/23/1943.

91   Miami in 1943: author's interview with Helen Stanton, July 1989, NYC.

92   "the long remorseless arm . . .": *A Writer's Capital*, 94.

92   "The idea spread . . .": *The Indifferent Children*, 410.

92   "not the cream . . .": LA to PSA, 12/5/1943.

92   Full lieutenant's duties and Mr. A: author's telephone interview with Chauncey Medberry, 1990.

93   LA liked by men: ibid.

93   "Get your trash . . .": *A Writer's Capital*, 99.

93   "one of the greatest factors . . .": Dwight D. Eisenhower, *Crusade in Europe*, Garden City, NY: Doubleday & Co., 1948, 53.

93   "With what still seems . . .": *A Writer's Capital*, 99.

94   "It's your bomb . . .": author's interview with LA, July 1990, NYC.

94   "Some tight . . .": LA to PSA, 6/12/1944.

95   LST under German fire: author's interview with Chauncey Medberry.

94 "moment of terrible . . .": LA to Ruth Jolly, 11/21/1974 and author's interview with LA, March 1991, NYC.

95 "without even transferring . . .": *False Gods*, ms. 244.

95 "They make a horrible . . .": LA to PSA, 7/31/1944.

95 "The city is beginning . . .": LA to PSA, 10/7/1944.

95 "The bells are ringing . . .": LA to PSA, 8/24/1944.

95 The captain's venereal record: author's interview with Chauncey Medberry.

96 "My life is . . .": LA to PSA, 8/2/1944.

96 "as the only war experience . . .": LA to PSA, 10/21/1944.

96 "At first I . . .": *A Writer's Capital*, 101.

96 "Despite the Battle . . .": ibid.

96 "was at her most typical . . .": LA to PSA, 10/7/1944.

97 "That buoy might . . .": *A Writer's Capital*, 105.

98 "I still haven't . . .": LA to PSA, 5/5/1945.

98 "We plowed our way . . .": "The Fall of a Sparrow," *The Romantic Egoists*, 75–76.

99 "We really are . . .": LA to PSA, 10/3/1945.

99 "the most significant novelist . . .": LA to PSA, 10/6/1945.

99 "I have no intention . . .": LA to PSA, 10/21/1945.

99 "I was awfully glad . . .": author's interview with LA, March 1991, NYC.

99 "not only because . . .": *A Writer's Capital*, 90–91.

100 "I continue . . .": LA to PSA, 2/23/1943.

100 "I remember Robin . . .": LA to PSA, n.d./1945.

100 "They were too drunk . . .": *A Writer's Capital*, 110.

101 "How do they . . .": LA to PSA, 11/30/1944.

101 "meant by the unforgettable intensity . . .": LA to PSA, 7/20/1944.

CHAPTER 6: LAW APPRENTICESHIP

102 "I can't help . . .": LA to PSA, n.d./1945.

102 "If S&C won't . . .": LA to PSA, 5/15/1945.

103 "I tell you . . .": author's interview with Ruth Jolly, July 1989, Dublin, NH.

103 "Hurry up, Maggie . . .": author's interview with LA, July 1989, NYC.

103 "Jolly, what have . . .": author's interview with Ruth Jolly.

104 "No. Fiancées are not . . .": author's interview with LA, July 1990, NYC.

104 "I don't know". quoted in Nancy Lisagor and Frank Lipsius, *A Law Unto Itself: The Untold Story of the Law Firm Sullivan & Cromwell* (New York: William Morrow and Co., 1988), 190.

104 "the hierarchical structure . . .": *A Writer's Capital*, 116.

104 "The nine of us . . .": author's interview with Richard Powell, July 1989, NYC.

105 "I liked that . . .": author's interview with LA, July 1990, NYC.

105 "I loved going . . .": author's interview with LA, March 1991, NYC.

105 "dry and juiceless": ibid.

105 "Rather scented . . .": ibid.

105 "Her standard . . .": ibid.

106 "He had a great . . .": Gore Vidal, "Real Class," *NYRB*, July 18, 1974, 12.

106 "I enjoy . . .": LA to PSA, 10/21/1944.

106   "I learned my lesson . . .": author's interview with LA, July 1989, NYC.

106   "I couldn't ever be": LA to PSA, 9/n.d./1945.

107   "Had I once . . .": *A Writer's Capital*, 110.

107   "to assume that . . .": ibid., 109.

107   "I got [the] two . . .": LA to PSA, 10/21/1945.

108   "to be confined . . .": *The Indifferent Children*, 145.

108   "that there wasn't . . .": ibid., 147.

108   "The day after . . .": LA to PSA, 9/25/1944.

108   "sense of never . . .": LA to PSA, 9/20/1945.

108   "Bottled up": author's interview with Judge Louis L. Stanton, July 1989, NYC.

108   "over-happy" and "button on . . .": *Hamlet*, act II, scene ii.

> HAMLET: Good lads, how do ye both?
> ROSENKRANTZ: As the indifferent children of the earth.
> GUILDENSTERN: Happy in that we are not over-happy. On Fortune's cap we are not the very button.
> HAMLET: Nor the soles of her shoe?
> ROSENKRANTZ: Neither, my lord.

108   "the most ridiculous . . .": *A Writer's Capital*, 108.

108   "afraid of girls": *The Indifferent Children*, 370.

108   "held her hand . . .": ibid., 261.

109   "he felt entirely relaxed . . .": ibid., 128.

109   "It would mean . . .": ibid., 303.

109   "in the end . . .": *A Writer's Capital*, 108.

109   "we'll never know . . .": *The Indifferent Children*, 423.

110   "a combination of . . .": LA to PSA, 10/21/1945.

110 "If you part . . .": "The Bookworm Turns," *The Panama-American*, August 4, 1947, 7.

110 "Here is a novelist . . .": William McFee, "A Remarkable Novel About the War," *The New York Sun*, May 27, 1947.

110 LA hiding work under blotter: Dinitia Smith, "The Old Master and the Yuppie," *New York* magazine, August 18, 1986, 34.

110 "A pseudonym . . .": Vincent Piket's interview with LA.

111 Kilgallen and Ventura columns: Kilgallen, *New York Journal American*, June 16, 1947, and Ventura, *New York World Telegram*, August 14, 1947.

111 "On the contrary . . .": *A Writer's Capital*, 116.

111 "You have trained . . .": ibid., 118.

112 "no objectivity . . .": author's interview with James Oliver Brown, July 1989, NYC.

113 "to emerge . . .": Brown's introduction to LA given at National Arts Club, 1968, box 23, James Oliver Brown Collection, Rare Book and Manuscript Library, Columbia University.

113 "in the consuming . . .": *The Injustice Collectors*, 34.

113 "Your apprentice days . . .": Walter Lippmann, 9/9/1950, LA scrapbooks.

113 "The conception of every . . .": Evelyn Waugh, 11/13/1950, LA scrapbooks.

114 "If you work . . .": author's interview with LA, March 1991, NYC.

114 "statistics of their states . . .": "Power of Suggestion," *Powers of Attorney*, 30.

114 "I *was* much disturbed . . .": LA to Ruth Jolly, 11/21/1974, courtesy Mrs. Jolly.

115 "very reluctantly": LA to author, 9/14/1989.

115 "I'll tell you . . .": Paul Holtman, *Lions of the Eighties* (New York: Doubleday, 1982), 159.

115 "ran out to get . . .": author's interview with Richard Powell.

116 "Eventually! . . .": *A Writer's Capital*, 117.

116 "I had to find out . . .": ibid., 119.

116 "they came around": Piket's interview with LA.

117 "Could love go further?": *A Writer's Capital*, 119.

117 "I'm always willing . . .": author's interview with LA, March 1991, NYC.

CHAPTER 7: A WRITER ADRIFT

118 "The nervous temperament . . .": LA to PSA, 6/23/1945.

118 LA's living room decor: author's interview with Ruth Jolly, July 1989, Dublin, NH.

118 "dinner party after dinner party . . .": author's interview with William Pedersen, July 1989, New Canaan, CT.

119 "he was always available . . .": author's interview with Ruth Jolly.

119 "As witty as . . .": ibid.

119 Jean Stafford pouting: ibid.

119 "contained so complete . . .": *Contemporary Literary Criticism*, vol. 62 (Detroit: Gale Research, Inc., 1991), 79.

120 "Right after the war . . .": Gore Vidal, "Real Class," *NYRB*, July 18, 1974, 12.

120 "I think I saw . . .": author's interview with LA, March 1991, NYC.

120 "He would not have . . .": quoted by LA in *A Writer's Capital*, 121.

120 "a Wall Street lawyer . . .": ibid., 120.

120–121 "Louis moved . . .": Vidal, "Real Class," 15.

121 "Isn't that sticking out?": author's interview with LA, March 1991, NYC.

121 "I almost always": ibid.

121   "The writers teased . . .": author's interview with Eleanor Elliott, July 1989, NYC.

121   "Poor Louis . . .": Vidal, "Real Class," 15.

121   "Everyone I remember . . .": author's interview with LA, March 1991, NYC.

121   "We gave Louis safe passage . . .": Tina Bourjaily to author, 7/12/1990.

122   "to be totally fair . . .": *A Writer's Capital*, 121.

122   "Here's a guy . . .": Vincent Piket's interview with Sam Shaw.

122   "Ah, but the woman . . .": LA, "My Mother, Priscilla Stanton Auchincloss," in *Family Portraits, Remembrances of Twenty Distinguished Writers*, ed. Carolyn Anthony (New York: Doubleday, 1980), 28.

123   "The Senior Partner's Ghosts": *Tales of Manhattan*.

123   "When you freely . . .": author's interview with LA, July 1990, NYC.

124   "her terror . . .": "Oberon and Titania," *The Partners*, 185.

124   "Louis is a remarkable . . .": author's interview with Robin Brewster, July 1989, NYC.

124   "We never know . . .": ibid.

124   "panicky from time . . .": Vincent Piket's interview with LA.

124   "I'm not going . . .": *A Law for the Lion*, 268.

125   White Horse habitués' assumption: author's interview with Vance Bourjaily, September 1990, New Orleans.

125   "The Nonsexual friendships . . .": Vincent Piket, *Louis Auchincloss, The Growth of a Novelist* (New York: St. Martin's Press, 1991), 68.

125   "Those women . . .": author's interview with Eleanor Elliott.

126   "I believe . . .": *Family Portraits*, 26–27.

126   "But mother dear . . .": LA to PSA, 3/30/1942.

127   "None of my . . .": author's interview with John Auchincloss, July 1990, NYC.

127   "I couldn't believe . . .": author's interview with Blake Auchincloss, March 1991, Boston.

127   "too much interested . . .": author's interview with Eleanor Elliott.

127   "her nutty theories . . .": author's interview with John Auchincloss.

127   "various nervousnesses": author's interview with Blake Auchincloss.

127   "She guarded her own . . .": ibid.

127   "she was absolutely . . .": author's interview with LA, March 1991, NYC.

127   "She didn't want . . .": author's interview with Adèle Auchincloss, July 1990, NYC.

127   "helped in every way . . .": Piket's interview with LA.

128   "Was there any point . . .": *A Writer's Capital*, 110.

128   "So often men . . .": ibid., 126.

128   "all sorts of things . . .": author's interview with LA, July 1990, NYC.

129   "My parents never . . .": "Amélie Rives" from page 2 of an unpublished portion of a biographical essay, Ms. Collection, Curtis Brown, Rare Book and Manuscript Library, Columbia University.

129   "the cobwebs of fears": author's interview with LA, July 1990, NYC.

129   "there was no tyranny . . .": "The Merger—II," *The Partners*, 244.

129   "his extraordinary inner compass . . .": author's interview with Patricia MacManus, July 1989, NYC.

129   "brought out on deck . . .": *A Law for the Lion*, 39.

130 Reese Parmelee: This character is based on Sam (Parky) Shaw. His thorough masculinity is what Auchincloss believed he had portrayed. Shaw sees it differently: "To some extent [LA] followed my life after the war when I left my wife and three children and Boston and came to New York. The character of the shithead who was the protagonist didn't seem too much like me. Louis is interested in predicaments, and my predicament was how does a man with a wife and three children respond." Piket's interview with Shaw.

130 "the world he resented . . .": *Pursuit of the Prodigal*, 58.

130 "What can happen . . .": ibid., 129.

131 "This is Mr. Auchincloss's . . .": John Barkham, *NYT*, September 27, 1953, 5.

131 "He is a fine stylist . . .": "Eight Dissenters," *Newsweek*, May 17, 1954, 107.

131 "I did want . . .": LA to Paul Brooks, n.d., Houghton Mifflin Collection, Houghton Library, Harvard University.

132 "Is it strictly necessary . . .": LA to Nina Holton, 3/29/1950, Houghton Mifflin Collection, Houghton Library, Harvard University.

132 "aversion to publicity . . .": James Oliver Brown to John Leggett, 9/19/1951, Houghton Mifflin Collection, Houghton Library, Harvard University.

132 "I just hope . . .": James Oliver Brown to Paul Brooks, 1/20/1954.

132 "the name Auchincloss . . .": James Oliver Brown to John Leggett, 11/20/1958.

132 "I am not happy . . .": James Oliver Brown to Paul Brooks, 10/13/1953, James Oliver Brown Collection, Butler Library, Columbia University.

132 Paul Brooks to James Oliver Brown, 10/15/1953, Houghton Mifflin Collection, Houghton Library, Harvard University.

132 "the agent Jim Brown . . .": interoffice memo, Paul Brooks to Connie Coyle, 12/19/1958, Houghton Mifflin Collection, Houghton Library, Harvard University.

132 "that she thought most . . .": LA to Dorothy Santillana, 12/12/1952, Houghton Mifflin Collection, Houghton Library, Harvard University.

133 "the little plot . . .": Piket's interview with LA.

133 "being tied up . . .": Lewis Nichols, "Talk with Mr. Auchincloss," *NYT,* September 27, 1953.

133 "A great step . . .": *A Writer's Capital,* 125.

133 "If a person . . .": *NYT Magazine,* October 10, 1983.

133 "He hopes . . .": "Abel Donner," *Fellow Passengers,* 185.

134 "rusted in his . . .": *A Writer's Capital,* 125.

134–135 Dialogue regarding LA's job search: author's interview with LA, March 1991, NYC.

135 "Returning to Wall Street . . .": *A Writer's Capital,* 125.

135 "When we went out . . .": author's interview with Eleanor Elliott.

136 "Would it be . . .": LA to Gore Vidal, n.d., Gore Vidal Collection, Wisconsin Historical Society, courtesy Vincent Piket.

136 "It was not hot . . ." to "one of the reasons . . .": author's interview with Eleanor Elliott.

137 "He's too social . . ." author's interview with Adèle Auchincloss.

137 "I can still remember . . .": ibid.

137 "It's the word . . .": ibid.

137 "Adèle was not . . .": author's interview with LA, March 1991, NYC.

138 "I am quite absurdly happy . . .": LA to Gore Vidal, 7/25/1957, Gore Vidal Collection, Wisconsin Historical Society, courtesy Vincent Piket.

139 "Thirty-nine years . . .": author's interview with LA, March 1991, NYC.

139 "I wasn't a good . . ." quoted in Dinitia Smith, "The Old Master and the Yuppie," *New York* magazine, August 18, 1986, 33.

139 "People think . . .": author's interview with Adèle Auchincloss.

CHAPTER 8: WRITER ARRIVED

140 "But what you . . .": *The Rector of Justin*, 53.

140 "I have told . . .": LA to James Donald Adams, 8/15/1963, James Donald Adams Collection, Harry Ransom Humanities Research Center, University of Texas.

140 "I like married . . .": LA to Gore Vidal n.d.1957, Gore Vidal Collection, Wisconsin Historical Society, courtesy Vincent Piket.

141 "You have to go . . .": LA to Gore Vidal n.d.1962, ibid.

141 "Adèle is planting . . .": LA to Gore Vidal, 3/12/1963, ibid.

141 "of an obviously intelligent . . .": quote on book jacket.

142 Beaux-Arts mansion at 7 East Ninety-first Street: The house is now part of the Sacred Heart Convent.

142 John Auchincloss's opinion about book characters: in Roy Newquist, "Louis Auchincloss," *Counterpoint* (Chicago: Rand McNally, 1964), 36.

142 "When I wrote . . .": LA to James Donald Adams, 8/15/1963, James Donald Adams Collection, Harry Ransom Humanities Research Center, University of Texas.

143 "vivid and colorful . . .": dedication of the book to Adèle Tobin.

143 "figures that kept . . .": LA quoted in "Notes and Comment," *The New Yorker*, August 13, 1960, 24.

143 "You have to be . . .": ibid.

143 "I never wrote a book . . .": author's interview with LA, July 1990, NYC.

144 "all such poor stuff . . .": ibid.

144 "the background had . . .": LA to James Donald Adams, 8/15/1963, J. Donald Adams Collection, Harry Ransom Humanities Research Center, University of Texas.

144 "it was one . . .": *The House of Five Talents*, 94.

144 "that every human . . .": ibid., 102.

145 "What's the good . . .": ibid., 128.

145 "What is . . .": ibid., 217.

145 "no less than . . .": ibid., 335.

145 "In this room . . .": ibid., 60.

145 "Aunt Daisy's was . . .": ibid., 31.

146 "their vast woebegone . . .": ibid., 60–61.

146 "It really had . . .": ibid., 38–39.

147 "We must have been . . .": ibid., 66.

148 "I worked very hard . . .": Vincent Piket's interview with LA.

149 "for the first time . . .": *Portrait in Brownstone*, 50.

149 "It's really only . . .": ibid., 51.

149 "In the first place . . .": ibid., 61.

150 "Poor grandma . . .": ibid., 62.

150 "Everybody in the family . . .": ibid., 64–65.

151 LA's use of first- and third-person narration: "I had first come across alternating first and third person narration in *The Mandarins* by Simone de Beauvoir," published in 1954. (Piket's interview with LA.)

151 "she learns from . . .": LA in *Literary Guild Newsletter*, Summer 1962.

152 "This book does seem . . .": LA to Dorothy de Santillana, 7/12/1962, Houghton Mifflin Collection, Houghton Library, Harvard University.

152 "I always reserved . . .": LA, "Writing *The Rector of Justin*," *Afterwords: Novelists on Their Novels*, ed. Thomas McCormack (New York: St. Martin's Press, 1988), 3–4.

153 "as a lazy . . .": *A Writer's Capital*, 149.

153 Auchincloss has said the reader will ask: paraphrase from "Writing the *The Rector of Justin*," *Afterwords: Novelists on Their Novels*, 5.

153 "Do we want . . .": *The Rector of Justin*, 318.

154 "It has always been . . .": ibid., 319.

154 "that Justin Martyr is like . . .": ibid., 324.

154 "to old Groton hands . . .": Frank D. Ashburn, *Peabody of Groton* (Cambridge: The Riverside Press, 1967), 320.

155 "the troubled story . . .": "Writing *The Rector of Justin*," *Afterwords: Novelists on Their Novels*, 4–5.

155 Years later, Auchincloss said: Piket's interview with LA.

155 "and she actually began to defend . . .": LA, "My Mother, Priscilla Stanton Auchincloss," in *Family Portraits: Remembrances of Twenty Distinguished Writers*, ed. Carolyn Anthony (New York: Doubleday, 1989), 31.

155 "the finest novel . . .": Orville Prescott, "In Loving Memory of a Noble Failure," *NYT*, July 13, 1964, 27.

155 "not only the best . . .": Maurice Dolbier, "Auchincloss's Best Novel," *New York Herald Tribune*, 23.

155 "passionately interesting . . .": Virgilia Peterson, "A Crucible Covered with Ivy," *NYTBR*, 1.

155 "The richest . . .": John Mason Brown, *Book-of-the-Month-Club News*, midsummer selection, 1.

155 "I was swept . . .": Granville Hicks, "Headmaster for Hero," *Saturday Review*, July 11, 1964, 28.

155 "I don't think . . .": J. Donald Adams, "Speaking of Books," *NYT*.

155 "with it Auchincloss . . .": Leon Edel, "Grand Old Man—Not What He Seems to Be," *Life*, July 17, 1964, 11.

155 Sales figures: New American Library *News* of 1966 and Houghton Mifflin records.

156 "As you see . . .": Paul Brooks to James Oliver Brown, 2/25/1965, JOB Collection, Rare Book and Manuscript Library, Columbia University.

156 "I write with . . .": LA to Gore Vidal, 5/3/1965, Gore Vidal Collection, Wisconsin Historical Society, courtesy Piket.

157 "Voices will no doubt . . .": Virgilia Peterson, "A Crucible Covered with Ivy," *NYTBR*, July 12, 1964, 1.

157 "Life in our better . . .": R. M. Adams, "Saturday Night and Sunday Morning," *NYRB*, July 9, 1964, 15.

157 Granville Hicks. Arnold D. Kates from NYC wrote a letter to the editor of *The Saturday Review*, March 5, 1966, expressing his opinion of Mr. Hicks's further comment as to the total irrelevance of LA's fiction in the world of the 1960s: "I wonder whether Mr. Hicks is aware how many educators and teachers have read this book and have been affected by it in their relationships with their pupils; of how many mothers and fathers who have been to preparatory schools have given the story attention and have thought of the implications, the advantages and disadvantages that their sons and daughters are subjected to; of how many students in all schools and colleges have read the book and what effect it had on them." Hicks's review was reprinted in his *Literary Horizons* (New York: NYU Press, 1970), 185.

157 "since 1776 . . .": Dixon Wecter, *The Saga of American Society* (New York: Charles Scribner's Sons, 1970, reprinted from 1937 edition) (introduction by LA).

157 "denying that a rich man . . .": *A Writer's Capital*, 122.

157 "small," and "narrow": James W. Tuttleton, "Louis Auchincloss: The Image of Lost Elegance and Virtue," *American Literature* (January 1972): 616.

157 "Baldwin's slums . . .": Virgilia Peterson, "A Crucible Covered with Ivy," *NYTBR*, July 12, 1964, 1.

158–159 George Whitney: To Whitney's credit, he repaid every penny, and in 1950, he became Morgan's chairman.

159 "What Dick Whitney . . .": Martha Whitney to LA, n.d./1966, courtesy of LA.

160 "an allegiance . . .": LA, "My Mother, Priscilla Stanton Auchincloss," in *Family Portraits*, 31.

160 "If any one person . . .": ibid., 32.

160 "based on a crime . . .": ibid.

162 "completely civilized . . .": Blanche Knopf to LA, 2/18/1966, courtesy of LA.

162 "The one premise . . .": John Mason Brown, *Book-of-the-Month-Club News*, March 1966.

162 "What James never . . .": *Reading Henry James*, 103.

163 "unfashionable and unrepentant": *Life, Law and Letters*, 102.

163 "strange, angry world": *Reflections of a Jacobite*, 149.

163 "I can best reply . . .": John O'Hara to LA, 11/1/1960, courtesy of LA; quoted in L. O. B. Bryan, "Under the Auchincloss Shell," *NYT* magazine, Feb. 11, 1979, 17.

164 "Her tragedy . . .": *Reflections of a Jacobite*, 57.

164 "Snobbishness reigns . . .": ibid., 111.

164 "*King Lear* strikes . . .": *Motiveless Malignity*, 25.

164 "among the ten . . .": *Reflections of a Jacobite*, 87.

164 "other object but . . .": LA in John Wakerman and Stanley Kunitz, *World Authors 1950–1970* (New York: H. H. Wilson, 1975), 93.

164 "I would not hesitate . . .": ibid. This statement was made before Alice Walker's *The Color Purple*, a contemporary novel in an epistolary form.

164 "I loved Albee's . . .": quoted in Mary Tannenbaum, "The Tastemakers," *Cue*, April 6, 1968, 14.

165 "You will be . . .": LA to Gore Vidal, 3/30/1967, Wisconsin Historical Society, courtesy of Piket.

165 "Still no new book . . .": ibid., 5/22/1967.

165 "the world to him . . .": LA, "Louis Auchincloss Tells About *A World of Profit*," *Literary Guild Magazine*, January 1969, 7.

165 "where there is no . . .": Toni Kosover, "Louis XVII," *Women's Wear Daily*, December 18, 1968.

166 "I have a big batch . . .": LA to James O. Brown, 12/19/1968, James Oliver, Brown Collection, Rare Book and Manuscript Library, Columbia University.

166 "a capital slump . . .": Piket's interview with LA.

167 "To have witnessed . . .": ibid.

167 "as much money . . .": LA to Gore Vidal, 1/17/1964, Gore Vidal Collection, Wisconsin Historical Society, Courtesy of Piket.

167 $200,000 in account: James O. Brown to Paul Brooks, 12/19/1969, James Oliver Brown Collection, Rare Book and Manuscript Library, Columbia University.

CHAPTER 9: LOUIS S. AUCHINCLOSS, LAWYER

169 "The world Auchincloss": Gore Vidal, "Real Class," *NYRB*, July 18, 1974, 12.

169 "Four decades . . .": LA in *Niagra*, 1990. (*Niagra* is a Russian journal devoted to American literature and published in Moscow.)

170 "There is nothing . . .": author's interview with John Pierrepont, July 1989, NYC.

170 "I never recovered . . .": author's interview with LA, July 1990, NYC.

170 "I think it's hurt . . .": author's interview with LA, March 1991, NYC.

171 "They have to . . .": LA quoted in Paul Hoffman, *Lions of the Eighties* (New York: Doubleday & Co., 1982), 137.

172 "Resigning Sullivan & Cromwell . . .": author's interview with LA, July 1990, NYC.

172 "He would have stood up . . .": ibid., 245.

173 "moved over . . .": author's interview with LA, July 1990, NYC.

173 "When a man's . . .": "The Kingly Crown," *The Partners*, 24.

173 "I rode a bonanza . . .": author's interview with LA, July 1990, NYC.

174 "great satisfaction . . .": Scott Rosenberg, "A Double Life in Perfect Balance," *American Lawyer* (February 1983), 43.

174 "the most boring . . .": "Dual Career," in "The Talk of the Town," *The New Yorker*, August 13, 1960, 23–25.

174 "I think my practice . . .": quoted in Jean W. Ross, "An Interview with Louis Auchincloss," *Dictionary of Literary Biography Yearbook: 1980* (Detroit: Gale Research, 1981), 7.

174 "that the imaginative . . .": "Dual Career," *The New Yorker*, 24.

174 "His Fabbri brief . . .": author's interview with Charles Kades, July 1989, Heath, MA.

175 "the greatest human . . .": *A Writer's Capital*, 35.

175 "a fortress . . .": Learned Hand, quoted in *New York Reports*, second series, 240. "It is true that in theory any document purporting to be serious and to have some legal effect has one meaning and no other, because the known object is to achieve some definite result. It is not true that in practice (and I know no reason why reason should disagree with the facts) a given word or even collocation of words has one meaning and no other. A word generally has several meanings, even in the dictionary. You have to consider the sentence in which it stands to decide which of these meanings it bears in the particular case, and very likely will see that it there has a shade of significance more refined than any given word in the wordbook." (Holmes, "The Theory of Legal Interpretation," *Harvard Law Review*, vol. 12 [1899]: 12.)

If words are a necessary simplification of actual experience, then it follows that we can hardly expect to make manifest to others what is "really going on" in our minds. We cannot say what we mean precisely, nor can we feel secure in our understanding of what someone else means. The concept of "intention" has proved to be awkward for both literary and legal minds, and for similar reasons. But only a literary man would have handled the Fabbri case this way.

176 "It was entirely . . .": ibid., 241.

176 Respondents' argument: ibid., 242–243.

177 "It takes . . .": Charles Kades to author, 9/13/1989.

177 "Sometimes we lawyers . . .": "Agreement to Disagree," *The Partners*, 152.

177 "On the phone . . .": author's interviews with Paul Golinski, July 1989, Brooklyn, and October 1989, New Orleans.

178 "Rarely would Louis . . .": author's interview with Charles Kades.

178 "You find out . . .": author's interview with LA, March 1991, NYC.

179 "It's precisely the push . . .": *The Rector of Justin*, 143.

179 "I have already . . .": LA to Paul Brooks, 5/23/1963, Houghton Mifflin Collection, Houghton Library, Harvard University.

180 "the most brilliant . . .": author's interview with LA, July 1990, NYC.

180 "I never had any . . .": ibid.

181 "judgment, kindliness . . .": author's interview with Donald Robinson, February 1991, NYC.

181 "He was a peacemaker . . .": author's interview with Ralph Brown, July 1989, NYC.

181 "he'd cut off . . .": author's interview with Charles Kades.

181 "He wasn't as . . .": author's interview with Paul Golinski.

182 "Louis wouldn't beat . . .": author's interview with Donald Robinson.

182 "Louis probably views it . . .": author's interview with John Pierrepont, July 1989, NYC.

182   "his belief . . .": address to American College of Probate Counsel, October 12, 1971, James Oliver Brown Collection, Rare Book and Manuscript Library, Columbia University.

182   "Derrick, as the . . .": *Portrait in Brownstone*, 97.

182   "in default of issue": ibid., 229.

182   "the rich untapped . . .": LA to Frank Cooper, 6/22/1965, James Oliver Brown Collection, Rare Book and Manuscript Library, Columbia University.

182   "What goes on . . .": address to American College of Probate Counsel, 10/12/1971.

183   "been bitten by the federal bug": "The Peacemakers," *The Partners*, 49.

183   "looked down on . . .": *The Great World and Timothy Colt*, 12.

183   "I had to do . . .": LA quoted in David Streitfeld, "Letters of the Law," *Book World*, September 9, 1990, 15.

184   "a group of gentlemen . . .": *The Great World and Timothy Colt*, 123.

184   "were the men who greased . . .": ibid., 109.

184   "I grew up . . .": author's interview with John Auchincloss, July 1990, NYC.

185   "capable of recalling . . .": "Power in Trust," *Powers of Attorney*, 4.

185   "Lloyd, in his near half century . . .": "Foster Evans on Lewis Bovee," *Tales of Manhattan*, 147.

185   "his policy to keep the spirit . . .": "The Double Gap," *Second Chance*, 160.

185   "You coolly manufactured . . .": ibid.

185   "Law firm is something . . .": ibid.

186   "the function . . .": ibid., 170.

186   "invoking the ideals . . .": *Diary of a Yuppie*, 58.

186 "The basic greed . . .": ibid., 94.

186 "a game . . .": ibid., 26–27.

186 "Richard Whitney was . . .": LA quoted in Dinitia Smith, "The Old Master and the Yuppie," *New York* magazine, August 18, 1986, 34.

186 "are largely hypocrites . . .": LA interview in *The Philadelphia Inquirer*, September 30, 1986, 56.

187 "Could lawyers . . .": "The Mavericks," a television play based on the 1963 story ("The Mavericks," *Powers of Attorney*) that WNET commissioned and then canceled during budget cuts.

187 "It's perfectly true . . .": LA quoted in Scott Rosenberg, "A Double Life in Perfect Balance," *The American Lawyer*, February 1983, 44.

187 "I guess it's the huggermugger . . .": "The Tender Offer," *Narcissa and Other Fables*, 86.

187 "On each side . . .": LA quoted in Sandra Salmans, "Business Wolves Stalk His Novels," *NYT*, October 28, 1985, D4.

187 "Even the vocabulary . . .": "The Tender Offer," 86.

187 "When people adapt . . .": LA quoted in Scott Rosenberg, "A Double Life in Perfect Balance," *The American Lawyer* (February 1983): 44.

188 "those people are . . .": ibid.

188 "I suspect the firm . . .": ibid.

188 "If ever you have . . .": "The Mavericks," *Powers of Attorney*, 147.

188 "I wish we could . . .": ibid.

189 "Well, did you and I . . .": "Power of Suggestion," *Powers of Attorney*, 44, and "The Senior Partner's Ethics," *Skinny Island*, 215.

189 "He's shifty . . .": LA quoted in Tom Stevenson, "Louis Auchincloss: Teller of Tales Out of Court," *Juris Doctor* (November 1973): 21.

189 "is nothing but another . . .": quoted in Rosenberg, *The American Lawyer*, 44.

189 "The tax system . . .": LA quoted in Tom Stevenson, "Louis Auchincloss: Teller of Tales Out of Court," *Juris Doctor*, November 1973, 21.

189 "What better seat . . .": "The Death of Ronny Simonds," *The Partners*, 29.

190 "The trouble in writing . . .": quoted in Stevenson, *Juris Doctor*, 21.

190 "no whisper of . . .": author's interview with Judge Louis Stanton, June 1989, NYC.

191 "loved the abstractness . . .": *The Great World and Timothy Colt*, 58–59.

191 "I think it is a profession . . .": LA quoted in Roy Newquist, "Louis Auchincloss," *Counterpoint* (Chicago: Rand McNally, 1964), 32.

191 "dressing up the world . . .": address to American College of Probate Counsel, 10/12/1971.

CHAPTER 10: THE PUBLIC MAN

193 "New York has . . .": "Auchincloss, a New Museum Head, Deplores Demolition," *NYT*, March 17, 1966, 1.

193 "What I've been . . .": "Literary Lawyer," *MD Literature* (March 1980): 104.

193 "very good company . . .": Lady Bird Johnson, *A White House Diary* (New York: Holt, Rinehart and Winston, 1970), 676.

193 "decided he wanted . . .": *Fellow Passengers*, 51.

193 "I have always . . .": "Louis Auchincloss Tells About *Portrait in Brownstone*," *The Literary Guild Review*, summer 1962, 4.

194 "a New York file": author's interview with Robert Macdonald, July 1989, NYC.

194   "evident love . . .": NYU commencement, 1974.

194   "A quiet but persuasive . . .": Ralph Miller's remarks at First Annual Literature Award Dinner honoring LA, National Arts Club, 4/24/1968, NYC.

194   "these geographical things . . .": author's interview with LA, July 1990, NYC.

194   "I have always dealt . . .": "The Novelist of Manners," *The Partners*, 154.

194   "the center ring . . .": interview of LA for "Bookmark," episode 108, WNET, NYC.

195   "the spirit of . . .": "Louis Auchincloss Tells About *A World of Profit*," *The Literary Guild Magazine*, January 1969, 7.

195   "I much preferred . . .": author's interview with LA, March 1991, NYC.

195   "To his achievement-oriented . . .": author's interview with James Oliver Brown, June 1989, NYC.

196   "It was only . . .": *The Partners*, 83–84.

196   "A mine of information . . .": "Beeky's Conversion," *The Partners*, 102.

196   "everything is based . . .": Vincent Piket's interview with LA.

196   "To get to the roots . . .": "Literary Lawyer," 104.

196   "money is power . . .": George Will, "Are Lawyers Ethical?" *Washington Post*, September 21, 1986, C7.

197   "New York is mesmerized . . .": quoted in Tom Stevenson, "Louis Auchincloss: Teller of Tales Out of Court," *Juris Doctor* (November 1973): 21.

197   "I'm very much . . .": quoted in Jean W. Ross, "An Interview with Louis Auchincloss," *Dictionary of Literary Biography Yearbook: 1980* (Detroit: Gale Research, 1981), 7.

198   "a travesty of . . .": LA, "Images of Elegant New York," *American Heritage*, October 1966, 48.

198 "that a record in painting . . .": ibid., 51.

199 H. B. Aldrich "made" him take the chairmanship: Patricia Linden, "The Museum That Saved a City," *Town & Country*, September 1987, 231.

200 "History is not only . . .": LA, foreword, Jerry Patterson, *The City of New York, A History Illustrated from the Collections of the Museum of the City of New York* (New York: Harry N. Abrams, Inc., 1978), 8.

200 "The noisy destruction . . .": *A Writer's Capital*, 29.

200 "whose buildings replace . . .": "Louis Auchincloss Tells About Portrait in Brownstone," *The Literary Guild Review*, summer 1962, 4.

200 "How many . . .": LA, "A City in Green," *NYT Magazine*, part 2, April 24, 1988, 15.

200 Index of NYC landmarks: Alan Burnham, *New York Landmarks* (Middletown, CT: Wesleyan University Press, 1963).

200 "a kind of fanatic . . .": LA to Jean Stafford, n.d., Jean Stafford Collection, University of Colorado Libraries.

200 "took long walks . . .": "The Landmarker," *Tales of Manhattan*, 234.

201 "Any casting director . . .": Linden, "The Museum That Saved a City," 230.

201 "if the past . . .": LA, foreword, Patterson, *The City of New York*, 7–8.

201 "had been the beneficiary . . .": *The Golden Calves*, 74.

202 "ancient rusted piece . . .": "The Prison Window," *Second Chance*, 126.

202 "take a new look . . .": ibid., 127.

203 "all of us . . .": quoted in Linden, "The Museum That Saved a City," 231.

203 "Louis took the trustees . . .": author's interview with Joseph Veach Noble, July 1990, Maplewood, NJ.

203   "Drug addiction . . .": *Arts Review* (Fall 1986): 9.

204   "A quick read . . .": author's interview with Robert Macdonald.

204   "I've directed . . .": ibid.

204   "The Museum of the . . .": author's interview with Jeff Rosenheim, June 1989, NYC.

204   "Louis came into the museum . . .": author's interview with Donald Robinson, February 1991, NYC.

205   "struck a theme . . .": interview of LA for "Bookmark."

205   "that the ends justify . . .": "Hermes, God of the Self-Made Man," *False Gods*, ms. 102.

205   Zoo trustee: "Charity, God of Our Day," *False Gods*.

205   "Of course, he wouldn't . . .": "The Foundation Grant," *The Partners*, 215.

205   "worship of artifacts . . .": Miriam Horn and Alvin Sanoft, "Worshipping False Idols," *U.S. News and World Report*, August 1, 1988, 55.

206   "You can't educate . . .": *Honorable Men*, 204.

206   "He did his friends' . . .": "The Takeover," *Skinny Island*, 219.

207   "If you see a tree . . .": *A Writer's Capital*, 66.

207   "One could do . . .": ibid., 18.

CHAPTER 11: THE PRIVATE MAN

208   "One's life . . .": *Honorable Men*, 171.

208   "Louis badly needs . . .": Joyce Hartman to Richard McAdoo, 11/16/1971, Houghton Mifflin Collection, Houghton Library, Harvard University. According to Jonathan Galassi, LA's editor for a short time, Louis was receptive to criticism. In this case, Hartman referred most particularly to "those awful Mummies and Daddys" that "he's adamantly set against changing." As the use of these terms by adults lessens, especially "Mummy" (used by Adèle for her own mother to the end), people react to them with unease.

208 "Peak and a dangerously large . . .": LA to J. Donald Adams, 8/7/1964, Harry Ransom Humanities Research Center, University of Texas.

209 "My life doesn't . . .": LA to Gore Vidal, 3/12/1963, Gore Vidal Collection, Wisconsin Historical Society, courtesy Piket.

209 "Routine . . . brought . . .": *The House of the Prophet*, 251.

209 "The boys did vacuuming . . .": Anthony Mancini, "Protector of the Parks," *NYT*, October 18, 1973.

209 "I've a little collection . . .": Agnes Murphy, "At Home with Mrs. Louis S. Auchincloss," *New York Post*, July 8, 1967, 43.

209 "Do you like . . .": author's interview with LA, March 1991, NYC.

209 "not one you . . .": author's interview with Blake Auchincloss, March 1991, Boston.

210 "Treated [her] like . . .": author's interview with Adèle Auchincloss, July 1990, NYC.

210 "I'm sitting on the porch . . .": Adèle Auchincloss to LA, 3/19/1972.

211 "She loved it . . .": Martha Sutphen's eulogy, AA funeral, Church of the Heavenly Rest, February 12, 1991.

211 "Two small orange . . .": James Oliver Brown Collection, accession 1, Box 15, Rare Book and Manuscript Library, Butler Library, Columbia University.

212 "Adèle was passionately interested . . .": author's interview with LA, March 1991, NYC.

212 "They have cutting edges . . .": Anthony Mancini, "Daily Close-Up," *New York Post*, October 18, 1973.

212 "We saw kids . . .": author's interview with Adèle Auchincloss.

212 "Don't ever think . . .": Murphy, "At Home With," 43.

212 "Adèle is now Deputy . . .": LA to Ruth Jolly, 11/21/1974.

213 "I learned how . . .": author's interview with Adèle Auchincloss.

213   "three times to . . .": author's interview with LA, March 1989, New Orleans.

213   "our most devoted . . .": John Adams's eulogy, AA funeral.

214   *Tongass Tides*: Fifty-five copies have been exquisitely printed by Academy Press, New York. Each copy includes twenty artist proofs.

214   AA's book jackets: She did jackets for the following books: *The House of Five Talents, The Rector of Justin, Powers of Attorney, The Embezzler, Tales of Manhattan, A World of Profit, Second Chance*, and *Reflections of a Jacobite*.

214   "Athletically he was . . .": author's interview with Blake Auchincloss.

215   "a certain amount of work . . .": author's interview with LA, July 1990, NYC.

215   "devoted himself . . .": author's interview with John Auchincloss, July 1990, NYC.

215   "We reclined . . .": *The House of the Prophet*, 125–126.

216   "I got a garden . . .": author's interview with Adèle Auchincloss.

216   Strongest influence on children: "Today the Strongest Force is Peer Pressure," Gannet Westchester Newspapers, November 25, 1978.

216   "My father is a . . .": author's interview with John Auchincloss.

216   "They resent . . .": *The Rector of Justin*, 129.

216   "admirably adapted . . .": ibid., 141.

216   "I realize . . .": John Auchincloss to LA, 8/31/1981.

217   "I write you . . .": John Auchincloss to LA, 4/11/1982.

217   "This must seem . . .": John Auchincloss to LA, 10/20/1982.

217   "Perhaps you will . . .": John Auchincloss to LA, n.d.

217   "My mother tended . . .": author's interview with John Auchincloss.

217 "from early on . . .": author's interview with Blake Auchincloss.

218 "a blend of a villa . . .": ibid.

218 "a bribe . . .": LA, "Wildcat Mountain," *Architectural Digest*, June 1989, 29.

219 "worked hard . . .": Martha Sutphen's eulogy, AA funeral.

219 "Writing is terribly . . .": author's interview with LA, July 1990, NYC.

220 "This book has not . . .": inscription in *Second Chance*, 12/16/1970, Southern Methodist University Library, Dallas, TX.

220 "As my twenty-second . . .": quoted in Tom Stevenson, "Louis Auchincloss: Teller of Tales Out of Court," *Juris Doctor* (November 1973): 21.

220 "Because I'm . . .": Vincent Piket's interview with LA.

220 "He's always . . .": author's interview with Robin Brewster, July 1989, NYC.

221 "from the beginning . . .": Gore Vidal, "Real Class," *NYRB*, July 18, 1974, 12.

221 LA's plays: Only one one-act play, *The Club Bedroom*, has been produced.

221 "A fine literary style . . .": *Sybil*, 276.

221 "The very moral . . .": LA speaking on "Bookmark," episode 108, WNET, NYC.

222 "They knew they were . . .": *The Book Class*, 210–211.

222 "The intensification . . .": *Edith Wharton, A Woman in Her Time*, 188–191.

222 "I do not . . .": statement made for writer's conference sponsored by Pepperdine University in Moscow, May 1990, published in *Niagra*, a Russian publication about American writing.

Acknowledgments

First and foremost, I want to thank Louis Auchincloss for his cooperation, which in no way should be construed as approval of what I have written; for introductions to family and friends; for access to such correspondence as he has saved; for permission to quote from the letters he wrote his mother during his naval service in World War II, which are deposited in the Manuscripts Department of the Alderman Library at the University of Virginia; for letting me photocopy more than two dozen oversized scrapbooks; for lending me privately printed family histories and genealogies; for guiding me through countless family photograph albums; and for answering questions.

Next, I want to thank Louis Auchincloss's editor, Joseph Kanon, for his time, for seeing to it that sales figures and other pertinent data from Houghton Mifflin's Boston files were photo copied and sent to me, and for permission to consult the Houghton Mifflin Collection at Harvard University; Ruth Jolly, who not only talked to me at length, but who also sent me letters she has received from Auchincloss over the past thirty years; Vincent Piket, who generously shared with me typed transcripts of his October 8, 1985 and July 2 and 8, 1987 interviews with Auchincloss, as well as copies of taped interviews he conducted with more than two dozen of Auchincloss's friends and business associates that he had made for his own book, *Louis Auchincloss, The Growth of a Novelist*; and to Gore Vidal for introducing me to Auchincloss's writing (his rousing essay "Real Class" was the stimulus for this book) and for answering questions.

I am grateful also to the Manuscripts Department of the Alterman Library of the University of Virginia (Waller Collection, Louis Auchincloss Collection, Amélie Rives Collection); Rare Book and Manuscripts, Beinecke Library of Yale University (several Auchincloss manuscripts); Rare Book and Manuscript Library, Columbia University (James Oliver Brown Collection, Allan Nevins Collection, Curtis Brown Collection); De Golyer Library of Southern Methodist University (Joseph Zeppa Collection); Groton School Archives; Houghton Library of Harvard University (Houghton Mifflin Collection); Special Collections, Mugar Memorial Library of Boston University (Stephen Birmingham Collection); New York Historical Society; Harry Ransom Humanities Research Center of the University of Texas (James Donald Adams Collection, Harper's Collection, Oliver La Farge Collection); Manuscripts and Archives, Sterling Library of Yale University (Gordon Auchincloss Collection, Walter Lippmann Collection, Dramat Archives, the Class of 1939 Papers); Rare Books Room, University of Colorado Libraries in Boulder (Jean Stafford Collection); and Wisconsin Historical Society in Madison (Gore Vidal–Louis Auchincloss correspondence); to Anthony Tassin, Director of Interlibrary Loan at the University of New Orleans; to Jackson R. Bryer for his published bibliography of Auchincloss's work through 1976; and to Anne Guice, Beatrice Calvert, and Elizabeth Arceneaux, who typed the manuscript.

I wish to thank the following people for their help: Harold Appel (LST 980), Adèle Auchincloss (Mrs. Louis), Andrew Auchincloss, Anne Auchincloss (Mrs. Gordon), Blake Auchincloss, Gordon Auchincloss, J. Howland Auchincloss, Jr., John W. Auchincloss II, Sarah Auchincloss (Mrs. J. H., Jr.), Thomas Baer, Stephen Birmingham, Bettina Bourjaily, Vance Bourjaily, Robert Brewster, Paul Brooks, Douglas Brown, James Oliver Brown, Ralph Brown, C. D. B. Bryan, McGeorge Bundy, Edith Crawford (Mrs. Donald Morse), Eleanor Elliott (Mrs. John), Jonathan Galassi, Loretta Golinski (Mrs. Paul), Paul Golinski, Marshall Green, Dan Hartman, Joyce Hartman (Mrs. D.), Mary C. Henderson, Richard Irons, Ruth Jolly (Mrs. Kenneth), Charles Kades, John Leggett, Frank Lipsius, Nancy Lisagor, Robert Macdonald, Patricia

MacManus, Robert McDonald, Chauncey Medberry, John B. Mitchell, Margot Finletter Mitchell (Mrs. John), Joseph Veach Noble, Priscilla Auchincloss Pedersen (Mrs. William F.), William F. Pedersen, Peter Pennoyer, Mark Piel, William Curtis Pierce, John Pierrepont, Doneden Powell (Mrs. Richard), Richard Powell, George Rickey, Donald Robinson, Jeffrey Rosenheim, Samuel Parkman Shaw, Helen Stanton (Mrs. L. Lee), Judge Louis L. Stanton, Ronald Steel, Roy Steyer, Leonard Stidle (LST 130), Roger Straus, Nan Talese, James Tuttleton, and Kathy Watts (Mrs. Charles).

And finally, I wish to acknowledge the careful copyediting of Carol Edwards, the fine book jacket designed by Ken Sansone, the perceptive and always helpful editorial direction of Peter Ginna, and the abiding encouragement of my agent, Elaine Markson.

Index

Auchincloss, John (great-grandfather),
5
Auchincloss, John Winthrop (grandfather), 5, 8–9
Auchincloss, John Winthrop (uncle), 9
Auchincloss, John Winthrop, II (son),
127, 184, 209, 212, 214–217
birth of, 139, 140
Auchincloss, Joseph Howland, Sr.
(father), 3, 5, 8, 9, 14–22, 25,
62–63, 126, 136, 161
charm of, 27–28
death of, 62
depressions of, 21, 122
education of, 9, 21, 52, 60
as father, 19–22
generosity of, 116–117, 122–123
Jews and, 29
LA's correspondence with, 89
LA's psychoanalysis and, 122–123,
129
LA's relationship with, 19–22, 34,
73, 129
LA's writing and, 70, 71, 102, 105,
116–117
as lawyer, 14, 17–18, 21, 108, 158,
183
marriage of, 9, 14, 22; see also
Auchincloss, Priscilla Dixon
Stanton
meticulousness of, 18
military training of, 16
music loved by, 14, 20–21
Peabody and, 39
social life of, 28
stroke of, 22, 210
temper of, 19–20
Whitney and, 158
wife's relationship with, 21–22,
27
World War II and, 86
Auchincloss, Joseph Howland, Jr.
(brother), 16, 23, 26, 34
education of, 53, 56–57
LA's relationship with, 19
marriage of, 39
Auchincloss, Louis Stanton:
acting of, 49, 68
anti–Roosevelt sentiment of, 42
anxiety of, 128

awards and honors of, 15, 49, 66,
112, 168, 194, 195
birth of, 16
book reviews of, 50, 77
"bottled up" emotions of, 108,
116
childhood of, 16–35, 125–126
discipline of, 72
doubts and insecurities of, 106
early writing of, 2, 49–50, 69–72,
102
education of, x, 30, 35–80, 85–86,
107
escapism of, 46–47, 64
European travels of, 50, 63, 93–97,
215–216, 218
family background of, 2–15, 125–
126, 128
family expectations for, 34–35, 47,
70, 71, 128
as father, 117, 209, 214–217
financial dependence of, 116–117,
122, 133
generosity of, 117
illnesses of, 46–47
indecision of, 116
kinship between dual careers of,
174–175
as lawyer, x, 79–80, 82–86, 102–
117, 133–135, 169–192
legal writing of, 76–78
literary criticism of, 162–164
marriage of, see Auchincloss, Adèle
Lawrence
military career of, 85–101, 107
musical interests of, 20–21
as observer, 107–108
as outsider, 32, 120–122, 161
pseudonym of, 106, 110–111
psychoanalysis of, 35, 122–129,
133, 135
psychological insight in work of,
110, 116, 123, 124, 129–131,
142–143
snitching of, 37
social interests of, 33, 64–65
speeches of, 38–39, 167–168, 191–
192
timidity toward women of, 125
writing problems of, 219–220